FOR REFERENCE ONLY

Gas Masks For Goal Posts

Football in Britain During the Second World War

GAS MASKS
FOR
GOAL POSTS
FOOTBALL IN BRITAIN DURING
THE SECOND WORLD WAR

ANTON RIPPON

FOREWORD BY SIR TOM FINNEY

SUTTON PUBLISHING

First published in the United Kingdom in 2005 by
Sutton Publishing Limited · Phoenix Mill
Thrupp · Stroud · Gloucestershire · GL5 2BU

British Library Cataloguing in Publication Data
A catalogue record for this book is available from the British Library.

ISBN 0-7509-4030-1

Typeset in 11/13.5pt Sabon.
Typesetting and origination by
Sutton Publishing Limited.
Printed and bound in England by
J.H. Haynes & Co. Ltd, Sparkford.

CONTENTS

FOREWORD

by *Sir Tom Finney*

When war was declared in September 1939, I was 17 years old and serving my apprenticeship as a plumber, while at the same time making my way with Preston North End. None of us knew how the war would affect our lives, but for me it meant a chance in Preston's first team a little sooner than might otherwise have been the case. I signed professional forms in January 1940, made my debut against Liverpool at Anfield at the start of the following season, and by the end of it was playing against Arsenal in a cup final. Facing players like Eddie Hapgood and Cliff Bastin at Wembley had been beyond my wildest dreams. For many other players, of course, the war had the opposite effect, ending their careers prematurely, robbing them of the last few years of their footballing days. Plenty of others, in their prime when war was declared, lost several years before picking up the pieces again in 1946. Some paid the ultimate price and never returned from the fighting. War changes the course of people's lives for ever. Footballers are no different from any other.

My memories of wartime football are many and varied. I saw active service with the Royal Armoured Corps but also had the opportunity to play alongside and against some of the game's finest players in services football, both at home and in the Middle East and Italy. My own club lost its ground for a couple of years and I can remember training on Tuesday and Thursday evenings at a Deepdale surrounded by barbed wire after it became a prisoner of war camp. It was an unusual time of regional football, guest players and many difficulties caused by travel restrictions and the like. Supporters would arrive at grounds not knowing who would be playing for their team. Sometimes they would have a pleasant surprise when a star guest had been enlisted for the afternoon. There are some hilarious tales of the lengths those players had gone to in order to play. Most of all, football was important to people. It kept morale high and helped give us a sense of normality in abnormal times.

It is a pleasure to provide the Foreword for Anton Rippon's fascinating account of this unique era in football's history. His book captures perfectly the atmosphere of the game in those difficult days from 1939 to 1945.

ACKNOWLEDGEMENTS

This book could not have been written without the help of a large number of people, not least the football historians who, since 1985 in particular, have published an astonishing wealth of information on their clubs; they should all be saluted. Their works are included in the Bibliography, but special thanks go to Scott Cheshire, Keith Farnsworth, Frank Grande, Martin Jarred, Robert McElroy, Fred Ollier and David Woods, all of whom were kind enough to answer specific queries. Where possible, I have gone back to original sources and this has sometimes resulted in my account differing from what has been previously published. Over the years, several former players, some of whom, alas, are no longer with us, have indulged me: Sam Bartram, Cliff Bastin, Frank Broome, Jimmy Bullions, Raich Carter, George Collin, Peter Doherty, Dally Duncan, Arnie Grace, Jimmy Hagan, Dennis Herod, Jack Howe, Tommy Lawton, Wilf Mannion, Jack Stamps, Bert Sproston, Ken Teasdale, Tim Ward and Jack Wheeler all gave me their time. Apart from answering my questions, Sir Tom Finney also did me the singular honour of providing the Foreword. Andrew Ward allowed me access to his own player interviews and also gave enormous support, encouragement and advice, as well as allowing me to use the description he coined: 'Football's Vera Lynns'. Geron Swann kindly made available material from his interview with Vic Barney. Thanks also go to Colin Bruce of the Imperial War Museum, Tim Challis of the RAF Personnel Management Agency, Carol Cooper of the Children and Families of Far East Prisoners of War, Peter Crocker of

Acknowledgements

the Royal Welch Fusiliers, Geoff Cushing, Peter Drake of Birmingham Central Library, Howard Fear, Jezael Fritsche of the Swiss FA, Brian Harris, Peter Lockett, Derek Lockton, Tom Mason, David Murphy of the Royal Scots Regimental Museum, Jonathan and George Plunkett, Gordon Rosenthal, Harry Shinkfield of 77 Squadron Association, and Eddie Whyte. Thanks also to my agent, John Pawsey, and to Sarah Bryce of Sutton Publishing, both of whom showed enormous enthusiasm for the book. And thanks to Pat, and to Nicola, for indulging me, as always.

1

A STIFLING AFTERNOON

Surely there couldn't be room for professional football in a world gone crazy? . . . I wound up my personal affairs, cursed Hitler and all his works, and, occasionally, sat down to think of what had been, and what might have been.

Tommy Lawton, Everton and England

There should have been plenty to talk about as football supporters all over Britain headed for the exits on 2 September 1939. On the second Saturday of the new season, Blackpool had beaten Wolves 2–1 at Bloomfield Road to lead the First Division with maximum points. Ted Drake had scored four times in Arsenal's 5–2 win over Sunderland. In the Second Division, Newcastle United had put 8 goals past Swansea Town. In the Third Division South, Bournemouth and Boscombe Athletic had scored 10 against Northampton Town. The Glasgow giants, Celtic and Rangers, had both won, but in Edinburgh there was a surprise when Albion Rovers, relative newcomers to Scotland's top division, beat Hibernian 5–3 at Easter Road. Yet on the trams and buses taking supporters home for their tea on that stifling, brooding afternoon, no-one said very much. It was the same in every dressing room. At the Baseball Ground, the Derby players who had just defeated Aston Villa decided to meet again that evening in a local pub, to discuss what the future might hold. At The Valley, the game between Charlton Athletic and Manchester United had been a tedious affair, the players' apparent lack of interest mirroring that of the 8,608 supporters who had bothered to turn up to a ground which, the previous year, had housed 75,000. Even a 2–0 home win had failed to spark any celebrations. The mood of the Manchester City players who had beaten Chesterfield was not helped by the sight of barrage balloons on the skyline around Maine Road. At Highbury, where the kick-off had been put back for two hours because of traffic congestion as the first of London's children were evacuated from the capital, the atmosphere was especially subdued. Even Ted Drake, rarely short of a few wisecracks, had little to say, despite his 4 goals. For once, the result of a football match seemed unimportant.

The previous day, Germany had invaded Poland. In Britain, military service had been made compulsory for fit young men between the ages of 18 and 41 – which, on the face of it, meant all professional footballers – and, for the second time in a generation, a world war appeared inevitable. At eleven o'clock the following morning at the Russell Hotel – half a mile from King's Cross and 'made of reinforced concrete', the establishment boasted not all that reassuringly – the defeated Sunderland team gathered around a wireless set to hear the Prime Minister's broadcast to the nation. When Neville Chamberlain reached the bit that everyone would remember – '. . . I have to tell you now, that no such undertaking has been received, and that, consequently, this country is at war with Germany' – Raich Carter's first thoughts were of how they would get back to Sunderland. Would the trains still be running now there was a war on? The Leicester City players who had beaten West Ham United at Upton Park the previous day were already safely home, but they had arrived back in Leicester late on Saturday evening to find the city's blackout already in force. Despite the inconvenience, they noticed that there were still plenty of people about. It appeared that no-one wanted to go home, despite a fierce thunderstorm.

The war had come as no surprise. The whole of the previous season had been played out against a backdrop of almost unbearable tension as diplomats bluffed, bargained and threatened. It had been the same for years, one international crisis after another. Like the rest of Britain, football had tried to carry on as normal. Yet as far back as 1934, footballers had been one of the first sections of British society to see for themselves what was happening in Germany. In May that year, Derby County made a four-match visit there. By train to Dover and then a cross-Channel steamer to Ostend, the Derby party eventually reached the German border to find a country swathed in the swastika emblem. After Hitler's success in the elections of March 1933, the Nazi State was firmly established. Dave Holford was a 19-year-old outside-left from Scarborough, excited to be included in the tour party despite his lack of experience: 'Everywhere we went, the swastika was flying. If you said: "Good morning," they'd reply with "Heil Hitler". If you went into a cafe and said: "Good evening," they would respond with "Heil Hitler". Even then, you could see this was a country preparing for war.' Derby lost three times and drew once. Twice they conceded 5 goals in a match and were surprised by the standard of their hosts' game. All agreed, however, that if the football had been hard work, overall the tour had been an enjoyable one. Good hotels and plenty of time to relax and enjoy the scenery were just the ticket after a strenuous English season. There was, however, one overriding blot on the collective memory. Just as the England team would be obliged to do in Berlin, four years later, the Derby players of 1934 were ordered to give the Nazi salute before each game. Full-back George Collin, who captained the side when Tommy Cooper left for England duty, remembered their dilemma: 'We told the manager, George Jobey, that we didn't want to do it. He spoke with the directors, but they said that the British ambassador insisted we must. He said that the Foreign Office were afraid of causing an international incident if we refused. It would be a snub to Hitler at a time when international relations were so delicate. So we did as we were told. All except our goalkeeper, Jack Kirby, that is. Jack was adamant that he wouldn't give the salute. When the time came, he just kept his arm down and almost turned his back on the dignitaries. If anyone noticed, they didn't say anything.'

Thereafter, every British team that visited Germany had a similar story to tell, although when Manchester City went there in May 1937, at the end of a season in which they had won the Football League championship, they decided on a collective response to Hitler's regime. Despite having just won the title, City, like Derby before them, found it hard going and won only one of their five matches. Peter Doherty, their Irish international inside-forward, brought back vivid memories of the trip:

> Most of their players seemed to be in the German army already and were sent away to special camps to prepare for the games. It was a shock. We'd just had a long, hard season and went there for a holiday. One of the games was against a German representative team in the Olympic Stadium in Berlin, which had just staged the 1936 Games. The entire stadium was swarming with armed guards, all wearing swastikas. We knew we'd be expected to give the Nazi salute before the kick-off, but when the time came we just stood to attention. Afterwards we were treated with enormous kindness, though, and the Germans just seemed to want to send us away with a favourable impression of their country. But you couldn't fail to see the military preparations everywhere. The whole country seemed to be one huge armed camp.

Frank Broome of Aston Villa had the unusual experience of being required to give the Nazi salute twice in as many days in May 1938. 'The Germans had invaded Austria the previous March and now there wasn't a separate Austrian international team – which had been one of the strongest on the continent – just one for "Greater Germany". England were due to play in Berlin, but the FA told the Germans that they couldn't include any Austrian internationals. They agreed on the proviso that Villa would play a German eleven the following day, and that could include Austrians. What struck me, though, was how the military was everywhere. You couldn't possibly have visited Germany and not realised that they were gearing up for war.' The FA's hope that Germany would not benefit from the *Anschluss* – the annexation of Austria – was realised. England won 6–3 in the Olympic Stadium, although one of the German goals was still scored by an Austrian, Hans Presser from Rapid Vienna. The following day, Aston Villa beat a German Select XI 3–2 before 110,000 spectators who sweltered in 90-degree heat at the Reichssportfeld. This German team contained no less than nine Austrian internationals. Broome scored in both games, only

24 hours apart. Again there had been the controversial issue of the Nazi salute. Villa, like Manchester City, kept their hands by their sides. England gave the full-flung version after Sir Neville Henderson, the pro-appeasement British ambassador to Berlin, persuaded the FA secretary, Stanley Rous, and committee man, Charles Wreford Brown, that there would be an international incident if they did not; and anyway, he pointed out, it was simply a courtesy to their hosts, not an endorsement of Hitler's regime. Perhaps most importantly, it would 'get the crowd in a good mood'. The England captain, Eddie Hapgood, wrote later: 'The worst moment in my life, and one I would not willingly go through again, was giving the Nazi salute in Berlin.'

Thus, sixteen months later, the nation's footballers could hardly be surprised when their livelihood was interrupted by war with Germany. Indeed, by September 1939 the whole country was prepared. Unlike the world situation five years earlier, when Derby County's players had been in a privileged position to see what was happening in Germany, now no-one needed a holiday on the Rhine before they realised the dangers. The 1939–40 football season was about to be interrupted, but it was surprising that the previous season had itself been completed. The international skies were already darkening as the first games were played on 27 August 1938, when Arsenal began their defence of the Football League championship with a comfortable home win over Portsmouth. By the time Derby County scored a surprise midweek victory at Highbury on 14 September, the world already knew that Hitler would invade Czechoslovakia if the Sudetenland was not annexed to Germany. The Nazi leader had made that much clear at a huge party rally in Nuremberg two days earlier. The fourth and fifth Saturdays of the new season were played out as Neville Chamberlain visited Hitler in Berchtesgaden and Bad Godesberg. Meanwhile, Everton put 5 goals past Portsmouth, and Liverpool beat Leeds 3–0, but even on Merseyside it was hard to concentrate on football.

There was enormous tension throughout the country. Gas masks were distributed, air raid shelters dug in public parks, and around London anti-aircraft batteries were sited to defend the capital in case of air attack. There was now every possibility that the next Saturday of the football season would see Britain at war. On Tuesday, 27 September, the Royal Navy was mobilised. The following afternoon, the Football League announced that the weekend's fixtures would be fulfilled unless the worst had happened by then. Few people would have put money on the matches taking place, but Chamberlain returned home from a hastily arranged meeting in Munich, clutching a piece of paper. He had agreed to all Hitler's demands. It was to be 'peace in our time'. The immediate crisis had passed and football could continue. On Saturday, 1 October, before the start of every Football League game, a service of thanksgiving was held 'to express thankfulness for the preservation of peace'. But if war had been averted for the time being, it was Easter before it could safely be assumed that the football season would be played to its natural conclusion. By then Hitler had occupied the rest of Czechoslovakia, and Everton were on their way to winning the First Division title. The Goodison club had begun the season with six consecutive victories, and even a sensational 7–0 defeat at Wolverhampton in February had not checked their stride. They had much the same team as the previous season, but this time their young centre-forward, Tommy Lawton, was receiving better service and would finish the season with 34 League goals. Portsmouth and Wolves, meanwhile, were looking forward to meeting in the FA Cup final.

Four days before the Wembley final, which Portsmouth would win 2–0, the Government announced the introduction of compulsory military service for men aged 20 and 21, limited to a period of six months' training. Summing up the season, W.M. Johnston, compiler of an annual review, commented: 'It is still too early to perceive the precise effect that this enactment will have upon the arrangements of [Football] League clubs, but at least it introduces a factor the consequences of which may be far-reaching.' None the less, the 1938–9 football season survived to provide a list of winners. For Everton there was the League championship, for Portsmouth the FA Cup, which they would now famously hold for seven years. Birmingham and Leicester City dropped out of the top tier of English football, to be replaced by the champions of the Second

Division, Blackburn Rovers, and the runners-up, Sheffield United. Norwich City and Tranmere Rovers disappeared into the Southern and Northern Sections of the Third Division respectively, while Barnsley, from the Third Division North, and Newport County, their southern counterparts, went up a division. Newport's achievements were especially pleasing. It would be their first time in the Second Division. They had gone three months undefeated, a spell broken, remarkably, by an 8–0 thrashing at the hands of Swindon Town on Boxing Day. But they had recovered and now this 'team without stars' sailed into new waters. They would have to wait seven years to get properly under way.

While football was settling its own issues, Hitler had turned his attention to Poland, whose affairs were dominated by the 1919 Treaty of Versailles, which had settled Polish frontiers to the displeasure of her neighbours. On 24 March 1939, Britain and France had agreed to resist any German aggression against Belgium, Holland and Switzerland. One week later, as regulars of Fratton Park and Molineux wondered what would be their chances of obtaining a cup final ticket, Britain announced that she would stand by France in guaranteeing Poland's frontiers. Football, however, had to go on. As soon as the 1938–9 season was over, the England team went on a three-match tour. At the rain-soaked San Siro Stadium in Milan, a German referee, Dr Bauwens, allowed an Italian goal, despite the ball being fisted into the net. An offer from the Italian Crown Prince to order Dr Bauwens to change his decision was politely declined by the FA, and the game ended 2–2 after a late England equaliser. After a long train journey to Belgrade, England lost 2–1 to Yugoslavia, and then Rumania were beaten 2–0 in an ill-tempered affair. When the referee blew his whistle to end the game in Bucharest, he brought down the curtain on England's pre-war international programme. For the next seven years it would be 'unofficial caps' only. That summer the FA's international committee toyed with the idea of organising a match against France in Paris for May 1940, but decided to defer the matter until a later date. It was a common-sense decision.

After Bucharest, the England party began the 24-hour train journey for home, across a Europe bracing itself for war. Just as the players of 1938 had seen for themselves the mood in Germany, so the 1939 team had, as they made their way through the streets of Milan towards the San Siro, witnessed the huge support for Mussolini. There could be little doubt in any of their minds that life would soon be changed irreversibly. At Basle, in the small hours of the morning, Tommy Lawton and Joe Mercer said goodbye to their teammates. They had agreed to travel on to Holland where their club, Everton, was making a short visit. On the steamer chugging across the Channel from Boulogne to Folkestone, Frank Broome lent alone on the ship's rail, watching the French coast disappear and wondering if he would ever see it again.

England were not that summer's only football tourists. Wales lost 2–1 in Paris on 20 May. Three days later, four English-based players – George MacKenzie (Southend United), Matt O'Mahoney (Bristol Rovers), Johnny Carey (Manchester United) and Jim Fallon (Sheffield Wednesday) – played in Bremen for the Republic of Ireland. As the local shipyard of A.G. Weser prepared to step up its production of U-boats, just down the road, a fine header from Paddy Bradshaw of Dublin's St James's Gate club earned the Irish a creditable 1–1 draw. From late May until early July, a strong FA team toured South Africa, winning all three 'test matches' but somehow managing to lose 1–0 to Southern Transvaal.

Back in Britain, while the FA XI was beating Natal 9–1, the Air Raid Precautions Department at the Home Office considered plans for closing all forms of entertainment upon the outbreak of hostilities. The FA, meanwhile, decided to convene a joint FA–League meeting as soon as war was declared. Essentially, it would decide 'what to do next'. Many players had already done their bit, however, and by the time an FA circular exhorting footballers to join the Territorials was doing the rounds towards the end of the 1938–9 season, several clubs had already seen their entire playing staff 'join up'. West Ham United had indulged in some forward planning; after the Munich Crisis of September 1938, the Hammers' chairman, W.J. Cearns, suggested that first-team players joined the reserve police, and reserve players signed up with the Territorial Army. This way, West Ham could be sure of a decent first team who, if war did come, would all presumably be stationed close by. To be fair to Cearns, his son also enlisted in the 'Terriers' and when war did come, many Hammers players joined the forces and served together in a searchlight unit of the Essex Regiment in East Anglia. Twenty-three of Brentford's thirty-man playing staff were in the reserve police, while Bolton Wanderers had signed up en bloc for the local Territorial artillery regiment.

Liverpool had been the first to join the Territorials as a club. Phil Taylor, a wing-half who had been transferred to Anfield from Bristol Rovers in March 1935, was one of them. He recalled a summer army camp in May 1939, when Liverpool had to send down their club trainer, Albert Shelley, to work on the footballers' feet, blistered from days of long route marches in ill-fitting army boots. Almost all Football League clubs saw players signing up with the Territorial Army, a trend which led to the League issuing a statement to the effect that clubs were not obliged to pay players who were undergoing military training, unless those players were going to be made available on match days. On the eve of the season, the FA waived their rule that stated that no player serving in the armed forces could be registered as a professional footballer. The game was going on a war footing.

By then football had already suffered its first war casualties. In July, Portsmouth's FA Cup final captain, Jimmy Guthrie, was seriously injured when the car he was driving crashed during a blackout practice near Harrogate. Everton's Billy Cook and John Thomson, who were attending the same coaching course as Guthrie, received relatively minor injuries but Guthrie's were life-threatening. Happily, he recovered and was able to watch some of Portsmouth's practice matches as they prepared for the new season, for sport was carrying on as usual. Even as late as 20 August 1939, a British track and field athletics team was meeting a German team in Cologne. Six days later, the new Football League season kicked off on schedule when a goal from Tommy Lawton earned the reigning champions, Everton, a 1–1 draw with Brentford at Goodison Park. There was the usual crop of early-season midweek games; at Highbury on Wednesday 30 August, Cliff Bastin's penalty was enough to defeat Blackburn Rovers.

At Anfield that evening, Phil Taylor, his blistered feet now recovered, scored twice as Middlesbrough were beaten 4–1. Portsmouth, the FA Cup holders, lost 2–0 at Derby, where Dally Duncan and new signing Billy Redfern, from Luton Town, both scored.

Nine hundred miles away, the 1939 Polish championship had been whittled down to a four-club play-off between Slask Swietochlowice, Smigly Wilno (from what is now Vilnius, the capital of Lithuania), Junak Drohobycz (now part of the Ukraine) and Legia Poznan, but the title was never decided. Warsaw was preparing itself for war. Trenches were being dug and power stations sandbagged and people had started to carry gas masks. In Danzig, now the flashpoint of the conflict, bands of Nazis attacked Polish shops in the city and smashed their windows. On Friday 1 September, the Luftwaffe bombed the Polish capital as German tanks crashed their way over the country's border. In Britain, theatres were closed, cricket matches abandoned, greyhound racing cancelled and the BBC wireless service changed to two wavelengths only. Many amateur football matches were cancelled, but the Football League pressed on for one more Saturday. The public were not sure what to do. Everywhere attendances were down. The first Saturday of the new season had attracted a total of 600,000 spectators to forty-four Football League games; seven days later, with the world teetering on the brink of war, the figure had slumped to well under 400,000. At only three grounds – Blackpool, Birmingham and Cardiff – was there an attendance in excess of 20,000. Arsenal's gate for the game against Sunderland, not helped by the late kick-off, was just over 17,000, less than half the normal attendance for Highbury. Newport County were caught up in traffic and arrived three-quarters of an hour late for their game at Nottingham Forest. Everywhere clubs had struggled to find enough players.

Liverpool's Territorials managed to persuade enough colleagues to stand in for them on sentry duty so that the players could travel to Anfield for the match against Chelsea. The Brentford match programme for the game against Huddersfield Town contained a cartoon of a man entering a turnstile, scowling over his shoulder at a storm cloud which bore the word 'Crisis'. The caption read: 'Let us forget our troubles for a while and see an honourable fight.' Honourably or otherwise, Brentford won the match 1–0. The Arsenal players clattered back into their Highbury dressing room to find a letter waiting for each of them. The message was unequivocal: in the event of war being declared, their contracts would be cancelled until further notice. It was almost eight o'clock and dusk was setting in by the time they left for home, the sight of a barrage balloon moored on the club's training pitch leaving them in little doubt that the afternoon's victory over Sunderland would ultimately count for nothing.

That night, the Derby players met at the Angler's Arms in Spondon, on the outskirts of the town. A violent thunderstorm was raging and one of the barrage balloons defending the Rolls-Royce aero-engine works near the Baseball Ground was struck by lightning and brought crashing down in flames. It seemed an appropriate, almost apocalyptic, backdrop. There was no chance of Germany withdrawing from Poland. 'We're out of a bloody job,' growled the Derby centre-forward, Jack Stamps. No-one disagreed. In Liverpool, Norman Greenhalgh was going to be annoyed for several years to come. He had played in every game of the previous season when Everton won the League championship. They were due to meet Portsmouth, the FA Cup holders, in the traditional FA Charity Shield game at Goodison Park on 4 October: 'We won the League and Portsmouth won the Cup, and we were supposed to play them. And what happened? Bloody Adolf Hitler stepped in, didn't he, and the bloody war was on, and I lost a medal. That was always a bone of contention with me.'

Jack Wheeler, a young goalkeeper with Birmingham, was not too worried, though. On the Sunday morning, as was his custom, he left his digs and went down to St Andrew's to take a shower and then enjoy a game of snooker with some of the junior players. On his way back home at lunchtime, someone told him that war had been declared: 'I wasn't really bothered. I was young, single and, let's face it, it would all be over by Christmas.'

11

2

PHONEY WAR, PHONEY FOOTBALL

The first season was very strange. It was quite enjoyable but a lot of the matches were played in a half-hearted manner. No-one knew what was going to happen in the war. It wasn't easy to concentrate on football.

Frank Broome, Aston Villa and England

On the second Saturday of the 1939–40 season, York City lost 1–0 at Rochdale in the Third Division North. In the early evening, the players travelled home across the Pennines from Spotland, wondering if they would still be playing Lincoln City in midweek. On the Monday morning, the York secretary, G.W. Sherrington, gathered the players in the home team dressing room at Bootham Crescent and told them what they already knew: as football had been suspended, the club had no prospects of any income and they were out of a job. Then he gave everyone their insurance cards, wished them luck and told them they could now go home. Lincoln City would have to wait. It was a scene played out at football grounds all over the country. In 1939, football's first reaction was a determination not to make the same mistake as in 1914, when the Football League and the FA Cup had been allowed to continue for a whole season and everyone connected with the game had been denounced as both unpatriotic and unproductive. In November 1914, *The Times* had carried a letter from the historian A.H. Pollard: 'Every club that employs a professional football player is bribing a much-needed recruit away from enlistment and every spectator who pays his gate money is contributing so much towards a German victory.' The FA responded by claiming that

500,000 recruits had already been raised by football organisations, that of 5,000 professionals, some 2,000 were already in the services, and that only 600 unmarried professional footballers had failed to heed the call.

Some people in the game had taken particular exception to claims that football was not supportive of the war effort. Frederick Charrington, the heir to an East End brewery fortune, who had renounced his inheritance and found his way into the Temperance movement, had been given permission by the FA to make a speech on wartime recruitment during the half-time interval of a match at Craven Cottage. For patriots like Charrington, footballers and their supporters were cowards. He was also seen by many people as one of those grim Victorian philanthropists for whom any entertainment was morally suspect. Alas, no-one had thought to inform the club that he had been given permission to air his views and as soon as Charrington began to speak, two Fulham officials set upon him, dragged him down a gangway and threw him out of the ground. Of course, there were fundamental differences between 1914 and 1939. The First World War had been fought largely by volunteer soldiers. Conscription, introduced in 1939, prevented a repeat of that. And there was now the imminent threat of air attack. Almost every family in Britain had been touched by the First World War, but largely through their menfolk away fighting on the front line. By 1939, the prospect of German air raids on British cities had been in the public mind for several years. Thus, one of the Government's first reactions after the declaration of war was to ban the assembly of crowds. That meant that all forms of public entertainment had to be suspended immediately. The *Daily Mail* of 4 September 1939 commented, 'For the moment, all sport has been brought to a halt. The concentration of Britain's whole effort on winning the war makes its continuance undesired and inappropriate.'

So, in contrast with the situation in 1914, football had no choice to make; the game could not carry on anyway. On 5 September, the Football League told all its member clubs to keep their players on standby. Then, after a hastily arranged meeting at Crewe, the League further informed clubs to release the players after all, paying them up to 6 September. Bonuses and any other additional payments should be settled at once, supporters would have to wait until it was decided what to do about refunding money for season tickets, and if the regular season could be resumed later, matches already played would count as cup games. As football hung in limbo, the players found themselves in a dreadful situation. The old retain-and-transfer system which was operating in 1939 – and which continued to do so until the 1960s – held all professional footballers in a feudal-like thrall. In the twenty-first century, when players and their agents rule the roost, it is hard to imagine a time when there was a maximum wage and a footballer could be tied to one club for life if that club so wished. That was indeed the case, but now, with a war on, the players were unceremoniously dumped by those same clubs. Their only immediate chance of earning a living was to join the armed forces. Even when, a few days after war had been declared, the Government lifted its ban on sporting activities outside highly populated areas such as London, Birmingham and Manchester, the players were not initially entitled to any payment above valid expenses, although they were insured under the Workmen's Compensation Act.

On 9 September 1939, the first wartime football match took place behind closed doors at Loftus Road, when Queen's Park Rangers put 10 goals past a hastily recruited army team. Just who the eleven servicemen were who were so roundly beaten, we shall never know: the army team was not published for 'security reasons'. Soon, the areas where matches could be played were extended provided that local police did not object. The first friendlies when spectators could be admitted took place on 16 September with twenty-eight matches involving Football League teams in England and three games in Scotland. Attendances ranged from 2,000 to 9,000, and altogether totalled 117,000. That day Nottingham Forest lost 4–3 to Peterborough United of the Midland League. As the FA had rescinded all contracts, it was the first time that Forest had fielded an all-amateur team since 1891. Derby County did not play that day but when they did give it a go, on 30 September, only 1,805 people turned up at the Baseball Ground for a friendly game against Leeds United. That was enough to convince the Derby directors to shut up shop. It would be 1942–3 before they joined the war league. Mansfield Town announced that they were also closing down. Chairman W.M. Hornby told the *Nottingham Evening Post*: 'We hope to come up smiling again and give Mansfield the sort of football it deserves.' Within a few weeks the club had started up again. Ipswich Town, elected to the Third Division South in 1938, had enjoyed only one season in the Football League when the competition was suspended. Ten days after the outbreak of war, the club's chairman, John Murray Cobbold, issued a statement on behalf of the board announcing that the club's activities would be suspended indefinitely. Supporters' representatives asked for a change of heart but at the end of the month, Cobbold told them, ' . . . it was decided in the interests of the club to close down all operations at Portman Road as and from 30 September 1939.'

By then, some restrictions had been relaxed. On 25 September, the stipulation that matches could be played only between clubs no more than 50 miles apart was altered to allow games where the away team could be 'there and back in a day'. Three days earlier, attendances of up to 8,000 in evacuation areas and up to 15,000 in safer centres were allowed. There were stipulations, however. The limit of 8,000 could be no more than half the capacity of the stadium. The bigger grounds in the non-evacuation areas could admit up to 15,000 provided that tickets were sold in advance, an arrangement which soon proved impractical. Nevertheless, football supporters began to see their local grounds quickly reopened, although had the local chief constable had his way, Birmingham would never have played a home match during the Second World War. When football was allowed to resume, Cecil Moriarty was having none of it. In his opinion the area around St Andrew's was a likely target for the Luftwaffe – as it turned out, he was right – and there would be the risk of serious loss of life if thousands of people were allowed to gather to watch football. The club did everything in their power to overturn his ruling and on 12 March 1940, Birmingham City Council passed a resolution asking the chief constable to reconsider. They argued that people who spent long hours working in munitions factories deserved some recreation, and that included watching football at Birmingham. The matter was raised in the House of Commons, but Home Secretary Sir John Anderson – after whom the cheap domestic air raid shelter had been named – declared that he could not intervene in such a local issue. A letter to the local *Sports Argus* accused Moriarty of 'killing people's Saturday afternoons', adding, 'He would change his views if he had to work in a factory for 50 or 60 hours a week.' Eventually, when it was pointed out that St Andrew's was the only football ground in Britain still closed, Chief Constable Moriarty, and the eight Birmingham councillors who had backed him, had no case. On 23 March 1940, the ground reopened and there was an attendance of 13,241 to see Birmingham play Walsall in a Midland Division game, for by then the wartime regional competitions were well under way.

The joint FA–League War Emergency Committee had announced its plans towards the end of September 1939. There were to be eight regional competitions. Two would be styled 'South', with divisions 'A' and 'B', and would comprise clubs from London and elsewhere in the south of England. The other sections would be East Midlands, Midlands, North-West, North-East, Western and South-Western. Six clubs decided not to take part: Aston Villa, Derby County, Exeter City, Gateshead, Ipswich Town and Sunderland. In Scotland there would be two divisions: East and West. As in England, six clubs declined: Brechin City, Edinburgh City, East Stirling, Forfar Athletic, Montrose and Leith Athletic. The Irish League decided to carry on as normal; the League of Ireland was unaffected because the Free State would remain neutral throughout the war. Players would be paid thirty shillings a match in England – where the maximum pre-war weekly wage had been £8 – and £2 in Scotland. Guest players would be allowed, provided the player's original club granted permission. Such a rearrangement of the Football League was bound to cause disaffection. Newcastle United found themselves in what was effectively a Yorkshire division with only lowly Hartlepool United and Darlington for company from the North East. Lancashire's clubs were also separated. In the North-West Division, Preston North End, Bolton Wanderers, Blackpool and Burnley had to play against Carlisle United and Barrow, while the Merseyside and Manchester clubs were put in the Western Division, which no doubt pleased the likes of New Brighton, Crewe Alexandra and Chester, who joined them there. Luton Town might have hoped for a place in one of the southern sections, but instead lined up with Wolves, West Brom and Birmingham in the Midland Division. Some divisions were so small that the clubs would have to play each other four times over the season instead of the normal two. This inevitably meant that interest waned as the season wore on.

The biggest fall-out, however, was in the south, where an acrimonious split soon developed. Over twenty clubs had wanted to play in the London area sections, the obvious attraction being matches against Arsenal, which would generate bigger gate receipts. But it was now nearly October and there was room for a maximum programme of only thirty-three matches. The answer was to split the south into two divisions, which displeased the clubs who were not in Arsenal's section. London clubs, meanwhile, objected to travelling to the south coast for matches when a perfectly workable competition could have been fashioned out of clubs from the capital alone. The London clubs pointed out that by taking just four clubs from outside their immediate area, they could have a competition where they each played twenty-eight matches. Also, they could not see why the Football League had to get involved. Such a league could be run by the London Combination and governed by the London FA. Eventually the eleven clubs from the capital agreed to the groupings – which provided two divisions with eighteen games for each club – provided that they could stage matches on consecutive playing days. This would allow them to run a similar competition in the latter half of the season, with the clubs shuffled around. This time the sections would recognise the pre-war divisions so that all the bigger clubs would be placed in the same section, the smaller ones in the other.

The new league season would begin on 21 October. In the meantime, friendly matches continued, although interest was minimal. Whereas an average attendance of 10,000 supporters had been watching each of the Nottingham clubs' indifferent form in 1938–9 – Forest finished third from bottom of the Second Division, Notts County eleventh in the Third Division South – only 4,000 turned up for the first wartime derby game between the rivals on 14 October. Forest triumphed 2–1, their winning goal scored by a Coventry City player, Ellis Lager. The same day, several clubs fielded two teams: Birmingham lost 1–0 at Wolves and 3–2 at Stoke; Charlton lost 2–0 at Watford and 9–2 at West Ham; West Brom won 4–2 at home to Coventry and 5–1 at Kidderminster Harriers. The BBC's wireless commentary of a friendly game between Blackpool and Manchester United was picked up by a French radio station and relayed to British troops of the BEF, who strained their ears for details of Blackpool's 6–4 win. They were unaware of the fact that, a few hours earlier at Scapa Flow, HMS *Royal Oak* had been torpedoed by a German U-boat and had gone down with the loss of 833 lives.

Three days before the regional leagues got under way, Aldershot staged the first representative game of the war when an FA team met a combined Aldershot and army side in aid of the Red Cross and St John Ambulance. There were a dozen international stars on display including the Arsenal full-back pairing of Eddie Hapgood and George Male for the FA team, and Leeds United's Wilf Copping and Eric Stephenson for the home side. The FA won 1–0, their goal coming from Barnet's amateur international outside-left Lester Finch, who had played for Great Britain in the 1936 Berlin Olympics. The previous season Aldershot had recorded only one attendance in five figures, but now a crowd of 10,000 raised over £350 for charity; such matches were to become an integral part of wartime football in Britain. The attendance proved one thing: that people would certainly turn out for games where there was an abundance of talent on display, even if there was no truly competitive edge to the affair. It also reinforced the Government's view that sport would have a beneficial effect on public morale. Even in the first few weeks of the war, Mass Observation, the organisation founded in 1937 to record public opinion, noted that the banning of competitive sports – and therefore the breaking of well-established routines – might have 'deep repercussions'. In 1940, Mass Observation would report: 'Sports like football have an absolute effect on the morale of the people and one Saturday afternoon of league matches could probably do more to affect people's spirits than the recent £50,000 Government poster campaign urging cheerfulness.' The organisation could not find one pre-war football supporter who thought that the game should be suspended for the duration of the war. Perhaps more significantly, they found that only 2 per cent of people not interested in football in peacetime were against sport being played in time of war. Alas, in 1940, Mass Observation also found that 65 per cent of supporters who attended pre-war matches could not now get to football because of Saturday shift work in factories, travel restrictions and family obligations.

When the first wartime league matches were played on 21 October 1939, the biggest attendance of the day was the 8,931 who saw tenants Arsenal beat Charlton Athletic 8–4 at White Hart Lane, to where the Gunners had removed on the outbreak of the war. Leslie Compton scored 4 goals, 3 of them from the penalty spot. Charlton's goalkeeper, Sam Bartram, conceded only one of Compton's spot-kicks. He left the field injured, to be replaced between the posts by the Torquay United left-back Ralph Calland, who was guesting that day. There was a crowd of 6,468 at Craven Cottage where 2 goals from Ronnie Rooke helped Fulham beat Portsmouth 2–1. At Griffin Park, 6,628 saw Brentford draw 2–2 with Chelsea. There were 4,000 at the Victoria Ground, Hartlepool, where the home side lost 2–1 to Newcastle United, despite the presence of seven Sunderland players in the Hartlepool team. The Manchester derby match at Old Trafford, where City won 4–0, attracted only 7,000. Perhaps the most surprising attendance on that opening day came at the far-flung football outpost of Carlisle. Accrington Stanley were the visitors to Brunton Park, where 4,500 watched a goalless draw between two clubs from the Third Division North. At the other end of the country, Plymouth Argyle's home game with their nearest neighbours, Torquay United, brought 2,866 to Home Park. The home fans were rewarded with a 4–0 win.

It was three weeks before the first five-figure attendance was recorded – the 12,000 who saw Arsenal draw 1–1 with Norwich City at Carrow Road on 11 November – but the following week, a crowd of 15,000 were present when Arsenal played Tottenham Hotspur at White Hart Lane, hardly surprising since this was the wartime home ground of both clubs. Generally, though, attendances were well down on pre-war figures. The forty-one regional wartime games of 4 November 1939 produced an aggregate attendance of only 101,000; a year earlier, forty-four Football League matches had been watched by a total of 685,000. Yet if attendances were down, people could still enjoy a flutter on the game. That month a new Unity Pools was formed combining Littlewoods, Vernons, Copes, Shermans, Socapools, Bonds, Jervis and Screens. The combined coupon saved paper and cut down on handling. The Edinburgh duo of Murphys and Strangs had started the ball rolling two weeks earlier with their own combined coupon. In January, a woman from Hull won a record Unity Pools dividend, with £8,059 for an outlay of one shilling and sixpence.

On 4 November, Goodison Park staged a representative match between the Football League and an All British XI. Both sides were packed with international stars. The League's forward line alone was worth the entrance money: Stan Matthews (Stoke City), Raich Carter (Sunderland), Tommy Lawton (Everton), Peter Doherty and Eric Brook (both Manchester City). The game ended in a 3–3 draw, and 15,000 spectators – the maximum allowed – raised over £1,200 for the Red Cross. The following week, the first wartime international was played between England and Wales at Cardiff. This time 28,000 spectators were allowed in, swelling Red Cross coffers by another £1,700. Seven days later another Wales–England game was played at Wrexham and 17,000 watched, with over £1,000 again going to the Red Cross. No-one could claim that football was failing to do its bit and newspapers did their best to remind everyone. They were more likely to print photographs of the leading players of the day if they were wearing military uniform.

On 22 November came a sign that the game was not falling to pieces when the first transfer of the war took place. Bobby King, a

20-year-old outside-right from Northampton Town, moved to Wolves for a fee of around £2,000. That the transfer market was still operating reinforced some people's opinion that the game's rulers had overreacted in cancelling the regular season. Some called it the Phoney War, others the Twilight War, but whatever title you cared to give it, life in Britain had taken on an almost surreal quality during the first few months of the Second World War. Everyone knew it would be different once it all began, and it was – but different in an entirely unexpected way. People expected Neville Chamberlain's announcement to be followed by wave after wave of German bombers. They had seen cinema newsreels of what had happened to the Poles. But nothing happened. There were no air raids, no bombs and no drastic changes between the state of war which now existed and the state of emergency which had lasted all summer. In reality, Hitler was hoping that after he had smashed Poland, Britain and her allies would sue for peace. Initially he forbade air attacks on British towns and cities; the appalling European winter meant a further delay.

So life went on pretty much as normal. True, posters everywhere exhorted people to 'Carry your gas mask at all times', but there was no apparent danger, and no food shortages either. Newspapers carried advertisements for whisky, meat, radios and furniture, and there were plenty of fresh vegetables. New potatoes were selling for one old penny per pound, and cauliflowers at twopence each. There were even plenty of oranges at threepence each. There was also plenty to grumble about. Getting about in the blackout was a serious problem. Street lamps were switched off and torches were in short supply. People fumbled about in the dark, apologising to lamp posts and pillar boxes. Fatal road accidents doubled in the last four months of 1939; on 18 November, the coach carrying the Bury team home from a match at Barrow knocked down and killed a 62-year-old man on Bolton Road, Bury. It was the town's first road fatality caused by the blackout.

Throughout it all, the football season meandered on, occasionally throwing up some remarkable statistics and some bizarre team selections. Don Howe, a guest from Bolton Wanderers, scored 5 goals for Newcastle when they beat York City 9–2; it was the only appearance he ever made for the Magpies. Nottingham Forest's 42-year-old manager, Billy Walker, turned out for Notts County in a friendly against Hull City and scored one of the goals in County's 5–4 win. Bury were ready to pull away from Gigg Lane for a match at Leeds but were still two players short. The club's trainer, David Robbie, was pressed into service, despite being 41, and the team bus then made a detour to the house of Robert Dalton, a local player with Bury Amateurs. Dalton was persuaded to turn out and the team, which also included George Griffiths, still a few days short of his seventeenth birthday, somehow managed a 2–2 draw at Elland Road. Preston North End enjoyed their biggest victory for many a year when they won 10–1 at Accrington Stanley. Coventry City's Tommy Crawley scored 8 goals in his side's 10–2 win over Luton Town; it avenged Coventry's 7–0 defeat at Luton three months earlier; West Brom's Harry Jones finished the season with 50 goals and along the way set a club record by scoring in eleven consecutive matches between 28 October and 30 December. Supporters of Queen's Park Rangers enjoyed a wonderful Christmas when their team beat Fulham 8–3 on Christmas Day and Portsmouth 5–2 on Boxing Day; a week later QPR scored 7 at Brentford. Twenty goals in three matches; it was almost enough to make you forget there was a war on.

In Germany, too, it seemed that football's role as a morale-booster was recognised. On 9 November 1939, the *Daily Express* ran a headline: 'Nazis Copy Our Soccer Scheme'. Reports emanating from Amsterdam claimed that German clubs would play in sectional competitions from 1 December, the winners of each section going forward to a knockout cup. The newspaper commented, 'The date and place of the final is optimistically set for Berlin on 16 June 1940.' Between 24 September 1939 and 22 November 1942, Germany played thirty-five official international matches against its allies and neutral states, winning twenty-two and losing only eight. In Italy, the regular championship continued until the summer of 1943.

In Britain, meanwhile, the wartime league season of 1939–40 was just about to run into difficulties: in early December the weather closed in. The British Isles were locked in the icy grip of one of the worst winters of the twentieth century. Indeed, the first three football seasons of the Second World War were notable for their harsh weather conditions. In 1939–40, however, not only was snow a significant problem, the winter also contained the longest-lasting ice storm (27 January to 3 February 1940) Britain had known. There was severe transport dislocation, and many injuries on the ice in a large area from North Wales across parts of the south-west Midlands to the South West and central-southern England. During the same period, a great snow storm with gale-force winds affected south-east England with drifts well above 15ft. January 1940 was the coldest of the century. To compound everyone's misery, food rationing – initially of butter, bacon and sugar – began on 8 January. Not surprisingly, the football season was severely disrupted by the weather. York City, for instance, played no competitive matches from Christmas Day until 16 March. On 3 February, only one match in Britain was able to be played, when Bristol City lost 10–3 at Plymouth. Less than 900 people turned up to watch. The previous week only seven of the scheduled fifty-nine games could be staged. One major problem for clubs was that weather forecasts could not be published for fear of aiding the enemy, so there were no opportunities to warn supporters that matches were going to be cancelled.

By the beginning of March, the clubs were asking for an extension to the season, not least so that a knockout competition, which they viewed as a potential money-spinner, could be fitted in. It was agreed that the season could run until 8 June and the preliminary rounds of the War Cup would begin on 13 April. A measure of how far behind the fixtures schedule had fallen came when the second round of the War Cup was played on 27 April, which would have been FA Cup final day had there been no war. Tranmere Rovers decided not to take part in the cup competition, but Sunderland and Gateshead, two of the clubs who had declined league football, each entered a team. The preliminary stage of the War Cup involved thirty-eight Third Division teams paired on a regional basis, each playing a one-off match. For the start of the first round proper, attendance restrictions were relaxed to 50 per cent of ground capacity with police permission. The sixty-four first-round matches – the ties were each played over two legs – attracted almost half a million spectators. The Manchester derby alone was watched by a total of 43,000. Cup football was obviously what everyone wanted.

For the third round, played on 18 May, the competition reverted to one-off sudden-death matches and there was one surprise when Arsenal lost at home to Birmingham. By then, however, the nature of the war itself had changed dramatically and the final games of the 1939–40 football season were played during a time of incredible international tension. On 9 April, Germany had invaded Denmark and Norway; the war in the west had started. Four weeks later, events took an even more dramatic turn and the first footballers to notice the difference were a lot nearer than most to the front line. For those servicemen who had been sent over to France in the autumn of 1939, the war had seemed almost as distant as it had for those who stayed at home. There was certainly plenty of football. In February, a strong British Army team played three games against the French Army, drawing 1–1 in Paris and winning 1–0 in Rheims and 2–1 in Lille. Near Limoges, Free Polish airmen fielded a regular Sunday-afternoon team, entertaining other sides at their camp. Early in 1940, Bury centre-half George Matthewson and Queen's Park Rangers centre-forward Tommy Cheetham were playing in corps matches at Douai, Lens and Lille. In March 1940, the 35th Anti-Tank Regiment played a match at Ostricourt and then went by lorry to the local coal mine for a shower. On 5 May, there were many British troops in the crowd when Racing Club of Paris beat Olympique Marseilles 2–1 to win the French Cup at the Stade Olympique de Colombes. Five days later, however, the army's playing days in France were brought to an abrupt end. Hitler invaded Holland, Belgium and Luxembourg; three days later France was attacked. On 12 May, twelve British football coaches working in Holland escaped on one of the last boats to leave that country. The Phoney War had ended. The football season, which had sometimes seemed almost as phoney as the war itself, was also coming to its conclusion – and for many the end could not come soon enough.

When Hitler invaded the Low Countries, Swindon Town were due to play Newport County, and with servicemen on standby for immediate posting, there were only seven players in the Swindon dressing room, with less than 30 minutes to kick-off. Eventually a full team was mustered and a player called Smith became an unsung hero with 2 goals in the draw. Football went on, but there was little appetite for the game, as Plymouth Argyle and Newport County illustrated in June 1940. By then Plymouth topped the South-Western Division and had two games to play, both away at Newport. Neither club had much desire to continue and asked if they could play just one game for four points. The War Committee insisted on the full programme being completed and thus Plymouth lost 6–3 at Newport on the Friday evening, and 5–2 on the same pitch the following afternoon, but still managed to win the title. The same month, the *News Chronicle* reported that the result of the Newcastle United–Bradford City game had officially been recorded as 4–3 to Bradford. There had been an argument over whether a shot from Albert Stubbins had entered the goal or hit the side netting. The referee had restarted the game with a goal-kick, but Newcastle sent in the result card with a 4–4 scoreline, insisting that a point was theirs. Clearly, they still cared on Tyneside. More so than at Leicester, where the last game of the season, against Northampton, attracted only 850 paying customers. That was better than Blackburn Rovers managed for their final game, against Rochdale on 3 June; the official attendance at Ewood Park was just 337. And at Elland Road, only 200 people turned up to see Newcastle United.

The War Cup, meanwhile, had progressed to a Wembley final between West Ham United and Blackburn Rovers. A crowd of over 42,000 saw West Ham win 1–0 and the curtain came down on the first season of wartime football. Arsenal and Queen's Park Rangers headed the final South Divisions, 'A' and 'B' respectively, and Tottenham Hotspur and Crystal Palace were champions of the competitions played in the latter half of the season. Wolves,

Chesterfield, Stoke City, Plymouth, Bury and Huddersfield Town won their respective divisions, while in Scotland, Rangers and Falkirk topped their sections. But did any of it really matter? The War Cup final had been played during the week of the BEF's evacuation from Dunkirk. Soldiers from the beaches were even in the crowd at Wembley. On 31 May 1940, the *Daily Express* reported that football might be closed down until peace was restored 'due to team raising and transport problems'. In a Britain on the brink of being invaded, finding eleven half-decent footballers and a bus in which to transport them was hardly a priority.

3

IN THE EVENT OF AN AIR RAID

Games in London were the worst. They were always being interrupted. I used to take my ukulele with me and when we came off, we'd have a singsong in the dressing room until the all-clear sounded and we could resume the game. George Formby numbers were particularly popular.

Jack Wheeler, Birmingham goalkeeper

'When the time comes to write the history of this war, it may not pass unnoticed by the chronicler that, as the Battle of Britain developed, the Football League launched a season of competitive football. It is, at all events, no small act of temerity on the part of sixty-eight of the League's flock of eighty-eight to embark in this new wartime enterprise in circumstances obviously more difficult than those last winter and early spring.' So commented the *Manchester Guardian* as the second wartime football season got under way in England on 31 August 1940. One month earlier, at the annual meeting of the Football League, plans for the 1940–41 season had been agreed. The competition would carry on with whatever clubs were prepared to play. They would be split into two large regional groups, north and south, and would arrange their own fixtures, although each club from the First and Second Divisions would to have play at least two from the Third Division. There would be no points awarded; positions would be decided on goal-average, by dividing the number of goals scored by the number of goals conceded. It was hoped that each club would play at least twenty matches. There would be no time for rearranged matches; where games were abandoned, the scores would stand. A Football

League proposal that players would not be paid was defeated; as in 1939–40 they would receive thirty shillings per match with no bonuses. There would be no trophies or medals for the winners. In Scotland, sixteen teams would compete in the new Southern League. Most significantly, the fixtures in both countries would be planned only up to the end of the year. With the German army massed on the other side of the Channel, no-one could look too far into the future.

Two weeks before these arrangements for the new season were announced, Hitler's plans for Operation Sealion, the invasion of Britain, had been issued to the German High Command. The new Scottish season opened on 10 August; five days earlier, the Battle of Britain had begun. On 13 August, the Germans launched 1,485 sorties against Britain. The Luftwaffe lost forty-five aircraft, the RAF thirteen. It became known as 'Eagle Day'. It was also an important day for football. In the *Daily Express*, Stanley Halsey reported, 'The entire Football League executive staff – secretary Fred Howarth and a fifteen-year-old office boy – wildly excited at being caught up in such vital football affairs, dashed from the Management Committee meeting in Manchester to League headquarters at Preston yesterday, to get busy with League plans for the coming season. Fortified by sandwiches, coffee and League decisions, they began the overtime job of ironing out the fix-your-own fixtures lists for next season, and tidying up the outstanding problems of wartime soccer.' Two days later, Germany launched their most intensive attack on Great Britain – 1,790 sorties. The Luftwaffe lost seventy-five planes, the RAF thirty-four. It was going to be an unusual sort of football season.

A clear indication of what was to follow came as early as the opening day. At The Dell, the League South game between Southampton and Brighton was held up for 30 minutes after an air raid warning. The attendance of just over 1,000 reflected people's caution at attending football matches on the south coast when the Luftwaffe was likely to appear at any time. The biggest attendances of the day were in the north of England, with crowds of 5,000 at Liverpool and Newcastle, and 4,000 at Manchester City. In the south, no club rivalled that kind of support on the first day of a season which no-one could guarantee would progress very far. The following Saturday, with only 60 seconds remaining at The Valley and the visitors, Millwall, leading Charlton Athletic 4–2, the air raid warning siren sounded. The raid was a heavy one with shrapnel from nearby anti-aircraft guns falling on the stadium. The 1,500 spectators took cover and when the all-clear sounded, the game resumed and the final minute played out. A week later, Charlton's match at Brentford was interrupted after 65 minutes. Again the players resumed the game, this time before the remnants of a crowd which had numbered only 600 at kick-off.

Playing football as the Battle of Britain raged overhead was a precarious – and sometimes tiresome – occupation. The Home Office had ruled that play must be stopped whenever the air raid alert sounded. Clubs attempted to counter this with a system of 'spotters'; even after the alert sounded, play would continue until the spotter on the roof of the stadium signalled the actual presence of enemy aircraft. The Government considered this too risky and refused its implementation, although eventually it was adopted. In the meantime, matches continued to be interrupted, occasionally for up to an hour. The players passed their time in various ways. Card games, singsongs, games of housey-housey, they all played their part in keeping footballers occupied while they waited for the all-clear. Some, however, got fed up and went home. When the referee went to round everyone up for a restart, often the teams could not be completed and so the game was abandoned. Not unnaturally, many supporters also decided not to waste their Saturday afternoons hanging around in air raid shelters waiting for the football to resume. For a club like Charlton, right underneath the air war, it was a particular problem. Attendances at The Valley dwindled to the low hundreds and the club was losing money every week. On 28 December 1940, their first round of fixtures completed, Charlton decided to close down for the rest of the season. Hull City also fell by the wayside, although their problems were a bomb-damaged ground and difficulty in raising a reasonable team. Hull struggled on into the second half of the season before calling it a day in early April, after an 8–0 home defeat by Middlesbrough.

In their different ways, most clubs suffered in 1940–41, not least when travelling to fulfil away matches. At the end of September, Reading's players had to stand all the way on a train journey to play Swansea Town. They arrived three-quarters of an hour late and lost 4–1. The following week, with a team that showed ten changes from their defeat at Swansea's rugby ground, Reading beat the Welsh club 4–0 at Elm Park. Whether the improvement in their fortunes was caused by the change of personnel or the short journey to their home ground was not recorded. Later in the season, Reading's manager, Joe Edelston, found himself pressed into service as a turnstile operator and unable to give his customary pre-match team talk. Southend United, already deprived of their home ground because of the dangers of bombing, were dogged by trouble week after week. On 14 September, their match at Clapton Orient was interrupted after only 8 minutes when the sirens wailed. The players returned after 75 minutes and began a match of 40 minutes each way, but just before the final whistle, another raid began and the game was abandoned. Seven days later, Southend had to call off a game at Portsmouth because they could not raise a side. Then in October, they had to play the first 30 minutes of their game at Norwich with only eight men. Sam Bell, Charlie Fuller and Frank Walton were delayed after the car in which they were travelling was involved in an accident. Southend lost 8–4. In November, Southampton's coach driver, returning from a game at Cardiff, became lost in the blackout, then he hit a brick wall, and finally the vehicle suffered a burst tyre. The players were forced to spend the night in the coach, arriving back in Southampton on the Sunday lunchtime. The players of Wycombe Wanderers had probably the worst experience. After a Great Western Combination game at Slough, the Wycombe team had to walk the 15 miles back to High Wycombe. The blackout also caused problems for players training after work. Harold Atkinson of Tranmere Rovers recalled the dangers: 'The part-time training was on a Tuesday and a Thursday and you ran around the ground at your own risk. We used to sprint down the side of the pitch in the dark, and there were more injuries caused by training in the blackout than there were in proper matches.'

League games were not the only form of football interrupted by the Battle of Britain. Ken Aston, who after the war made his name as an international referee, recalled the day he took charge of a services game, with a steel helmet and a gas mask on his chest:

> I was a gunner on a gun site on a bomber station in 1940 when bomber stations were being heavily attacked by German aircraft, and a match had been arranged between the RAF personnel and the gunners who were operating the low-level-attack guns. There was this match, being played near my gun site. For that reason I was allowed to referee the game. In the middle of the game we hear a low droning sound. It was a day of low clouds. We look up at the aircraft and it is a Ju-88, a German light bomber. And so I raced to my gun, whipped on my steel helmet and respirator which we had to wear – you never knew when there was going to be a gas attack – and manned the guns in refereeing kit. We had to abandon the game.

Finding enough referees for the war leagues was a constant problem. And even when an official turned up, clubs could not be guaranteed that he could stay until the game was decided. On 15 March 1941, the cup tie between Grimsby Town and Barnsley stood at 1–1 after 30 minutes' extra time. 'Sudden death' was ordered – the match would continue until another goal was scored – but after a further 50 minutes' football there was still deadlock. Then the referee, Flying Officer McKenzie, was called away for RAF duties. The game was abandoned and duly awarded to Barnsley because of their higher league position. Football's rulers had made some attempt to ease the difficulties faced by the game. The chronic shortage of referees was addressed by allowing them to wear spectacles, thus widening the pool of available officials. In early September, the ban on Sunday football was lifted so that war workers could take part in local amateur matches on their only day off. A suggestion that matches in the regional competitions might also be played on the sabbath was instantly rejected. Sunday play for Football League clubs was still thirty years away.

On Christmas Day 1940, several teams played two games, with some remarkable results. Leicester City lost 5–2 at Northampton in the morning and then the whole show moved on to Filbert Street, where Leicester, with only one team change, extracted instant revenge by winning 7–2. On the same afternoon, Southampton fielded two teams: one beat Portsmouth 2–1 at Fratton Park; the other hammered Clapton Orient 9–3 at Chelmsford. Watford drew 2–2 with Luton Town at Vicarage Road; after lunch, Luton beat the same opponents 4–1 at Kenilworth Road. Tommy Lawton recalled the time he played for Everton against Liverpool at Anfield on Christmas morning 1940, and for Tranmere at Crewe in the afternoon. 'The Tranmere people just came into the dressing room and asked if anyone wanted to play as they were a couple of men short. I said: "Go on, I'll help you out." And I did.' The same day, Len Shackleton played two away matches, one for each Bradford club. In the morning he turned out for Park Avenue at Leeds; in the afternoon he scored for City at Huddersfield. But the most remarkable scoreline that day came at Norwich and questioned the very point of wartime football. Brighton arrived with only five players and their team was completed with Norwich reserves and spectators. Norwich won 18–0, 6 of their goals coming from centre-forward Fred Chadwick. Eleven days earlier Chadwick, who was on the books of Ipswich Town, had scored four times in a 10–1 win over Aldershot. In late October, West Ham had been 8 goals up at half-time against Southend United and eventually won 11–0. Only 500 people watched the game. The same afternoon, Cardiff City beat Swansea Town 8–0, and Mansfield Town and Walsall fought out a 6–6 draw. Two weeks later, Walsall beat Notts County 11–4 before 427 spectators, the lowest attendance at Fellows Park during the war. League football was often being reduced to a farce.

Three days after the Christmas pantomime between Norwich and Brighton, the final round of scheduled matches in the regional leagues was played. Attendances were still poor, averaging less than 2,500. The biggest crowd of the day was at Luton, where 8,000 saw Arsenal win 8–1. More importantly, the invasion of Britain had not happened. The fixtures had been arranged only until Christmas but now the season could continue. The issue was not straightforward, however: the discontent of the southern clubs was boiling over. A second round of matches had been arranged to start in the New Year, including those for a War Cup competition. This would be played on a home and away basis, and regionalised into north and south right up to the semi-finals, thereby creating a north v. south cup final at Wembley. There would also be a London Cup, which drew howls of anguish from those southern clubs who were left out of this supplementary competition. They suggested an alternative format to include themselves. London's clubs rejected it, instead forming their own cup competition. Then Bournemouth, Brighton, Portsmouth, Southampton, Southend United and Watford created their own South Regional League, soon to be joined by Luton Town and Norwich City, who argued that this competition could not include the word 'south' in its title unless they were included. Anarchy was in the air.

Elsewhere, matters were much less contentious but almost as complicated. In both north and south, some games counted towards two competitions. Leicester City, for instance, played six matches to win the Midland Cup; the games also counted towards the overall League South. There were also regional knockout competitions for Lancashire and the West Riding, and Sheffield (which included all South Yorkshire's clubs), and even a Cheshire Bowl, between Crewe Alexandra and Stockport County. And every game counted towards the League North. This football merry-go-round kicked off on 4 January 1941 with the usual high scores and low attendances. A Bolton Wanderers player, Jim Currier, scored 5 goals as Manchester City beat Rochdale 9–1 in a League North/Lancashire Cup game watched by 2,000 supporters at Maine Road. The following week Currier scored another 5 against Rochdale when City won the return game at Spotland 6–1 in front of 1,000 spectators. By the end of the season, Currier had rattled up 47 goals in 42 games for his adopted club. If Rochdale were sick of the sight of Jim Currier, Clapton Orient must have been utterly fed up with Jackie Gibbons, Tottenham Hotspur's amateur international centre-forward. On consecutive Saturdays, from 21 December to 11 January, Gibbons scored hat-tricks against Orient as Spurs won 9–0, 7–0, 3–0 and 9–1. There were big scoring feats everywhere, including one which set a record for football in the British Isles. On 25 January, Peter O'Connor scored 11 of the 13 goals which Belfast Celtic put past Glenavon in the Northern Ireland Regional League. After carrying on as normal in the first wartime season, Ulster's footballers had also introduced wartime competitions. O'Connor's tally that day has never been equalled in a senior league game in Britain or Ireland. When he retired from playing, O'Connor became Glasgow Celtic's scout in Ireland and sent them Charlie Tully, Sean Fallon and Bertie Peacock before emigrating to America during the 1950s.

As the second half of the football season gained momentum, clothes rationing was introduced in Britain. The rules applied to everyone and the Government would not allow clubs to purchase replacement kit without coupons; it was now left to supporters to donate their own precious coupons. The rationing of clothes was just another item in a catalogue of bleak war news. Heavy bombing continued night after night as the Luftwaffe pounded all the nation's big industrial centres as well as the capital. German and British forces clashed for the first time in the Western Desert, where Erwin Rommel's Afrika Korps captured Benghazi and besieged Tobruk. Greece and Yugoslavia were invaded. A day earlier, the Football League had announced an extension of the season to 7 June 1941. By then the Blitz had ended. The last of the heavy air raids on Britain took place on 10 May. Slowly a beleaguered nation began to realise that the nightly wail of the warning siren was over. True, there would be many more air raids to come, but the incessant raids, night after night spent down the shelter, not knowing what would greet you in the morning, had come to an end. More important for football, daylight bombing raids had ended. The Battle of Britain had been won and there would be less disruption to games from now on.

Preston North End and Arsenal contested the second Wembley cup final of the war. Over two legs in the third round, Preston had beaten Tranmere Rovers 12–1 and 8–1. Arsenal, meanwhile, could count a 15–2 victory over Clapton Orient in the London War Cup among their triumphs. Leslie Compton scored 10 of the Gunners' goals that day. Ironic then, that when Arsenal and Preston drew 1–1 at Wembley, Compton missed a penalty. The sides met again at Blackburn, where Preston took the trophy with a 2–1 win. Preston also topped the League North, and Crystal Palace the League South. Brighton were champions of the eight-club South Regional League. Reading won the London Cup, Rangers the Southern Scottish League and the Cup after a replay. If it was goals that were required, however, the neutral spectator could have done no better than follow the Hampshire Combination Cup. In one of the semi-final matches, Portsmouth found themselves 3–1 down at half-time against Aldershot, pulled back to 5–5 by the end of normal time, and scored another 5 in extra time to win 10–5. In the final they beat Southampton 8–1. A week earlier, Aldershot had achieved some revenge with a 9–2 win over Pompey in a league game. So the football season, which many thought would never be completed, finally drew to a close. It had been an odd affair, but if attendances had been disappointing, football was still an essential part of wartime Britain. Indeed, there were so many Canadian servicemen playing the game at camps all over the country that eighty-four teams were divided into six sections to compete for the Canadian Armed Forces Soccer Tournament that season.

The 1941 London Cup final between Reading and Brentford at Stamford Bridge had been watched by only 9,000 spectators, but this disappointing support for the breakaway competition did not dissuade London's clubs from open rebellion during the close season. When the Football League announced the fixture list for 1941–2, the eleven London clubs, including Charlton who had decided to start up again, refused to accept them; they did not see the point in travelling to places like Swansea, Norwich and even Luton. At various stages of the row, the London rebels were joined by Aldershot, Brighton, Portsmouth, Reading and Watford. Crewe Alexandra also found themselves in dispute with the Football League after being bizarrely included in the League South. Crewe offered to play in the northern section but in the end would not take part in any Football League competition that season. The sixteen

'London clubs' were expelled from the League, which could have meant dire consequences when peacetime football was eventually resumed. But the League, having made its point, and realising that it was stoking up major difficulties for itself, decided to put a different spin on matters. As far as they were concerned, they had not expelled the clubs; the clubs had expelled themselves. Common sense prevailed. The rebels could get on with organising their own London League, administered by the pre-war London Combination and affiliated to the London FA, and the Football League would allow the guest player system to continue, with players moving freely between the London competition and the League's own.

The make-up of the 1941–2 season was the rebel London League – with a normal programme of home and away games giving each club thirty matches to the end of the season – and the official Leagues North and South. League North comprised thirty-eight clubs each playing eighteen matches up to Christmas; the truncated League South – which had also lost Birmingham, who joined Aston Villa in the Birmingham and District League – was made up of thirteen clubs mainly from the Midlands, Wales and the south coast. They would play no more than eighteen matches each, with those playing fewer having their points calculated on the average they would have won had they played eighteen games. Pocket calculators were more than a generation away. Supporters now had to brush up their arithmetic, or wait for the newspapers to publish league tables. After Christmas, a War Cup would begin with the northern and southern sections now combining in a qualifying competition where each club would play against five others on a home and away basis, these small pools being selected by the Football League. All the cup games would also count towards the championship's 'second period', the top thirty-two teams would then go into a straightforward knockout competition and there would be extra league matches to make up the 'second championship'.

In Scotland, the Scottish Southern League continued, but a North-Eastern League, which included a second Rangers team, was started. And just in case anyone thought that the bitterness between the two Glasgow giants would be put aside as bigger battles were fought, when Rangers and Celtic met at Ibrox in early September, a riot broke out. The police made two baton charges into the Celtic supporters, and bottles were thrown and two players injured. A year later, Rangers goalkeeper Jerry Dawson was carried off during a game against Hibernian when he was hit by a bottle thrown from the crowd. The season also saw the demise of one of Scotland's oldest clubs. They did not know it at the time, but when St Bernard's lost 3–2 to East Fife on 16 May 1942, they had played their last game. Meagre support meant that the Edinburgh club decided to close down for the duration. Alas, the following year one of the directors died and the executors of his will demanded the return of money he had loaned the Saints. It was a huge blow to a club that had first played in the Scottish League in 1893. Although some efforts were made to revive St Bernard's after the war, the club had died during it.

Another bad winter would eventually see the English season extended to the end of May, but when the campaign began on 30 August it was in glorious weather. Jack Rowley scored seven times as Manchester United beat New Brighton 13–1, Stoke City beat Everton 8–3, Sunderland won 7–1 against Sheffield United, and Reading were 8–3 winners at Clapton Orient. The 5,000 spectators who went to see West Brom play Cardiff City at The Hawthorns were soon back into the swing of things when Albion scored five times in the first 11 minutes. Such is the nature of football that the flood of goals abated somewhat and the final score was only 6–3. Nevertheless, it was apparent that the days of high scoring were far from over. Neither were the days of matches being disrupted by the war. In November 1941, Queen's Park Rangers and Norwich City were just about to take the field at Loftus Road when the air raid warning sounded. The teams waited in the dressing rooms for the all-clear, but eventually the referee decided to abandon the game. The Norwich players set off back for East Anglia without kicking a ball. A week later, Norwich were waiting for the arrival of Nottingham Forest when, just before the scheduled kick-off time, they received a telegram to say that Forest were somewhere in Lincolnshire. They had boarded the wrong train at Peterborough.

A seven-a-side match between Norwich players was staged instead, and most of the 3,000 crowd stayed on to enjoy the action.

Occasionally the weather intervened. Just before Christmas, Clapton Orient's match with Charlton Athletic had to be abandoned after 57 minutes when fog enveloped the ground. And as if all this were not enough, a London League game between Portsmouth and Aldershot had to be ended 13 minutes from time when a goalpost snapped. For clubs like Southampton, playing in the remnants of League South following the mass desertion of the London clubs and their allies, it was difficult to arrange sufficient fixtures. Midlands teams did not want to make the difficult wartime journey to the south coast, so the Saints were restricted to only five opponents: Cardiff City, Luton Town, Bournemouth, Swansea Town and Bristol City. Their league programme did not begin until the season had been under way for almost a month; by Christmas they had played only nine league games and filled in their spare Saturdays with friendly matches against army, police and naval teams. Southampton eventually managed ten league matches; Swansea Town could arrange only nine, Norwich City only eight. After the final matches were played on Christmas Day, Leicester City headed the table with seventeen games played and 26.4 points, calculated on eighteen games. Blackpool were champions of the League North first championship. The London League, of course, was still in full swing.

Just over two weeks earlier, Japan had attacked the US naval base at Pearl Harbor. This was now truly a world war. British troops bound for the Middle East were diverted to defend Singapore. Among them were many pre-war professional footballers, several of whom would never return. The garrison at Singapore surrendered on 15 February 1942. The previous day Arsenal beat Millwall 10–0. Football went on despite the deepening gloom, but the fall of the Malayan peninsula had one unexpected effect on the game, when the supply of rubber began to diminish. Controls were introduced in Britain and the manufacture of football bladders was one of the first non-essential processes to suffer. Clubs were already struggling to maintain their playing strips; now they were forced to use the same ball for several matches. Goalnets were already in short supply and in October there had been a series of incidents in the London League game between Portsmouth and Brentford at Fratton Park. After Bill Rochford had scored a second goal for Pompey, Brentford's players protested that the ball had entered the goal through a hole in the side netting. Indeed, the net was in such poor condition that the referee took the players off the pitch. Eventually they persuaded him to continue the game, but within seconds there was more controversy. Jimmy Guthrie appeared to miss a penalty kick for Portsmouth but claimed that the ball had beaten goalkeeper Sam Bartram before going clean through the net into the crowd. His protest fell on deaf ears, although Pompey still won the game. Seven months later, in a Wembley cup final, Brentford would more than avenge that league defeat.

When the qualifying competition for the League War Cup started on 27 December, there was a small but significant improvement in attendances. Once more it was clear that cup football was the real attraction, although, again, there were some scorelines which posed the question: how valid was wartime football? On 28 February, Jock Dodds scored three times inside as many minutes to record probably the fastest hat-trick of the war. More than that, Dodds scored seven times before half-time as Blackpool beat Tranmere Rovers 15–3. On the same day, Hearts' Andy Black, guesting for Portsmouth against Clapton Orient, scored half his side's goals in a 16–1 victory against a side whose stand-in goalkeeper had been hastily recruited from a nearby army base. The following Saturday, Dodds scored another 5 as Burnley were hammered 13–0, while Jack Rowley of Manchester United turned out for Wolves and scored 5 in an 11–1 defeat of Everton. There could surely have been little pleasure for anyone in such mismatches. Nevertheless, support grew steadily and on 2 May there were some remarkable attendances which rivalled many seen between the wars. At Goodison Park, where West Brom scored a surprise 5–1 win over Everton in the second leg of the League War Cup quarter-finals, over 34,000 paid for admission. At Stamford Bridge there was a crowd of 41,154 to see Arsenal and Brentford draw 0–0 in the semi-final of the London War Cup.

In the two-legged League War Cup semi-final, a total of 64,000 saw Wolves beat West Brom 7–0 on aggregate, while the replayed London semi-final drew a crowd of 37,600, who saw Brentford go through.

Wolves faced Sunderland over two games to lift the League War Cup, 6–3 on aggregate. There were 34,776 at Roker Park for the first game, 43,038 at Molineux for the second. The London final was played at Wembley, where Brentford beat Portsmouth 2–0 in front of 71,500 spectators. Jimmy Guthrie missed another penalty for Portsmouth, although this time he could not blame the shoddy condition of the goalnet. It was A.V. Alexander, the First Lord of the Admiralty, who suggested that a showpiece match between the London Cup winners and the League War Cup winners should be staged in aid of the King George's Fund for Sailors. Chelsea offered their ground free of charge, the clubs paid their own expenses, and even the Government chipped in by waiving Entertainment Tax on the gate receipts. Alas, despite glorious weather, what should have been the ultimate cup final drew only 20,174 to Stamford Bridge. Most of the crowd were supporting Brentford; day trips to London from the Midlands were difficult to arrange. Nevertheless, the fixture would become a regular feature of wartime football.

The season ended on a controversial note as far as league football was concerned. Arsenal were undisputed winners of the London League, but the Football League decided that their own 'second championship' should exclude any club that had played fewer than eighteen matches, which meant well over half the fifty-one that had taken part. Points for the rest were 'rounded up' to a notional twenty-three games played, which saw Manchester United, who had played only nineteen, declared champions. In Scotland, Rangers did a league and cup double and even managed to win the first-half-of-the-season championship of the North Eastern League in which their other team played. In July they also won the Summer Cup against Hibernian, although that victory came about through the toss of a coin after 120 minutes of football had produced no goals and only two corners apiece. Not everyone was pleased, but this was wartime and life was far from perfect.

In the summer of 1942, Britain's newspapers could report only the gloomiest war news. On 21 June, Rommel captured Tobruk and with it 35,000 British troops and a priceless array of military equipment. Winston Churchill called the defeat 'a disgrace'. The Luftwaffe had already opened a new phase of the air war, bombing Exeter, Norwich, Bath and other historic cities. On the Eastern Front, Sevastopol was under siege and the Germans poised to advance on Stalingrad. Despite some American successes, it seemed that the war in the Far East would rage on for years to come. On 29 June, however, at the Football League's annual meeting in Nottingham, Birmingham tabled a motion calling for the formation of an advisory committee for 'matters appertaining to postwar football' comprising representatives of nine clubs in full membership of the League together with three members of the competition's management committee. Birmingham's proposal was withdrawn when the management committee announced that it would seek the club's assistance in forming such a committee 'as and when it deems it necessary to do so'. The war was far from being at the stage where anyone could begin to think about what to do when peace was restored.

The League had a more pressing matter to occupy it: how to reassimilate the renegade London clubs. The dispute between the Football League and its members from London was officially settled in June, although as far back as the previous season it had been agreed that the clubs could be allowed back into the fold on the understanding that they apologised in writing and accepted a nominal fine of £10 each. It was a small price to pay for peace. In December 1941, the Football League offices in Preston had been requisitioned by the Office of Works, forcing the League to move into new premises nearby. Coupled with all the other problems of running the competition under wartime conditions, the tiny staff were already overwhelmed. Coming to an agreement with the London clubs meant one less worry. Effectively, those clubs were allowed to continue with their own competition, but under the auspices of the Football League and now known as the League South rather than the London League. The London clubs were joined by Aldershot, Brighton, Luton Town, Portsmouth, Reading, Southampton and Watford, bringing their league up to a relatively small competition of eighteen clubs each playing twenty-eight matches. The league would end on 27 February, whereupon there would be a qualifying competition of four mini leagues, the winners of which would provide the semi-finalists for the League South Cup.

In the rest of the country it was much as before: a League North of forty-eight clubs for the first part of the season; then a qualifying competition for a War Cup with matches also counting towards a second championship. The sheer size of League North meant that the competition would also revert to the fixture-making of 1939–40, with small localised groups of clubs playing each other but all games counting towards an overall table. The position of clubs in South Wales and the South West posed a particular problem because simply playing between themselves would not provide enough matches. So Bath City, from the pre-war Southern League, and two Welsh League clubs, Aberaman and Lovell's Athletic, were drafted in, making up a six-team League West with Cardiff City, Swansea Town and Bristol City. In the first half of the season they would play each other between two and four times each to give an eighteen-match programme. After Christmas they would all take part in the League North War Cup, and therefore the League North's second championship. And there would also be a League West Cup. There was a lot for supporters to keep their eyes on.

Norwich City and Bournemouth were both left out of the southern section because of the additional travelling their inclusion would have created, but there were still more clubs than ever before taking part in the Football League's wartime competitions. Aston Villa and Derby County competed for the first time and Coventry City, Birmingham and Notts County all rejoined after sitting out the 1941–2 season. All five clubs found themselves in the Midlands group and when the season kicked off on 29 August, Derby were straight into top form with a 6–1 win at Notts County. In November, however, Derby lost 8–1 at Wolves, all their opponents' goals coming from one man, the guest from Manchester United, Jack Rowley; two months later Derby themselves hit 10 goals past

Mansfield Town. On consecutive Saturdays in September, Blackpool beat Bury 9–1 and 11–1. On the next two Saturdays they beat Stockport County 6–0 and 6–2. It was going to be that sort of season again. Indeed, come 5 December, thirty-six league matches yielded 200 goals, an average of 5½ per game. The crowd at the Chelsea–Brighton encounter must have felt cheated that day: they witnessed the only 0–0 scoreline of the afternoon.

In November there was little wartime camaraderie on display at Ninian Park, where Cardiff City were playing Lovell's Athletic in a League West game. Full-blooded tackles were coming thick and fast when a section of the home crowd invaded the pitch and surrounded the Lovell's players. The referee took both teams off the field, made them shake hands with each other and then resumed the game. His actions calmed tempers both on the pitch and in the crowd, for there was no further trouble as Lovell's won 1–0. There were 3,500 spectators at Ninian Park that day, one of Cardiff's bigger attendances of the season, and overall crowd figures had shown an improvement on previous wartime seasons. The opening day had produced a total figure of around 145,000 from thirty-six games, with the biggest attendances at Villa Park (15,000), The Valley (14,000) and St James's Park, Newcastle (10,000). On Christmas Day, a crowd of 34,455 watched the Sheffield derby between United and Wednesday at Bramall Lane. By Boxing Day, when the cup qualifying matches started in the north, thirty-five games attracted well over 300,000. The average attendance had more than doubled to over 8,000 since the start of the season. Even allowing for the greater attraction of cup football and the traditional boost to attendances over the Christmas holidays, it was an illustration that the game was pulling in bigger crowds, helped no doubt by lessening dangers from the air.

Blackpool lifted the League North first championship with a record of sixteen wins and only one defeat. Not only were they the most successful team, they were probably the most attractive. Having a major RAF station nearby helped, not least when it enabled the brilliant Stoke City and England winger Stanley Matthews to play in two-thirds of their games. Lovell's Athletic, with a surprisingly strong team for a non-League club, won League West. When the fixtures in League South were completed, Arsenal sat on top of the table. In the second half of the League North season, Liverpool were the front runners, eventually winning the title from Lovell's, who were now experiencing the sort of heights they could only have dreamed about before the war. Blackpool added the League North Cup to their league title, beating Sheffield Wednesday 4–3 on aggregate. Arsenal cruised to victory in the League South Cup final, beating Charlton Athletic 7–1 at Wembley. In the final between the north and south winners, Blackpool completed a treble with a 4–2 defeat of Arsenal at Stamford Bridge. In Scotland, Rangers did another league and cup double, although their cup final victory over Falkirk came only when the game was decided on corners after a final score of 1–1. Attendances at the cup finals had given great heart to those trying to keep the game alive throughout the war. The two legs of the northern cup final had been watched by 70,000, and there were 75,000 at Wembley for the southern final, and over 55,000 to see the north–south finale.

The war news was also much more encouraging. After Montgomery's victory at El Alamein in November 1942, Winston Churchill had told the Lord Mayor's luncheon at the Mansion House, 'Now this is not the end. It is not even the beginning of the end. But it is, perhaps, the end of the beginning.' Sure enough, on 7 May, as Manchester United prepared to meet Liverpool in the Lancashire Cup final, the German army in North Africa surrendered. In January the Germans had surrendered to the Russians at Stalingrad. In the February the Americans had driven the Japanese from Guadalcanal in the Solomon Islands. The Allies were now preparing for the invasion of Sicily. Small wonder that the Football League felt confident enough to spend £36 on the purchase of a special trophy, ready for the victory that was surely now in sight. At the annual meeting of the League in June 1943, the focus was firmly on postwar plans. Everyone seemed to agree that, once peace was restored, a transitional season would have to be played while football sorted itself out.

The Football Association, meanwhile, had issued a memorandum on the problems facing the game after the war. Both the League and the FA recognised that at least one of the compromises necessary to keep the game going during hostilities had opened up an avenue down which they would rather not tread in peacetime. The guest player system was their cause for joint concern and, in July 1943, the FA attempted at least to prevent players flitting back and forth across national boundaries. Service players would not be allowed to play for clubs outside their own association unless stationed permanently in the area. Players registered with English clubs, for instance, could not play in Scotland if they were on temporary military attachment or simply on leave. The FA also made some radical suggestions for the postwar period. The appropriate government department should be approached and a central fund set up from part of the proceeds of football pools betting. The money would be used to provide football grounds, gymnasia, sports centres and recreation rooms. The association urged an increase in international football for schools, clubs and leagues, pointing out that this would be made possible by the development of air travel in the postwar world. A full-time England team manager was mentioned. Hitherto, the FA had steadfastly refused to countenance such a post, although even now their idea of an England manager was one who would 'assist' in the selection of teams rather than have sole charge. Still, it was a step in the right direction. Transfer fees were also addressed: the FA was concerned that over-inflated fees might cripple the game's finances and that a cap might work. Ivan Sharpe, editor of the *Athletic News Football Annual*, had a better idea: 'I . . . pray the day of the inflated fee is over. Club poverty – strange to relate – won't end it. The only remedy is an undefeatable ban.' Sharp also wanted a British League: 'Such a league is bound to come sooner or later.' Sixty years later we are still waiting.

The Football League, buoyed by the changing fortunes of the war, announced that its management committee, augmented by representatives of six clubs, would look at arrangements for the transitional season. Guest players would have to be phased out, there would be a Victory Cup, but no promotion or relegation, the League would institute a clearing house to oversee the payment of transfer fees still owing from 1939, and players' wages would be increased to a figure decided by the clubs 'as circumstances warrant'. Doubts, though, were expressed about reintroducing the pre-war bonus scheme. Ivan Sharpe commented, 'This is a welcome development, since the £-a-point system takes the fee all too near the field of play and makes for temper.' The most pressing matter, though, was the forthcoming season. For 1943–4, players' wartime match fees were increased from thirty shillings to £2. Winners of league and cup competitions would receive a bonus of £5, runners-up £3. The season's competitions would continue in the same format as the previous campaign; again there would be no place for Norwich City or Bournemouth, among others.

Seventy-one of the League's complement of eighty-eight clubs took part and were soon producing the usual bizarre scorelines. In September, Wrexham beat Tranmere Rovers 9–0 (Archie Livingstone scoring 7) but a week later lost 6–0 to the same opponents. By then, Wrexham supporters were already used to such results. On the opening day of the season, the Welsh club had beaten Chester 8–4, then lost 8–0 to Liverpool a fortnight later. November was a particularly good month for supporters seeking goals. Billy Price scored 7 of Huddersfield Town's 8 against Crewe Alexandra; Cyril Done also scored 7 in Liverpool's 9–0 defeat of Chester. The following week Liverpool again won 9–0, this time against Southport. Everton played four games that month, beating Tranmere 9–2 (Tommy Lawton scoring 5) and 6–2, then Crewe 8–0 (a Lawton hat-trick), and finally making a 5–5 draw with Crewe, when Jimmy McIntosh, a guest from Preston North End, scored all their goals. One week before Christmas, came perhaps the most remarkable match of the season when Lincoln City beat Notts County 8–5, all of County's goals coming in the second half, 7 of Lincoln's being scored by one man, Cyril Lello, who would star with Everton after the war. The Christmas Day matches brought yet more goals, including 9 for Northampton Town against Nottingham Forest and 8 for Coventry City against West Brom.

With the League North first championship completed, Blackpool were again the champions. They had enjoyed a superb run of home form stretching right back to Christmas Day 1941. The League North second championship was headed by Bath City and Wrexham on equal points; Wrexham claimed the title because they said they had played against a better standard of opponents, which no-one could dispute. In League West, Lovell's Athletic again topped the final table, and in the League South, which this time went through to May, Tottenham finished five points ahead of West Ham. Blackpool could not manage another league and cup double, however, losing the League North final to Aston Villa over two legs. Charlton won the League South Cup, 3–1 over Chelsea at Wembley. There had been big crowds for the later stages of the cup competitions. The second-leg quarter-finals of the northern cup saw attendances of 52,836 at Newcastle and 39,552 at Birmingham. In the second legs of the semi-finals, 48,483 assembled at Bramall Lane, and over 50,000 at Maine Road. The south final at Wembley attracted 85,000, the second leg of the north final at Villa Park a crowd of 54,824. On 20 May 1944, when Aston Villa and Charlton drew 1–1 in the north–south final at Stamford Bridge, the attendance was 38,840. People's confidence was returning and two weeks after Charlie Revell's late equaliser had saved the day for Charlton against Villa, the Allied invasion force landed in Normandy.

On 25 August 1944, the French 2nd Armoured Division entered Paris. Twenty-four hours later, British and American forces were greeted by tens of thousands of liberated Parisians. That afternoon the new football season kicked off in England with the biggest opening-day attendances of the war. At Villa Park, 25,000 watched the home side defeat Stoke City 4–0. The Sheffield derby at Hillsborough drew 20,000 fans. There were gates of 15,000 at Everton and Sunderland, and five-figure crowds also at Leicester, Portsmouth and Nottingham Forest. Attendances were bigger, the atmosphere brighter, than at any time since the Football League had closed down five years earlier. The format for what would be the last season played in wartime – although not the last 'wartime' season – was relatively unchanged from the previous two seasons. Accrington Stanley, Hull City, Port Vale and Preston North End returned to the fray but there were still no places for Bournemouth and Norwich City, nor for Plymouth Argyle, Exeter City and Torquay United, Barrow and Carlisle United, all of whom were considered too far-flung to be absorbed into the regional sections. Bournemouth's plight was particularly sad. At only 33 miles from Southampton, under ordinary circumstances the town could hardly be considered remote; but it was 33 miles too far for London's clubs, who had all the football they wanted right on their doorstep.

The annual meetings of both the FA and the Football League had been postponed until the autumn, rather than held in the immediate aftermath of D-Day, when the country was consumed by the opening of the Second Front and all the transport and logistical problems that went with it. At the League's annual meeting in October, the Post-War Planning Committee put forward its proposals both for the transitional season and for the 'normal' seasons which would follow. Everything, though, depended on the success of the Normandy invasion, and only one week after D-Day a new threat from the air had arrived. Just when Londoners were beginning to get accustomed to the RAF's supremacy in the skies, the first V1 'doodlebug' – a pilotless monoplane powered by a jet motor and carrying a 1-ton warhead – descended upon them. On 18 June 1944, one scored a direct hit on the Guards Chapel in London; the chairman of Ipswich Town was among 119 people killed. On 12 September, the first V2 rocket fell on London. Again it had a 1-ton warhead but could fly at supersonic speed, making it impossible to intercept and shoot down. By March 1945 nearly 9,000 civilians had been killed by flying bombs. The attacks created enormous panic and tens of thousands of people left the capital, but despite the threat of death and destruction raining down on the South East, the 1944–5 football season continued. The 'spotter' system was used again, although what use it was against the V2 in particular is hard to imagine. West Ham's Upton Park was hit by a V1, which severely damaged the pitch and terracing. Fortunately there was no match in progress, otherwise the loss of life would have been catastrophic.

The committee planning football's postwar future had every reason to temper its suggestions with a large dose of caution. Indeed, Britain entered 1945 in low spirits. After the D-Day landings, everyone was hoping that the war might be over by Christmas – that phrase again – but far from that, in December the Allies had suffered a serious reverse following a German counter-offensive in the Ardennes. The Battle of the Bulge began on 16 December. That same foggy day, at Stamford Bridge, a crowd of 24,492 saw Chelsea lose 2–0 to Brentford. Despite the doodlebugs, the first half of the football season was progressing to its close. A week later, Huddersfield Town, far outside the range of any secret weapon the Nazis had invented, won League North, while Cardiff took League West. The southerners played on until May, when Tottenham were again confirmed as champions with West Ham runners-up. By then Chelsea had won the League South Cup, the Wembley final against Millwall attracting 90,000 spectators. Derby would take the League North second championship, and Bolton Wanderers the northern cup, on aggregate from Manchester United. More importantly, the last of the flying bombs had buried itself in a Hertfordshire sewage farm at the end of March, Hitler had committed suicide at the end of April, and the Post-War Planning Committee could begin its work in earnest.

On 9 May, several clubs arranged matches to mark VE Day, which had been celebrated twenty-four hours earlier. Most of the games were local affairs – Derby and Nottingham Forest, Newcastle and Sunderland, Sheffield United and Sheffield Wednesday – although Aston Villa made the unusually long journey to Portsmouth. At Derby, magistrates fined a coal merchant for 'misuse of petrol'. His crime? He had driven his son to the Baseball Ground to watch Derby County. Another local tradesman had employed a foolproof idea throughout the war: transporting a piano from Belper to Derby and back every time the Rams played at home. Had the police stopped him, he had the perfect excuse: he was delivering a piano. The law never challenged him, but the piano covered hundreds of wartime miles, just in case. Harold Bell, whose long career with Tranmere Rovers began in wartime, remembered a similar incident when the entire Tranmere team were transported by furniture van: 'It was a funny thing travelling in the war because you weren't allowed petrol and couldn't have coaches. We had a chap on the committee whose job involved moving furniture about. He brought this wagon one day when we were playing at Chester. There were no seats or anything. We all got in with our bags and were dropped in an isolated part of Chester and then walked in as though we'd come on the train.'

The final match of the season came on 3 June 1945 at Stamford Bridge, where Bolton Wanderers beat Chelsea 3–1 in the fourth north–south cup final of the war, a match which the north had never lost, incidentally. It had already been announced that 1945–6 would be a transitional season. The FA Cup would return but the Football League would be run on a regional basis for one last time. Normal football, the kind interrupted by Hitler in 1939, would pick up the pieces on 31 August 1946. It already seemed an awfully long time since spectators had first been told what to do 'in the event of an air raid'.

4

WHO'S PLAYING TODAY?

You never knew which team was which because blokes were coming
home on leave and then couldn't get . . . I've been at Goodison and it's
come over the Tannoy: 'Any footballers in the crowd?' Some fans used
to go to the game with their boots.

Harold Atkinson, Tranmere Rovers

'So to tomorrow's semi-finals with the Fulham–West Ham
clash the greatest wait-and-see match of any consequence
ever played. What with some of the players in the army and others
of them in the national workshop effort, there's no way of
knowing just what a bunch of lads is likely to trot on to that field.'
The *Daily Express* of 31 May 1940 neatly summed up the
problems facing those responsible for selecting football teams
during the Second World War. Five years later, the war almost at
an end, the situation was no better, even for matches of great
consequence. On 7 May 1945 Chelsea, with eight guest players,
met Millwall, who fielded four, in the Football League South Cup
final at Wembley. Between them Millwall's four guests – Sam
Bartram and 'Sailor' Brown (both Charlton Athletic), Stan
Williams (Aberdeen) and George Ludford (Spurs) – had totalled
only eighteen appearances for the Lions that season, and Bartram
and Brown had each played only once before. Three of Chelsea's
guests – John Harris (Wolves), George Wardle (Exeter City) and
Danny Winter (Bolton Wanderers) – could be classed as semi-
regulars, but Ian Black (Aberdeen), George Hardwick
(Middlesbrough), Leslie Smith (Brentford), Len Goulden (West
Ham United) and John McDonald (Bournemouth) had managed

only thirty-one appearances between them. Smith and Goulden were making their debuts; Smith would never play for Chelsea again.

It was enough to make *Sunday Express* reporter Frank Butler almost apoplectic: 'Chelsea won the League Cup South yesterday, beating Millwall before 90,000 in the craziest and poorest final ever staged at Wembley. This final became a farce more than a week ago when both clubs began competing to secure star players from other clubs. The result was that Chelsea won this lease–lend cup final with only three of their own players. Millwall had seven local players and four guests. Blame it on the war if you like, because it just couldn't happen in normal times – 90,000 people, including the King and Queen, flocking to Wembley to see Third Division football. If this game had been staged on the Millwall or Chelsea grounds before perhaps 15,000 it would have passed a crowd in not too critical a mood, but for Wembley it became a misfit . . . There were long periods when there just wasn't a single cheer. There were so many strangers on the field that perhaps the fans didn't cheer because they couldn't recognise the players!'

The irony was that while on the one hand Butler was criticising Chelsea and Millwall for chasing star players for the cup final, on the other he was complaining about the poor standard of football in the Wembley showpiece. It appeared that this pursuit of outside talent had not been entirely successful. Nevertheless, by the time of the 1945 'lease–lend' cup final there had been hundreds of examples of clubs conducting an undignified scramble for star guests to boost their chances and their gate money. Peter Lockett was 8 years old in December 1939 when word got out that Stanley Matthews was to play for Lockett's local club, Crewe Alexandra, that Saturday. 'At the time, the average attendance at Gresty Road was about 1,500 but when people heard that Matthews was playing against Manchester City, the interest was enormous. There were over 5,000 there. I was given a shilling to go to the match, which covered my bus fare, admission and a programme. It was amazing to see Stan Matthews playing in a Crewe shirt.' In peacetime Crewe were a Third Division club; being able to field a player of the calibre of

Stoke City's England winger was an impossible dream. In wartime it seemed that anything was possible.

It has to be said that whatever the ethics of clubs trying to improve their fortunes by importing star players each week, without the guest system organised football would have collapsed almost immediately. The problem was that while it had been introduced of necessity to keep the leagues running, some clubs were using it to give them an even greater advantage. Securing star guests, often at the expense of a club's younger, less-experienced registered players, was hardly in keeping with the spirit of the arrangement. Arnie Grace was in his late teens and playing amateur football when Derby County noticed him; but even though they were keen to sign him as a professional, he was quickly cast aside every time an experienced guest was available: 'Local lads were the last to be considered for team selection. Many's the time that, having been already selected, come half-past-two on a Saturday afternoon, a stranger would be brought into the dressing-room and I'd be quietly asked to step outside and told that I'd have to stand-down in order to give the stranger a game. It didn't help when the teams were announced before the game and when the names of local lads were read out, there were always loud groans of disappointment and boos from the crowd.'

Some clubs, usually the smaller ones, were habitual offenders; a handful, better off for top talent in the first place, tried to do without guests. When the war ended, it was claimed that Aston Villa had used only three guest players throughout the conflict. Vic Potts, from Doncaster Rovers, later joined Villa on a proper transfer, but Dicky Davis of Sunderland made the most impact with eleven hat-tricks between 1940 and 1943. The other Villa guest was Bob Scott of Wolves. Northampton Town and Aldershot, meanwhile, regularly turned out teams made up entirely of guest players. In Aldershot's case it was almost inevitable. The Hampshire club had on its doorstep a huge military base which included the Army School of Physical Training. Upon the outbreak of war, dozens of professional footballers enlisted in the school through a scheme devised by the Football Association. Thus Third Division Aldershot could call upon the likes of Joe Mercer, Tommy Lawton and Cliff Britton, all of Everton, Wilf Copping and Eric Stephenson of Leeds United, Frank Swift of Manchester City, Stan Cullis of Wolves, Liverpool's Matt Busby and Jimmy Hagan of Sheffield United. This was how little Aldershot could boast the famous half-back line of Mercer–Cullis–Britton, considered by many to be the finest of all time. Northampton's use of guests – in 1941–2 alone, two-thirds of their players came from the ranks of other clubs – produced an interesting character. In January 1944 they gave a chance to young man called Hess, of all names, who claimed to have played for one of Austria's leading clubs before the war. He turned out on the right wing in a 3–0 defeat at Walsall. He was quite awful but Northampton were stuck with him for the whole 90 minutes. Then they said their farewells and Herr Hess disappeared from Northampton Town's history quicker even than he had entered it.

Northampton were not the only club so duped. In the chaos of wartime football there were plenty who saw an opportunity to earn a few extra shillings; for others it was simply the chance to play in exalted company. And in the days before substitutes – always assuming that an extra player could be found – managers had little option but to allow impostors to remain on the pitch. A young man turned up at Chelsea claiming to be a well-known Motherwell player. The manager, Billy Birrell, had only ten men and even though the stranger looked an unlikely footballer, Birrell had little option but to play him. After only a few minutes Birrell's worst fears were confirmed. The crowd were also quick to spot that the new man had hardly played the game. All Birrell could do was leave him on the pitch and tell the rest of the Chelsea team not to pass the ball to him. In 1941–2, Jimmy Baxter, who went on to make over 500 appearances for Barnsley and Preston North End after the war, was a young man working down the pit and playing for Dunfermline Athletic in the Scottish North-Eastern League. He trained two nights a week, learning a tremendous amount from experienced footballers like Blackpool's goalkeeper Jock Wallace and Liverpool's Jim Harley as well as future Arsenal star Jimmy Logie, all of whom guested for Dunfermline while stationed at the nearby Rosyth naval base. Baxter recalled the chaos of the guest system: 'Players would claim that they'd played for Aldershot, get in the team and earn thirty shillings, but they often turned out to be useless.'

In October 1943, the Charlton manager, Jimmy Seed, had to apologise to supporters: 'I feel that it is somewhat necessary for me to attempt some sort of apology for introducing the outside-right, Rogers, in our last home game. This player was introduced to the club as the old Arsenal–Newcastle United–Chester player. Being short of players we were forced to play this man with unfortunate consequences. I have now found out that we were hoodwinked, although his inept display was sure evidence of his inability to play. We will leave it at that.'

The guest player system also created problems among established stars. The one occasion that Derby County stuck by their young player Arnie Grace resulted in one of the most miserable afternoons of his career: 'Raich Carter, who was a great pre-war name at inside-forward with Sunderland and England, was stationed at a nearby RAF camp and was guesting regularly for Derby. He turned up with an RAF mate and insisted that he should play, but for once Derby stuck by me. Raich was furious and spent the entire afternoon making me look a fool out on the wing. In a way I admired him. He was such a great player that he could actually make a team-mate look daft by just under-hitting passes in a way that no-one else spotted. Just the opposite of Peter Doherty, who liked to help the young lads and would come back on his own to train with us.'

Irish international Doherty was livid when he was included at the expense of another:

I had a free afternoon and had gone along to watch Blackpool play Liverpool. George Kay, the Liverpool manager, asked me if I'd turn out for them and I agreed. Afterwards I found out that George Ainsley of Leeds United was expecting to play but had been left out at the last minute when Liverpool knew I was at the ground. I was furious. The guest system had to be implemented, otherwise there would have been no proper league football, but it had a lot of pitfalls. It was one of the reasons I fell out with

Manchester City. I was still managing to play the occasional game for them and one week when I knew I had a free Saturday, I sent a telegram to the manager, Wilf Wild, asking him to send the details to my home in Blackpool. When I got there I found a letter telling me that Albert Malam of Doncaster Rovers had already been selected. That was fair enough because he'd been playing regularly, but what really annoyed me was the fact that I'd made a long overnight journey to play and City wouldn't even pay my travel expenses.

Doherty lost count of the number of clubs he played for during the war: 'Many clubs used so many guests that they were hardly recognisable. Once I played for six different League clubs in little more than a week. After I was posted to a camp at Skegness, for instance, I played for Lincoln and Grimsby, switching between the two quite regularly. I can't imagine how the fans felt. Some weeks there were so many changes that it was hardly worth printing the team sheets.'

The Irishman sometimes had to miss club football altogether when military duties called: on 13 November 1943, the *Daily Express* reported, 'Lincoln have to do without guest Doherty, who is playing for the RAF in a "Warships" match at Skegness.' So did others. In January 1943 it was reported that the RAF versus National Police match at Upton Park was causing real problems for London clubs. Chelsea, for instance, had George Hardwick, Frank Soo and Billy Liddell playing for the RAF, and Dick Spence for the police team. Ironically, the first three named were only guesting for Chelsea in the first place. Meanwhile, Blackpool's good fortune in having an RAF camp full of first-rate professional footballers on their doorstep backfired on Easter Monday 1942, when they were due to play Manchester City in the first round of the War Cup knockout stage. Blackpool were favourites to win the trophy but a military order banning servicemen from leave over the holiday weekend meant that ten of the Seasiders' team, all RAF personnel, were unable to play. Only goalkeeper Alex Roxburgh, who was in the National Fire Service, was available. Later in the season it was

Blackpool who benefited when Everton could not raise a side for the Lancashire Cup semi-final, Blackpool receiving a bye into the final. Raich Carter and Peter Doherty were prime examples of how wartime football affected some clubs' postwar fortunes. Both men were guesting for Derby County; luckily for Derby both fell out with their respective clubs and so the Rams were able to sign them permanently. Carter commented later, 'You could say it was the war that won the FA Cup for Derby County.'

The war also hastened the development of young players, even if spectators hoping for star guests groaned in disappointment when the names of local lads were announced. Leicester boy Jack Smith was working at an electrical factory and playing amateur football when the war started. In 1940–1, at the age of 17, he found himself in Leicester City's first team, playing inside-right to a little right-winger called Billy Wright, whose own club, Wolverhampton Wanderers, had closed down for that season. Smith, of course, had no idea that his right-wing partner would one day win a record number of England caps from the half-back line:

A lot of the Leicester players had joined up and that gave opportunities to youngsters like me. I made my debut in May 1940, against Wolves, and managed to score twice, but my best memory was playing against Stanley Matthews in a snowstorm at Stoke. It was beyond my wildest dreams to play against someone like him and I had the war to thank for it. I was just a baby really. The biggest problem was getting time off to play. I was working three shifts and it was awkward, especially for away games or early evening matches at the beginning and end of the season. Eventually I got my call-up papers and went into the Royal Navy. I was based near Southampton and got a few games for Southampton Reserves in 1944. Then I was posted abroad and played in India, against Army and RAF teams, all of which were stacked with pre-war professionals.

Henry Walters, who after the war played almost 500 games for Walsall and Barnsley, signed for the Wolverhampton Wanderers nursery club, Wath Wanderers, in 1939 when he was still at school. He was only 17 when he made his first-team debut for Wolves, at Villa Park in August 1942, playing with and against players who were still his heroes. At half-time, Walters was unable to speak; he was so out of breath that he thought he would never make it to the final whistle. Later he was sent to London to work on repairing bomb-damaged property. It was his first experience of staying away from home. He had to work on Saturday mornings, shoring up derelict buildings in the East End, and then made his way to guest for Clapton Orient, his boots and shinpads carried in a Gladstone bag. He was a home-loving boy, far away from his family. Football was just something that brightened up his weekends.

Wolverhampton Wanderers were ever keen to introduce young players: Billy Wright and Jimmy Mullen, two of Wolves' great postwar stars, both made debuts while still in their mid-teens. On 27 September 1941, Wolves fielded their youngest-ever first team. The average age of the side which lost 2–0 at Leicester was 17; the team's veteran was 19-year-old full-back Derek Ashton. Almost exactly a year later, on 26 September 1942, Wolves included Cameron Campbell Buchanan, barely 14 years old, against West Bromwich Albion. Buchanan, the youngest-ever footballer to compete in a first-class competitive match in Britain, came from a Lanarkshire mining village. In October that year the FA told Wolves that, while they were not in the wrong to play him, it was surely not in the best interests of a boy so young to take him so far from his home to play football. Buchanan did not play again for Wolves until April 1944 and never appeared for them in peacetime, although he did enjoy a reasonable career with Bournemouth in the early 1950s. A few of the youngsters given an early opportunity because of the war did go on to prosper spectacularly after it. Nat Lofthouse was in the Bolton Wanderers first team in March 1941 when he was only 15 years and 207 days old. Lofthouse, who scored twice that afternoon, went on to become one of England's greatest players. So did Tom Finney, the plumber's apprentice who came through Preston North End's visionary youth scheme. When Preston achieved a league and cup double in 1940–1, Finney, barely 18 years old, was the only player to appear in every match. Unlike Lofthouse, however, Finney was not too far off the Preston first team anyway. After signing as a part-time professional in January 1940, he played regularly for the next two seasons before being called up.

For others, football meant simply an extra wartime wage, not something which would replace a secure job in peacetime. In November 1942, Ken Teasdale was working as a postman when Bradford City asked him to play in goal for them. For the next three seasons he was their regular goalkeeper, often having to change his shifts in order to play. 'For home games I'd work from five in the morning until one o'clock. For away matches I switched to nights, which often meant arriving in Bradford just in time to go back to work. In the beginning I played as an amateur but after I was established, City paid me.' On the opening day of the 1943–4 season, Bradford City's amateur goalkeeper trooped off the Valley Parade pitch after a defeat by Newcastle United. As an amateur, Teasdale was entitled to have his initials before his surname in the match programme and he had noticed one amateur in the Newcastle line-up too. As they left the pitch, Teasdale asked his fellow amateur how long he had been playing for Newcastle. 'It's my first game today,' replied one J. Milburn. 'Wor Jackie' was to become one of the greatest players in the Magpies' history. Yet even playing in that company failed to encourage Teasdale to make a career out of football after the war. 'When I signed on as a part-timer I got two pounds a week which almost doubled my wage as a postman. When the war ended and the Football League started up again, City asked me to sign full-time but I had ten years in at the Post Office by then and a decent pension starting to build up. If I'd chucked it all in to play football, I'd have been out of a job within five years.' So Teasdale continued to pound the streets of Bradford and indulged his passion for football by becoming a local referee. He was taking charge of matches well into his 70s.

While full-time workers like Teasdale played football as an extra job, there was criticism of pre-war players who were found work near their clubs. In 1940 it was reported that one factory at Oldbury in the West Midlands was employing no less than eighteen West

Bromwich Albion footballers. It was not long before a question was being asked in the House of Commons as to whether these fit young men were receiving preferential treatment to keep them away from military service. And in May that year, the Secretary of State for War was being questioned in the House about the apparent ease at which professional footballers serving in the forces had been released from their units to play in the previous week's cup games. Notwithstanding that, in November 1942, George Allison, the manager of Arsenal, complained that when it came to getting players released from military duties, southern clubs got less cooperation from the armed forces than those in the north. Southend United goalkeeper Ted Hankey certainly felt so. He sneaked away from his Royal Artillery unit to play under an assumed name for the reserves against Reading and lost his sergeant's stripes when his deception was discovered. Liverpool's Billy Liddell had better luck. Posted to an RAF camp at Heaton, near Manchester, he discovered that personnel were not allowed out until 4.30 p.m. on Saturdays. Liverpool were playing Manchester City at Maine Road and when Liddell's application to be released at midday was refused, he climbed over the wall and joined up with his teammates at the railway station. Military police were checking passes outside the station but they ignored the party of footballers and Liddell, who later became a JP, got away with it.

Sometimes the manager himself had to turn out to make up the numbers. On 20 January 1940, Swindon Town found themselves with only ten men at the Aero Engines Company Ground at Kingswood for their match against Bristol City. Swindon's manager, Neil Harris, 43 years old, his previous competitive match over nine years earlier, was forced to turn out in borrowed boots too small for him. Swindon lost 5–2 and Harris lost two toenails. In November the same year, Clapton Orient manager Bill Wright had to play in goal against Queen's Park Rangers when he was three players short. Wright, a centre-half who had played only one League game before the war, would turn out several more times for Orient during wartime emergencies. In January 1941, Nottingham Forest's 43-year-old manager Billy Walker kept goal in a cup game at

Lincoln. A few weeks later, Walker, a forward who had won his first cap for England in 1921, was playing on the left wing for Forest. Yet another manager who found himself called upon to keep goal was Derby's stand-in boss, Jack Nicholas. With first choice Frank Boulton stuck in Birmingham, the Rams called on their reserve goalkeeper but he arrived at Derby bus station just in time to see the team coach disappearing up the road to Barnsley, where Nicholas, normally an outfield defender, performed valiantly and restricted the opposition to a 2–0 win.

In December 1944, Reading and Watford were both a man short for their match at Elm Park; to make matters worse, the referee had also failed to arrive. An appeal over the public address system brought forth an army cadet who volunteered to play for the home side, and even someone prepared to take charge of the game. None of the 3,000 crowd, however, fancied a game for the visitors. That left Watford's 44-year-old manager Bill Findley no choice but to play. The best days of his playing career had been with Leicester City in the 1920s. Findley had kept Watford going almost single-handedly throughout the war, when his skills as a qualified physiotherapist were also put to good use. To Bill Voisey, however, must surely go the honour of being the oldest manager forced back into action. In the same month that Billy Walker was keeping goal for Nottingham Forest, Voisey selected himself as Millwall's outside-right for their London War Cup match against West Ham United. Voisey had played in the Millwall half-back line from 1908 to 1923. During the First World War, as a sergeant in the Royal Artillery, his bravery under fire on the Western Front had earned him the MM, DCM and Croix de Guerre. At the age of 50, he was pressed back into service as a footballer when his side had only ten men for the game against the Hammers. Voisey had tried his best to manage with local players rather than enlist guests, unlike his successor, Jack Cock, who was only too ready to call upon strangers after his appointment as Millwall's manager in November 1944.

The wholesale use of guest players often bewildered spectators, and events at Northampton Town during 1940–1 were typical. In October, the team that Northampton selected to play at Arsenal comprised eleven guests, but when two failed to turn up, Town were forced to include two of their own players. One of them, Bill Barron, scored a hat-trick in Northampton's 5–4 defeat. The following month, when Arsenal were the visitors to the County Ground, the Northampton manager, Tom Smith, received a telephone call to say that four of his players were still in Rugby and were hiring a taxi. Smith decided to begin the game with only seven men but when the missing quartet had still not appeared by half-time, he made an appeal for any professional footballers in the crowd. The second half started with Pursglove of Barnsley, Towl of Hull City, Hart, a Northampton junior, and Bob Pryde, the Arsenal twelfth man, making up the side. Alas, the damage had already been done. Arsenal were leading 7–0 at the interval; with Northampton up to strength, the game ended 8–1. The previous season, John Pritchard of Manchester City played against Northampton for Leicester City, and seven days later scored Northampton's winner against Luton. Such events, becoming commonplace all over the country, moved one Northampton supporter to say later, 'It was great seeing all these internationals but I never accepted any of them as a Cobblers player because they could play for you one match and against you the next.' Getting suitable guest players on to the field was not always easy, however, even if they themselves were desperate to play. In October 1940, York City wanted to field Aberdeen's Andy Cowie in their home game against Rotherham United. Aberdeen, who had pulled out of the Scottish wartime league for 1940–1, agreed provided York insured the player for £5,000; the English club decided to look elsewhere for a right-back.

The influx of Allied servicemen and refugees from other nations gave English clubs an early taste of foreign footballers. Dazajna Stankowski, a Polish goalkeeper, played for Brighton. Another Pole, an airman called Pawlaw, played a few games for Lincoln City in 1944–5, scoring the winning goal in a 5–4 victory over Notts County in September. A forward from the Belgian Army, Ed De Busser, scored on his debut for Queen's Park Rangers, against Chelsea in August 1943, while another Belgian Army player, Hadelin Yielleyoye, appeared for QPR against Tottenham in

December that year. Emilio Aldecoa, an evacuee from the Spanish Civil War, was a regular with Wolves for two seasons. He later played for Coventry and Barcelona, was capped for Spain, and returned to the Midlands to work with Birmingham City in the 1960s. The J. Scott Lee who played wartime games for Everton was a Chinese graduate of Manchester University. Southampton had two Spaniards on their books when the war started. Raymond Perez and Sabin Barinaga were both Basque refugees who arrived in England in 1938 and appeared in the Saints' nursery team. Sixteen-year-old goalkeeper Perez made three first-team appearances in the Football League South 'C' Division in 1939–40. At the end of the season both men returned to Spain. In 1943–4, Reading gave a debut to Od Rojahn, a Norwegian serviceman who had been picked out after playing in a services match at Elm Park. In Scotland, two Polish servicemen, Alfons Lesz and Feliks Staroscik, impressed enough to begin full-time professional careers after the war, with St Mirren and Third Lanark respectively. Lesz began his wartime football career in Scotland with Forres Mechanics in the Highland League and newspaper reports of the time often referred to him simply as 'the Polish outside-left'. There was difficulty with the names of several Polish players in the area.

The most famous example of a foreign player making a name for himself in Britain after the war is that of Bert Trautmann, a paratrooper who was captured near the Dutch border shortly after D-Day. In June 1945 he was moved to a POW camp at Ashton-in-Makerfield in Lancashire and began playing for the camp team. In 1948, Trautmann signed for St Helens, later marrying the club secretary's daughter, and a year later Manchester City saw him as the natural replacement for Frank Swift, their England goalkeeper who was on the verge of retirement. Trautmann overcame considerable, and understandable, prejudice from City's Jewish supporters to become one of the greatest names in the club's history. In October 2004 he was awarded an honorary OBE for his work in fostering Anglo-German relations through football.

Trautmann, though, did not play in wartime Britain, when it was the truly bizarre events that perhaps best encapsulated the problems of getting eleven decent players on to the pitch. In December 1940, Manchester United entertained Blackburn Rovers in a North Regional League game at Stockport. Blackburn turned up with only seven men, and four spectators were recruited to complete their team, the criterion for selection being based, not on footballing ability, but on possessing the correct size of feet to fit the available boots. At least one stand-in appeared never to have played the game before and, not surprisingly, United won 9–0. On Christmas Day 1941, Bristol City set off in three cars to play Southampton at The Dell. By kick-off time, only the car carrying the kit and two players had arrived. The match eventually kicked off one hour late, with the Bristol team completed by five Southampton reserves, the Saints' trainer and three spectators. Twenty minutes into the game, the missing Bristol players arrived, crammed into one car. The other vehicle had broken down en route. At half-time Southampton were winning 3–0 and one of the spectators in the Bristol team decided that he could not carry on. City decided to slip on one of the late arrivals, Ernie Brinton, who changed into the dirty kit and rubbed mud on his knees before trotting out for the second half. Within seconds of the restart, a linesman spotted the ringer and Brinton had to leave the field. In the circumstances it was surprising that Southampton won by only 5–2. In September 1944, when that season's League South champions, Tottenham Hotspur, played at Reading, their goalkeeper, Harry Dukes, a guest from Norwich City, had to run all the way to Elm Park from the railway station. The previous week, the entire Fulham team had to walk from the station to the Reading ground when no transport was available.

Very occasionally an unlikely hero would emerge from the ranks of those who had come only to watch. In November 1941, Sergeant Major Bill Bryson, a member of the army's Aldershot-area team, came out of the crowd at Ewood Park to score the winner for Blackburn Rovers against Burnley. Harry Hunt, a player from the local RASC depot, scored on his debut for Sheffield United against Sheffield Wednesday on the opening day of the 1944–5 season. In September 1943, a young marine called Arthur Shepherd scored 6 goals for Liverpool against Wrexham; in 1945–6 Shepherd was guesting for Wrexham and after the war scored 10 goals in thirty Third Division North games for New Brighton. In January 1944, a young forward called Cuthbert Tatters was drafted into the Everton team to meet Liverpool at Anfield. Tatters had played once previously, against Chester earlier in the month, but against Everton's fiercest rivals he had a brilliant game, helping his side to a 4–1 victory. Jim King, later chairman of Everton's supporters' club, regarded him highly: 'One of the finest players I ever saw play for Everton was an inside-forward called Cuthbert Tatters. It was at Anfield and this lad came out. He was only small and he looked nothing, but when he got the ball he turned Liverpool inside out. No-one's heard of him since.'

For those who had been selected, just getting to the ground in the first place often proved an ordeal. In March 1945, Charlton Athletic goalkeeper Sam Bartram, guesting for York City while serving in the RAF at Harrogate, decided to thumb a lift to a game at Hartlepool. It was snowing heavily and eventually a fire engine picked him up, but Bartram arrived at the Victoria Ground to find that the game had started without him. It was an awful lot of trouble to go to, just to be a spectator. In October 1941 Tommy Olsen, who had enjoyed a good career with Swansea Town before being transferred to Bury just before the war, made a superhuman effort to get to Gigg Lane in time to play against Oldham Athletic. After hitching lifts from seven different lorry drivers, he arrived moments before kick-off, pulled on his kit and scored twice in Bury's 5–0 win. A week later, full-back Les Hart walked all the way from a Manchester railway station to Bury in the small hours of the morning in order to play against Burnley.

Sheffield United's party arrived at Villa Park in April 1944 for the first-leg match of their League North Cup semi-final, to discover that they were a star man short. England's Jimmy Hagan had just arrived at Birmingham's New Street station, his train having suffered one of those inevitable wartime delays. Hagan hurried out of the station to find the taxi rank deserted and long queues for the trams. Eventually he persuaded the conductor of a tram already full to capacity to take him as near to Villa Park as it could. He had to walk the last 2 miles to the ground, but late in the game it was Hagan's magic that gave United hope when they pulled 2 goals back after trailing 3–0. When Southern League Yeovil and Petters United – later to become Yeovil Town – arranged a wartime Boxing Day friendly match against a strong Royal Marines team from Exmouth, it attracted a large holiday crowd. An hour after the scheduled kick-off, however, there was no sign of the visitors and most of the angry spectators drifted away. Then a military lorry turned the corner and out fell the Marines team, much the worse for wear after overindulging in the Christmas spirit. Small wonder that Yeovil won a farcical game 9–0. Lending players to opponents could sometimes backfire. On the first day of the 1941–2 season, Brighton loaned their Scottish centre-forward, John Davie, to Queen's Park Rangers; Davie netted a hat-trick to send his regular club on their way to a 5–2 defeat. When Charlton Athletic arrived with only ten men at Elm Park in December 1944, Reading allowed centre-forward Dick Yates, who had been guesting for them from Chester, to make up the visitors' numbers. Yates promptly scored against his 'own' club, who went on to lose 3–2.

Keeping up with team changes was difficult. Beyond mentioning that a well-known name was expected to play that Saturday, local newspapers practically gave up publishing line-ups in advance. Supporters craned their necks to see the chalkboard carried around the pitch announcing the teams, and the match programmes bore much crossing-out and amendments. Sometimes fifteen or more of the names printed in the programme had to be changed. 'A.N. Other', 'S.O. Else' and 'A. Newman' made regular appearances. Even the players themselves were not always sure in which team they would be appearing, even as they arrived at the ground. In 1941, Derby County's Tim Ward, by then serving with the 15th Scottish Division, was guesting for Hamilton Academical. He was asked to fix up Tommy Lawton with a game; the England centre-forward was on a brief honeymoon in Scotland. Ward did as he was asked, but two days before the game, at Greenock Morton, he was surprised to see that Lawton was not in the team. He asked the Hamilton manager why this was; after all, he had promised Lawton a game. The answer was simple: as the game was at Morton, it would make better financial sense if Lawton played for the home side, thereby ensuring a bigger attendance. He did more than that, scoring twice against the club that had originally invited him to play.

The guest system was vital, but this free-flowing pool of players was unlike anything professional football had ever known. The freedom that footballers now enjoyed deeply troubled the League. Before the war, and up to the 1960s, players belonged to clubs in the strictest sense. The League liked to say that it was players' registrations that were owned by the clubs, not the players themselves, but the effect was the same. If a club so wished, it could keep a player on its books for ever and a day. On the other hand, if it wanted to get rid of him, he could be sold – or simply dumped at the end of the season. That much had not changed, but the game's rulers hated to see footballers swanning around the country, playing for this club one week, that club the next. It was the one thing that they were determined to eliminate just as soon as it was practical. Back in August 1940, Stanley Halsey had reported in the *Daily Express* that players living and working in England away from their registered clubs would be allowed to play elsewhere provided their club gave permission and the player's temporary move was reported to League headquarters: 'This means that the League, without inflicting hardship, will be able to compile a "Who's Who" in soccer and curb the nomadic nonsense which blotched last football season . . . Moreover, the player will have to stay – except in special humane circumstances – with the club to which he has been temporarily transferred. The day of the "flitterbug" is over.' It did not quite work out like that.

5

SPOILS OF WAR

After the war, the Inland Revenue came down on me for tax on money I was supposed to have been paid by Derby for playing when I was hundreds of miles away. So there was something dodgy going on in wartime as well.

Jack Stamps, Derby County

In the summer of 1939, after a season throughout which they had been haunted by the threat of relegation, First Division Brentford paid £12,000 to strengthen their team. Goalkeeper Frank Clack came from Birmingham, full-back Jimmy Anderson from Queen of the South, wing-half Tom Manley from Manchester United, and inside-left Percy Saunders from Sunderland. Although gate receipts had dropped by £1,500 in 1938–9, the Bees still had a surplus of almost £16,000 on that season's transfer dealings. Spending most of it on strengthening their playing staff in order to avoid another relegation fight in 1939–40 seemed a sensible idea. The new players were all in their mid-twenties and all had several years of football ahead of them, or so it seemed. There was one vital flaw in Brentford's thinking: it ignored the fact that the world was on the brink of war and there had been times in 1938–9 when the season seemed unlikely to reach its conclusion. By the time the Bees played their first home game of the following season, that war was only twenty-four hours away. The visit of Huddersfield Town on 2 September 1939 attracted a crowd of barely 13,000 spectators, the club's lowest-ever attendance for a First Division match. Neither Clack nor Anderson played again for Brentford in peacetime; neither did Saunders, who lost his life in 1942 while trying to escape the

Japanese. Only Manley reappeared for the Bees after the war. Brentford would never see a return on their 1939 investment in new talent and by Christmas 1940 the club's very future was in doubt. Gate receipts had tumbled to around £40 a match and only 400 people had watched the visit of West Ham United in November. Ersatz football, played when the air raid warning siren was likely to pierce the air at any time, was threatening the existence of dozens of football clubs. Brentford were one of those most at risk.

Two unconnected developments eventually eased the West London club's financial plight. The Battle of Britain was won and the daylight raids that had so disrupted Saturday-afternoon football came to an end. Attendances increased as a result. On a more mundane note – but one which had a significant effect on football's finances – cup football was introduced. The idea of knockout matches following a qualifying league appealed to supporters. More important still for Brentford, they were quite good at it. The Bees reached the final of the London War Cup in 1942, before a crowd of 71,500 at Wembley. Brentford's share of the gate receipts from the semi-finals and final had rescued them. By 1945–6, the club's average attendance was around 15,000 and, although their financial situation was far from stable, they had survived to enjoy the postwar soccer boom which lay ahead.

Brentford's story is fairly typical of the financial plight in which many clubs found themselves during the Second World War: it started badly and slowly got better. Swansea Town lost £5,452 on the 1939–40 season 'wholly due to the outbreak of war'. Their debit balance was fourpence short of £10,500, and their bank overdraft – secured by the club's assets and directors' guarantees – stood at £18,399. In 1947 it was reported that Swansea were 'without any of the old bank overdraft', despite spending most of the war out on a geographical limb in the Football League West. Thanks to some inspired transfer dealing, not least the sale of star centre-forward Trevor Ford to Aston Villa for £10,000, and hugely increased attendances as the transitional season of 1945–6 in the League South progressed, the Welsh club had also survived intact. For Blackpool, the war was responsible for wiping out their bank overdraft of £33,704. The rent paid by the War Office for the use of Bloomfield Road, and the Seasiders' playing success, which brought in big crowds for league matches and a share of several cup final takings, helped the club to become solvent once more. By 1947, Blackpool could afford to spend £11,500 to bring their star wartime guest, Stanley Matthews, permanently to Bloomfield Road.

Towards the end of the 1939–40 season, Charlton and Fulham could attract only 776 spectators to The Valley – the absentees would rue missing a 7–5 home win – and when Charlton entertained the FA Cup holders, Portsmouth, only 895 spectators felt it worth turning out to watch. Given the admission fee of 1*s* 3*d*, and that children and servicemen were getting in for half-price, neither game would have yielded as much as £25 in gate receipts. Less than a year later, Charlton's average attendance was down to below 500 and average receipts around £15. Progress to the 1943 League South Cup final against Arsenal brought in a welcome cheque for almost £3,000 as Charlton's share of the takings. Blackburn Rovers had a similar tale to tell. Thanks to their share of the 1940 War Cup final and the rent from hiring out Ewood Park, they showed a profit of £334 where they would otherwise have posted a big loss. By 1942 the club was still £22,000 in debt, however. The first season of the war was always going to be difficult. No-one knew what to expect from the new regional leagues, the problems of raising teams, and the huge difficulties, both for players and supporters, in travelling to games. That one of the worst winters in living memory then descended on Britain served only to worsen an already dire situation and there were stark warnings from boardrooms around the country. In 1939, Exeter City's chairman had told supporters, 'Unless something drastic happens I cannot see how this club is to continue. Unless we get some assistance we shall have to put up the shutters.' Because of their geographical position, Exeter did indeed put up the shutters, for five years.

In February 1940, Reading were being asked to repay a £4,000 loan guaranteed by the former board of directors. In April, the Midland Bank threatened to wind up the club, but a saviour appeared in the shape of chairman Bill Lee, who agreed to take over the guarantees. A loss of £1,882 on the season led to suggestions that the club should close down, but the Reading faithful soldiered on. At a home game in 1942, the club's junior players staged a collection which raised 280 clothing coupons to obtain kit. In June 1940, the *News Chronicle* reported that a meeting of Leicester City shareholders and loanholders heard that the past season had been 'disastrous', resulting in a £7,000 loss. The meeting decided that all accrued interest should be cancelled and all loans be interest free for the duration of the war, except certain loans from players. Large creditors were being asked to 'forget' about their claims until after the war. The previous month Swindon Town had reported a loss of £2,500. Other losses on the 1939–40 season included Port Vale (£2,000), Sheffield United (£6,440), Bury (£4,309), Middlesbrough (£8,000), Aston Villa (who did not play – £11,751) and York City (£435). For many clubs this was the picture throughout the war, although by 1941–2 Bury were doing better, losing only £495. Nevertheless, the final home game of the season, despite being against attractive neighbours Bolton Wanderers, saw an attendance of only 1,222 at Gigg Lane. That season Bury's illustrious Lancashire neighbours Manchester City lost £1,688. In 1943, Port Vale, now over £5,000 in debt and with the executors of their late president calling in debentures of £3,000, appealed to the FA for help. The same year, Wolves announced that they had lost nearly £25,000 since 1939. By 1946, Manchester United, with no ground and no manager for the previous seven years, had a £15,000 overdraft. In 1943–4, Arsenal lost £4,514 and had an overdraft of £25,000. At the same time the Gunners' landlords, Tottenham Hotspur, made a profit of £3,848. Gate receipts at White Hart Lane were £27,000 in 1943–4, although Entertainment Tax claimed £9,000 of that.

In any era, success on the field brings financial rewards and after Preston North End did the wartime league and cup double in 1940–1, they turned a loss of almost £11,000 the previous season into a profit of £2,500. As with Brentford the following season, the War Cup helped Preston's finances, and indeed those of many clubs. Every club which took part had an equal share of the cup pool, which rose from £160 per club in 1939–40 – a 'nest egg' was how the *News Chronicle* described it – to over £400 by 1944. The most successful clubs also shared bigger and bigger gate receipts as they progressed through the competition. The 1945 League South Cup final between Chelsea and Millwall at Wembley realised £26,000. Each club received £4,000, as did the cup pool, and £2,000 went in expenses. The real winner, however, was the Government, pocketing £12,000 in the hated Entertainment Tax which by that stage scooped up a swingeing 45 per cent of gate receipts. Introduced as a 'wartime measure' in 1917, the tax had been a huge thorn in football's side throughout this second war. Indeed, it was to last much longer than that, until 1957 when it was abolished. Reaching cup finals was one way of improving finances but there were other success stories, and some surprising ones at that. In 1942, Walsall, a pre-war Third Division South club, made a profit for the first time since 1921, thanks largely to being included in a regional division with their bigger, more glamorous neighbours. They not only enjoyed higher attendances at Fellows Park but also took a share of bigger gate receipts when they played away from home. In the North East, Gateshead, who had played in the Third Division North before the war, now enjoyed regular league matches against the likes of Newcastle United, Sunderland and Middlesbrough. In 1942, Gateshead made a profit of more than £1,500, as much as that of Newcastle.

For others, too, the tide began to turn. Beginning with a modest £27 in 1940–1, for York City five of the seven wartime seasons produced a profit. York reached the 1943 League North Cup semi-final, twice breaking Bootham Crescent's wartime attendance record along the way. Gross receipts from eight cup games were £9,156 and the year's profit £2,188. Reading's 1943 annual meeting heard that a profit of £782 had been made. Reading had received £389 from the Football League pool, and although they had contributed £425 to it in the first place, manager Joe Edleston described it as 'a very fair and democratic arrangement'. In 1940–41, Swindon, despite not playing, made a profit of £361, and small profits followed, although towards the end of the war the club's overdraft still stood at £1,045. Occasionally a club was fortunate enough to have wealthy benefactors to hand. When Ipswich Town, who had closed down on the outbreak of war, held their annual meeting in January 1943, they reported a loss of £1,080 on the year ended 31 May 1941 and a further loss of £1,070 for the following twelve months, leaving the club with an overall debt of £14,195. The directors simply paid off the debt, with the chairman, John Murray Cobbold, picking up a lion's share of £11,195. It was either that, said Colonel Cobbold, or allow Ipswich Town to go into liquidation and throw away all the years of hard work which had culminated in Football League membership in 1938. Sometimes it was left to everyday supporters to pitch in. In 1945, Exeter City still showed a deficit of £19,000 and an appeal for £5,000 was launched 'to enable the City to make a successful comeback'. Attendances of 10,000–11,000 in 1945–6, and the sterling work of a newly formed supporters' club, which at one stage was raising £1,000 a month, helped Exeter back on the road to recovery.

For two League clubs, their grounds posed differing challenges. Hull City were facing financial oblivion before the war when, in 1938, the resignation of the chairman and a fellow director reduced the club's guarantors, making the bank extremely nervous about Hull's £8,500 overdraft. The crisis was averted when several new directors were appointed, but meagre attendances in the early days of the war exacerbated the situation. When Barnsley were Hull's visitors in December 1940, the gate receipts amounted to only £27. In 1941, their ground out of commission, Hull decided to close down for the duration. There was a brief revival on a local rugby league ground in 1944 but it was the end of the war that saw a virtual rebirth of the club, with a new ground and new owners in the shape of the Needler family. With their purpose-built stadium and massive support, Hull City were indeed one club which rose from the ashes of war. In 1940, Bristol Rovers, with liabilities of £20,000, sold their Eastville ground for £12,000 to the greyhound racing company that had hitherto rented it. The club then decided to close down until normal football could be resumed. When, in the summer of 1942, the greyhound company urged them to enter a team in the Football League West – they would even meet the club's financial obligations for 1942–3 – Rovers said no. In September 1944, two members of the greyhound company joined the Rovers board, with a cash injection of £3,000, and doubling the share capital. But even after selling their ground, Rovers still owed £600 to the bank, £700 to other creditors and £4,700 to directors and supporters who had loaned them money. Another £1,000 was lost on an aborted revival for 1944–5. Eventually the two directors of the ground's new owners became chairman and vice-chairman of the football club and many of the loans were written off by lenders who had the club's best interests at heart.

By 1945, with a new dawn being heralded in the nation's affairs, football shared in this renewed public confidence. Supporters began flocking to matches again, the FA Cup returned and the uncertainty of the wartime game was fast disappearing. In 1945–6, after transferring Tommy Lawton to Chelsea for £11,500, Everton made a profit of £21,557. Aston Villa's profit was £18,185; over 850,000 people watched football at Villa Park that season. Bury's attendances were up considerably, helped by an FA Cup run which brought 13,248 to one tie against Rochdale. Bury ended the season with a bank balance of £1,752. The following season, the first postwar campaign, Huddersfield Town announced a profit of £21,542, due mainly to record season ticket sales. By 1946 many football clubs were in better shape than at the beginning of the war. There had been a dramatic increase in attendances but overheads, particularly players' wages and travelling expenses, had not caught up. When Aston Villa met Derby County in the sixth round of the revived FA Cup in March 1946, a record crowd of 76,588 paid £8,651. That week's wage bill covering the twenty-two players on the pitch was less than £200. The transfer market was also swinging back into action; in August 1945, Chelsea paid West Ham United £4,500 for the former England inside-forward Len Goulden, who had been a guest player at Stamford Bridge. More players would move as the last wartime season unfolded.

All this signalled the start of a boom which would last for the remainder of the decade, and by 1948–9, more than 41 million people would pay to watch League matches in England. If the war had done one thing for football, it had created an enormous appetite for the 'normal' game and the legacy would be enjoyed for several years to come. The Football League and the Football Association could both be pleased with the way that the game was recovering, but the FA, in particular, had good reason to rejoice. The organisation's many commitments had seen it lose heavily during the war's early years: £13,337 in the first season, £9,287 the following year, £3,703 in 1942. The Football League had managed a small profit each season, but still looked forward to the day when the fixture list abandoned in 1939 could be reprinted.

Whatever the problems of running the game in wartime, they had not deflected either the League or the FA from tracking down and punishing clubs who had been less than honest in peacetime. In December 1939, Crystal Palace were investigated after it was alleged that vouchers entered as directors' expenses had been used to cover up illegal payments to players, including inducements to sign for the club. Director R.S. Moyes, who had taken over as manager, and three other directors were suspended for twelve months, another director for six months, two players fined and the club secretary cautioned. In May 1940, Leicester City were found guilty of paying signing-on fees and bonuses in excess of those allowed, and of making illegal payments to amateur players. Their former manager, Frank Womack, was suspended for twelve months, while current or former directors were also banned, with the sentences ranging from one year to *sine die* suspensions. At the beginning of the following season, twelve current or former players were also suspended for twelve months. At one stage the Leicester club considered going into liquidation, its financial situation already critical even before the war halted normal football.

In August 1941, Derby County became yet another club to be punished for pre-war financial irregularities. In the 1930s, Derby had surprised football by attracting some of the country's top players in the face of competition from more glamorous clubs. In wartime their supporters discovered the reason. Manager George Jobey was suspended permanently, four directors were suspended *sine die* and a former director similarly treated. Another former director was suspended for three years and the club secretary severely censured. Derby were also fined £500. 'Under-the-counter' payments had been balanced by some inventive bookkeeping. Derby apparently did not learn from being found out. In 1949 the club was again fined and saw its directors and secretary suspended after more illegal payments were uncovered for the period from March 1945 to July 1946. Not every offence was as serious, however. In September 1942, Aston Villa were in dispute with the Football League because they were charging 1s 6d as the standard entrance fee instead of 1s 3d. They pointed out they were letting servicemen enter the ground for free instead of charging 7d. In October the club also began admitting women free. In November, the League ordered Villa to drop their price. Brighton, meanwhile, were banned from admitting servicemen free over Christmas; they got round the problem by making everyone wearing military uniform a guest of the directors.

The game had certainly made an enormous effort to look after servicemen and if clubs' finances ebbed and flowed during the Second World War, the one institution which benefited consistently was charity. As early as October 1939, a committee was formed to benefit the Red Cross and St John Ambulance organisations. Football played its part to the full, with hundreds of matches, from full-blown internationals to scratch games between service teams, raising tens of thousands of pounds for dozens of charities including Wings for Victory, the Spitfire Fund, Battleship Week, Mrs Churchill's Aid to Russia fund as well as support organisations for soldiers, sailors, airmen, merchant seamen, prisoners of war, civil defence and children's homes. In September 1941, Bloomfield Road, Blackpool, staged the first inter-league game of the war when the Football League beat the Scottish League 3–2 in front of a 20,000 crowd who contributed towards RAF charities. The England–Wales game at Wembley in February 1943 raised £12,500 for POWs and the Aid to Russia fund.

A week after England's 3–0 victory over Scotland at Wembley in January 1942, Sergeant Major Stan Cullis received a letter from Clementine Churchill: 'I am writing to thank you very much for the part you played in making the representative match at Wembley on

Saturday, 17 January such an outstanding success. The magnificent donation, which will be received by my "Aid To Russia" Appeal as a result of the match will enable the Red Cross and St John War Organisation to procure many of those supplies which are so urgently needed in Russia to alleviate the sufferings of her soldiers and civilian population.' The note always remained a treasured item in Cullis's collection of football mementoes. Representative matches at Wembley alone contributed £140,000 to war funds between 1939 and 1945, but gate receipts were not football's only contributions. The 75,000 crowd at the England–Scotland international at Wembley in October 1942 were asked to place their unwanted ticket stubs and programmes into special bins so that the paper could be recycled for the war effort. In October 1944, Aston Villa held a mock auction for the War Cup they had won the previous season. The trophy remained in the cabinet at Villa Park, but £450 was soon on its way to the Red Cross. Even a game as modest as Sunderland Police against the Gordon Highlanders raised £30 for the Mayor's Boot Fund for Children, although it should be noted that the police team enjoyed the services of the England forward Raich Carter, whose presence put a few on the gate.

As the war drew to a close, one section of football remained disaffected: the players. Cast aside by their clubs as soon as war was declared, then quickly snatched back when it was realised that there was to be some football after all, they had been paid thirty shillings a match, later to be raised to £2. Although this was now an additional wage to that which they were earning in the forces or in factories, most footballers could not forget that before the war they were being paid £8 per week in the season and £6 in the close season. When peacetime football was restored they were not prepared to return to the conditions of 1939. Players' Union activist Jimmy Guthrie described footballers as 'whipping boys'. He wrote, 'We wanted a satisfactory minimum wage, a contract dated to cover the summer months to restrain the annual blackmail of family men, larger bonuses for achievements that made money for our masters.' In 1945, the players threatened to go on strike, eventually squeezing from the clubs a rise of £1 on the old maximum weekly wage.

In December that year, an anomaly arose regarding players still in the services. They were entitled to a fee of £5 per match, whereas non-service players were on a flat weekly wage, drawing the same money no matter how many games they played. With three games in almost as many days over the Christmas holidays, players still in uniform suddenly found themselves considerably better off than their full-time teammates. It was resolved only when the service match fee was eventually abolished.

After the 1946 Budget gave clubs partial relief from Entertainment Tax, the Football League reluctantly agreed to raise the maximum wage to £10 (winter) and £7 10s (summer). It compared favourably with the lot of London's milkmen, who in June 1946 went on strike for a minimum weekly wage of £5 4s 6d, but for Guthrie the struggle was far from over. In 1948 he became the union's chairman and continued his fight both for better wages and freedom of contract. Three years earlier, in October 1945, Brentford's England winger, Leslie Smith, had signed for Aston Villa when he could have chosen a number of clubs after the Bees fancied the £7,000 transfer fee. The newly married Smith went to Villa not for what extra he could earn – this was still the era of the maximum wage – but because he could not find suitable accommodation for himself and his young wife in war-ravaged London. It was the promise of a new bungalow which lured him to Birmingham. The spoils of war came in many guises.

6

GROUNDS FOR WAR

If there was an air raid, we watched for any incendiaries dropped around the ground. Then we'd go down and put them out with buckets of sand. A big one dropped on Anfield cemetery . . . it didn't come into the ground but it shattered the glass and knocked down the cemetery wall.

Gordon Watson, Everton

On the Monday morning of 4 September 1939, with the Second World War less than twenty-four hours old, Arsenal's captain, Eddie Hapgood, made the usual trip to his place of work. The scene that greeted him, however, was far from familiar: 'Workmen were already there, with pneumatic drills roaring, making air raid shelters. Highbury was putting on its war paint.' Supporters of the north-London club were about to experience what many football followers would feel over the coming years, when the bond between them and their local club was loosened by the closure of the ground to which they made their fortnightly pilgrimage. Over the next six years of war – and, in one prominent case, well into peacetime – several clubs would lose their grounds, either because the stadiums had been handed over to the military or had suffered bomb damage. Some clubs, with nowhere to play, would close down altogether; others would share a rival's ground. In either case, supporters would feel a sense of disconnection as wartime football gathered momentum.

Arsenal's stadium was one of the first major grounds to be turned over to the war effort, when a first-aid post and an ARP centre were established there in the hours following Neville Chamberlain's broadcast. A blast wall was erected just inside the main entrance, the dressing rooms became a casualty clearing station and air raid wardens reported to their post in the Main Stand. The ARP personnel included England winger Cliff Bastin, who was excused military service because of his deafness, the Gunners' trainer Tom Whittaker and England full-back George Male, both awaiting their call-up to the RAF, and assistant trainer Billy Milne. Not surprisingly, the 'Arsenal Arps' usually won their football matches against other wardens' posts. The West Stand became a clearing centre for foreign evacuees and also an air raid shelter. Early in the war, some 1,500 people used the communal shelter and, later on, cubicles were created to allow families to sit through air raids together. Large porcelain sinks were installed under the stand so that wounded people could be washed, and a gas-decontamination room and accommodation for medical staff were also built. Arsenal even lost their nearby training pitch, which was requisitioned by an RAF barrage balloon unit. Highbury, already unavailable to Arsenal because of the war effort, was also damaged by enemy action. In October 1940, the roof of the North End was destroyed by incendiary bombs, and Milne recalled the sight of both sets of goalposts burning merrily. In April 1941, a 1,000lb high-explosive bomb scored a direct hit on the training pitch, killing two RAF men and badly damaging part of the Highbury terracing.

Arsenal, meanwhile, had decamped to White Hart Lane, where Tottenham Hotspur had rolled out the welcome mat. Spurs were returning a favour from the First World War, when the Ministry of Munitions closed their ground and turned it into a factory where 11 million gas masks were manufactured. From 1916, Tottenham had played half their games at Highbury and half at Clapton Orient's Homerton ground. In the Second World War, White Hart Lane escaped the bombing and the Gunners remained at the home of their greatest rivals for the duration. Nonetheless, Spurs' home was still put to war work. Part of the ground again became a factory producing gas masks, while the top of the East Stand was set aside for a grim task, a mortuary for air raid victims.

London's other clubs had mixed fortunes. Millwall's immediate problem once football resumed in September 1939 was to persuade the Metropolitan Police Commissioner, Sir Philip Game, to lift the potentially crippling 8,000 limit on attendances. Eventually the limit for all London grounds was raised to 15,000. Each turnstile would be issued with a limited number of tickets; when they ran out it was up to the police to decide whether to admit more spectators. The Den was badly damaged either side of the London Senior Cup final between Tooting and Mitcham United and Dulwich Hamlet, staged at Millwall on Easter Monday, 26 April 1943. In the early hours of Monday the 19th, a lone raider dropped two bombs. One fell on waste ground, the other on The Den's North Terrace, near the Old Kent Road. A half-ton crush barrier was thrown 200 yards, the terrace and part of the penalty area were cratered and debris was strewn across the pitch. The fact that the Luftwaffe had hit Millwall's North Terrace was ironic since in September 1940 the Germans had released a propaganda photograph of a Heinkel He 111 supposedly over the Surrey Docks. In fact it was a fake, given away by the lack of the North Terrace cover at The Den, which had been roofed since 1938.

Amazingly, Millwall cleared up sufficiently for the cup final to go ahead but fate had not yet finished with the club. Within 30 minutes of the final ending, the Main Stand was engulfed in flames, the likely cause being a discarded cigarette. After surviving the Luftwaffe, Millwall had been beaten by a spectator who carelessly chucked away a still-burning cigarette end. They were now forced to play home matches at The Valley, Selhurst Park and Upton Park before celebrating their return to The Den with a 5–0 victory over Portsmouth in March 1944. In November 1943, Charlton had the unhappy experience of losing 5–2 to Millwall at The Valley and, to add insult to injury, were also the 'away' team, despite playing at home. Millwall eventually received compensation from the War Damages Commission but, because of building restrictions, it was not until after the war that they obtained the licence to rebuild. In fact, work was not completed on a new Main Stand until September 1962.

Chelsea's Stamford Bridge suffered some damage, two bombs falling on the West Terrace, but the ground was never closed and football continued uninterrupted throughout the war, thanks in no small part to an act of extreme bravery – or foolishness – on the part of manager Billy Birrell. When a police constable told Birrell that the bomb disposal units were so busy that he would have to wait until after the weekend to have an incendiary removed from the terracing, the manager decided to take matters into his own hands. Birrell apparently picked up the device and moved it himself, thus saving that Saturday's fixture from postponement. The conflict also affected Stamford Bridge in another way. After years of doing little to improve a ground which had once staged FA Cup finals and full international matches, but which was now considered in desperate need of modernisation, in the summer of 1939 the Chelsea board embarked upon building a North Stand. It was an ambitious project and was originally intended to be extended to provide an upper deck to the original East Stand. But the war intervened and it was the autumn of 1945 before even the first stage was completed. Chelsea's West London neighbours, Fulham, received some damage to their Craven Cottage ground but it caused little disruption. Those parts of the ground affected by bombs falling in the surrounding area were simply roped off and spectators stood around the damage. When the pitch was hit, it was repaired within a few hours. Matches at Brentford's Griffin Park were constantly interrupted by air raid warnings; in September 1940, a delayed-action bomb fell in Braemar Road, forcing the cancellation of the Bees' match against Chelsea. By 1945, Brentford faced the first postwar season with a ground that had fallen into a state of disrepair. Some twenty-five years after the war, however, Brentford were benefiting from the conflict. In 1970, they were receiving £1,500 annually by renting out for storage the air raid shelters which had been installed at the ground during the early part of the war.

In 1939, West Ham United's landlords, the Archdiocese of Westminster, offered the club the Upton Park ground for a yearly rent of only £1; but the Hammers had to take on the responsibility for preparing the stadium for the military, who would use the forecourt for drill, and other parts of the ground for practice ranges. The arrangement was acceptable to West Ham, although the club later had to battle with the local rating authority, who had increased their valuation of Upton Park by over 50 per cent. Their ground was hit during the early days of the London Blitz and the West Stand had to be evacuated. The club set up offices in the Green Street House pub – the legendary Boleyn Castle – but all the Hammers' pre-war records had been destroyed, as had those for the first twelve years of the London FA, which had just moved into temporary offices at Upton Park. Then, in the late summer of 1944, a flying bomb fell on the south-west corner of the pitch, extensively damaging the South Bank. West Ham were then forced to play a number of their 'home' League South matches on other grounds. Later that year, when the Hammers wanted to begin repair work, the Ministry of Works refused them a licence. The club wanted to know why the local cinema up the road could be repaired but the football ground could not. They also pointed out that Clapton Orient had been given permission to roof a concrete terrace with asbestos sheeting (the dangers of asbestos as a building material were not then known). West Ham also tried to sound socially aware, pointing out that there was no covered accommodation for supporters who could afford to watch from only the cheaper parts of the ground, and the wooden terracing was deteriorating rapidly. Nevertheless, it was the autumn of 1947 before the club was finally given permission to begin repair work and improvements.

The Valley, the cavernous home of Charlton Athletic which in its pomp could hold 75,000 spectators, was hit several times in the first year of the war. After all, the Battle of Britain was being fought literally overhead and Hitler's blitz on London had started. Four bombs fell on the terraces, the penalty spot received a direct hit from one of two bombs to fall on the pitch, and an ambulance hut was destroyed. Later in the war, Charlton's North Stand received a direct hit. The ground escaped being requisitioned by the military, however, and only a small part was used as an ARP centre.

Southend United's pitch at Southend Stadium became so overgrown late in the 1939–40 season that matches were rendered almost meaningless. Perhaps the groundsman knew something. By August, the Government had decided that playing football there was too risky, given Southend's position at the mouth of the Thames. With the continued presence of warships moored off its pier, the military garrison at Shoebury and the EKCO radio factory, Southend was declared a restricted zone and many of its children were evacuated. Southend Stadium became a centre for training army officers and Southend United asked West Ham United if they could share Upton Park. The Hammers refused, claiming that this would interfere with their own junior teams; instead United went to play at Chelmsford City's New Writtle Street ground. It was only sensible since Chelmsford, who had turned professional in the season before the war, were effectively Southend's nursery team. Unfortunately, no-one told Tottenham outside-right Tom Paton, who in December 1940 turned up expecting to play at Southend Stadium, only to discover that the home team had moved 20 miles down the road. In October 1941, Southend decided to close down for the duration. They owed Chelmsford £310 in rent and were travelling long distances even for home games, and attendances were low. It was October 1944 before they played again. In the meantime, Southend Stadium had branched out from being just an army training camp. The Royal Artillery beat Southend Police in a charity match there, and then Alex James, the great pre-war Arsenal and Scotland inside-forward, who was now stationed at Shoebury, appeared in an Army v. Royal Navy match. There was a softball game in aid of Merchant Navy Week, a boxing tournament, a rugby match and a 1-mile race. But no Southend United.

As in London, where Tottenham accommodated Arsenal, Manchester was another city where the spirit of wartime cooperation between hitherto deadly rivals was a shining example to others. Manchester United felt the presence of the war at Old Trafford as early as 5 September 1939, when the military moved in. Like Arsenal, United also lost their training ground to an RAF balloon squadron when The Cliff at Lower Broughton was commandeered. Old Trafford, set in the middle of the vitally important Trafford Park industrial area, could have expected to be troubled by enemy action, and so it turned out. On 22 December 1940, United's ground suffered some damage but it was on 11

March the following year that the war took its full toll. The Main Stand was completely destroyed by one bomb, while another wrote off much of the terracing. The pitch was also rendered unplayable after it was badly scorched. United went to play their home games at City's Maine Road stadium in Moss Side – and were still doing so until August 1949. The reserve teams of United and City shared The Cliff for their Central League games, once the military had relinquished it towards the end of the war. United's offices had been relocated to the Cornbrook Cold Store, owned by the club's chairman, James Gibson.

Ironically, when it was opened in 1910, Old Trafford had been one of the great stadiums in British football, but so little money had been spent on it between the wars that by the time the Luftwaffe partially destroyed it the ground was no longer one of the Football League's outstanding venues. The War Damage Commission eventually granted United over £22,000 to remove the debris and rebuild the ground, and the club initially had dreams of a 120,000-capacity stadium; then financial realism took over and only the Main Stand was replaced. This was no quick job, however, and it was November 1944 before United were granted a licence even to remove the remains of the old stand so that work might one day begin on the new. Manchester United's tenure of Maine Road for the first three years of peacetime football set them on the road to being the number-one club in that city, according to one theory. Before the war, Manchester City had been the leading club. FA Cup winners in 1934 and League champions in 1937, City had been relegated in 1938. United, meanwhile, had won nothing of note since 1911 and had returned to the top flight only in 1938. Although City were themselves promoted in the first postwar season of 1946–7, United, under their new manager Matt Busby, the former Liverpool, Manchester City and Scotland half-back, were about to embark upon a glorious chapter in their history. Servicemen returning from the war, and young boys growing up after it, went to Maine Road week after week – but it was United, not City, who caught their imagination.

The Manchester clubs' poorer neighbours Stockport County escaped both enemy action and significant military occupation, so they could play landlords to Broughton Park rugby union club, who used Edgeley Park after their ground was taken over by the army. Wigan Athletic, then a humble Cheshire League club, saw their ground closed completely, Wigan had long harboured dreams of joining the Football League but, when the war ended, Springfield Park was in a poor state. The pitch was overgrown, major repairs were needed to the stand which ran the length of the playing area, and the popular terracing needed to be reroofed. Volunteers set to work and Wigan were soon ready for peacetime football. Blackpool's Bloomfield Road was used as an RAF training centre and a storage depot. The ground escaped bomb damage but, by the time the military had finished with it at the end of the war, it was in need of major repairs. Blackpool could hardly complain, however: the rent they had received more than paid off the club's bank overdraft. Football had continued there; the rent was simply an additional income.

Preston North End, who missed two seasons of wartime football, were another club to rent their ground to the War Department, receiving £250 per annum. They even rented out their car park for £5 a year. In 1942, Deepdale was taken over by the military and used as a reception centre for prisoners of war. Alas, the legend that Oberleutnant Franz von Werra, the German flyer who eventually escaped from Allied captivity in Canada and was immortalised in the film *The One That Got Away*, was imprisoned at Deepdale is just that. The nearest von Werra got to the home of Preston North End was POW Camp No. 1 at Grizedale Hall in the Lake District before he was moved to Swanwick in Derbyshire. Bolton Wanderers, another club from the cradle of professional football, found a stand at their Burnden Park ground crammed with food after it was taken over by the Ministry of Supply. The local education authority also moved in. During the week they used the pitch on which, in March 1946, the dead bodies of thirty-three spectators were laid out after the tragic events of the FA Cup game against Stoke City. Looting was an ever-present problem in wartime Britain and when the thousands who were locked outside began to scale the walls, the police had been reluctant to call up reinforcements from the officers guarding stockpiled food in the Burnden Stand.

Sitting near to Liverpool docks, Goodison Park, home of Everton, was hit during the air raids on Merseyside and the club received £5,000 from the War Damage Commission. Everton wing-half Gordon Watson remembered the part which some of the club's staff played in preventing more serious damage: 'We started firewatching. There was me and Jackie Grant, and Bill Borthwick, who was one of the trainers. Theo Kelly, the manager, also took a turn. Two of us were on every night.' Nearby Anfield was more fortunate, Liverpool FC escaping serious damage to their stadium. It was Tranmere Rovers, the third and poorest of the Merseyside clubs, who had the worst of it. They lost a stand roof during one of the many raids on Birkenhead and suffered the effects of burning oil as their car park was used as a base for sending up smokescreens in an attempt to foil the Luftwaffe. Outside, in Borough Road, huge tank traps were set up. After the war, Tranmere gave the local council six feet of land behind the Borough Road side of Prenton Park – it was wanted for widening the pavement and providing bus loading bays – and in return the local authority helped Rovers lift the 10cwt tank traps into the ground to provide a base on which to raise the banking on the Kop end. New Brighton, members of the pre-war Third Division North, played the first three seasons of wartime football at their Sandheys Park ground before air raids on the Wirral rendered it unusable. Then, in 1944, Wallasey Corporation requisitioned the site for urgently needed housing. New Brighton re-established the Tower Grounds – where New Brighton Tower FC had played around the turn of the century – as a Football League venue. But it was in a sorry state. The stands had collapsed, the pitch was a morass after US military vehicles had been parked on it, and there were weeds everywhere. It took over £1,000 and a huge effort on the part of supporters to make the Tower Grounds ready for the first postwar season.

In the North East, Sunderland's Roker Park escaped the attentions of the Luftwaffe until the night of 14–15 March 1943, when the Germans scored a direct hit on the pitch as well as dropping bombs just outside the ground, where a policeman was killed. Two months later, on 16 May, a 500kg bomb fell on Sunderland's car park, badly damaging their clubhouse at the corner of Roker Baths Road. Newcastle United's St James's Park escaped serious bomb damage but the ground was put to use in various ways for the war effort and by 1946 was in need of repair. At the start of the war, Ayresome Park, Middlesbrough, boasted a new South Stand and there were plans to cover the Boys' End (or East End). These were soon shelved and the South Stand itself was closed from 1939 to 1945. At York City's Bootham Crescent, a tunnel at the back of the Popular Stand was utilised as an air raid shelter for staff and pupils at the nearby Shipton Street School. In April 1942, German bombs fell on houses in Shipton Street and the football ground suffered slight damage.

Anlaby Road, then the home of Hull City, suffered several direct hits as Hull joined London, Plymouth and Coventry in the dubious distinction of being the most heavily bombed of all British cities during the Second World War. In 1941, Hull City decided to suspend operations until the end of the war, the Tigers' chairman, Alderman Arthur Shepherd, announcing that it would cost at least £1,000 to repair the damage – and then there was every possibility that the Luftwaffe would strike again. Just as significant was the fact that the club's landlords, Hull Cricket Club, had given them notice to quit. When the football club sought to dismantle their grandstand and remove the turnstiles, the cricketers took out an injunction to prevent them. Eventually the matter was resolved but, nonetheless, Hull City were gone. After a season at the Boulevard rugby league ground, they reappeared in 1946–7 at their new ground, Boothferry Park. Anlaby Road, meanwhile, continued to stage football of one sort or another until April 1965, when British Rail put a section of track through the ground. During the war it had staged several services matches. Even Hull's new ground had suffered during the war. The Boothferry Road site had been earmarked for development as a multi-purpose sports complex as early as 1932 and, although progress was painstakingly slow, Hull City looked forward to moving in for the 1940–1 season. The war put an end to those aspirations, not least because the Home Guard used the site, and later on tanks were repaired on the pitch area. At the end of the war, building restrictions and the lack of materials also affected progress but, after a race against time, Hull City were able to move into their new stadium in August 1946.

Although Grimsby Town's Blundell Park is situated in neighbouring Cleethorpes, it was considered too dangerous to have people congregating there in large numbers during the early part of the war. The fans themselves must have agreed with this assessment because, once football resumed, attendances were very poor. In November 1940, the Mariners removed to the Old Show Ground where Scunthorpe United, a Midland League club who had recently failed in their bid to join the Football League, welcomed the attraction of a team then in the top division of English football. The puzzle was that as Scunthorpe was helping to keep the wartime steel industry at full tilt, the town seemed at least as inviting a target as a seaside resort 30 miles up the road. In 1941–2, Grimsby returned to Blundell Park for one match, against an RAF XI, but when it was suggested that they might return home permanently for the 1943–4 season, the League asked them to remain at Scunthorpe, giving the rather mysterious reason that opposing clubs found it easier to reach. On New Year's Day 1944, Grimsby's final return to Blundell Park was marred by controversy when half-back Ginger Hall was sent off a few minutes from the end of a game against Doncaster Rovers. Hall refused to leave the field and the match was abandoned. For followers of football in Scunthorpe, it was a sad day when Grimsby left for home. In 1942, nearly 12,000 had squeezed into the ground to see Town play Sunderland in the League War Cup. Now there was nothing to do except lock up the Old Show Ground and await the peace.

Lincoln City's Sincil Bank was requisitioned as soon as war was declared. The South Park Stand was taken over by the ARP and tons of sand were heaped on the seated area above to provide protection from incendiaries. The players' recreation room was made ready as a decontamination centre. The St Andrew's Stand was later used to store air raid shelters before their distribution around the city. It was 1947 before the ARP cleansing centre was converted back to the players' use, this time as modern dressing rooms.

Bramall Lane, home to Sheffield United and also a venue for Yorkshire County Cricket Club, suffered badly during December

1940, when the steel-making city was the target of a massive German air attack. Ten bombs fell on the ground itself, destroying a large section of the John Street Stand. The visitors' and referee's changing rooms, along with the club's medical room and about one-third of the ground's seating were lost. The roof of the Kop was also destroyed and there were two craters in front of the goal at the Bramall Lane End, and one at each end of the cricket pitch. The *Sheffield Telegraph* announced simply that the forthcoming game against Newcastle United had been cancelled – wartime censorship forbade the newspaper to explain that enemy action was to blame – and, indeed, there was no more football at Bramall Lane that season. United moved their home games to Sheffield Wednesday's Hillsborough stadium and, as is the strange nature of these things, their first 'home' match was against Wednesday. In the meantime, United raised £35 from the sale of reclaimed timber from the damaged stand. The Blades returned to Bramall Lane in September 1941, the damage cleared up. (But forty-three years later, the Luftwaffe had still not finished with Sheffield United: in 1984, a home match against Oldham Athletic had to be postponed when an unexploded German bomb from the Second World War was found close to Bramall Lane during building work.)

Bradford City's Valley Parade was soon requisitioned for military use. By 1944 the ground was available to the club only on Saturday afternoons and by the time League football resumed two years later, City were forced to appeal to supporters for contributions to the ground repair fund. Bradford Park Avenue, meanwhile, became the only club to set a ground record attendance in wartime when 32,810 packed in to see Blackpool – guest player Stan Matthews and all – in a League North Cup quarter-final match on 8 April 1944. The main stand of Doncaster Rovers' ground at Belle Vue was converted into kitchens to prepare meals for the British Restaurant situated in the Corn Exchange. The area opposite the ground was converted into a prisoner of war camp, housing first Italian, then German, prisoners.

Derby County's Osmaston Stand was badly damaged during an air raid on the town in January 1941. Like so many football grounds, the Baseball Ground was situated in a prime industrial area, next door to a foundry producing munitions and alongside the main railway line connecting the north-east of England with the south-west. The Rolls-Royce factory producing Merlin aero-engines, which powered Spitfires, Hurricanes and Lancasters, was also close by. The ground stood little chance during Derby's heaviest air raid of the war. The Rams board had closed down the club in September 1939 – local militia and Home Guard used the pitch for training – so the bomb damage did not interrupt football. When Derby County resumed on Christmas Day that year with a game against the RAF, the Baseball Ground was considered safe enough to allow spectators into its undamaged parts. The only change – and then visible only to a chosen few – was in the boardroom, where the army had made some structural alterations. When Derby entertained West Brom in an FA Cup tie in January 1946, the attendance of 31,795 was the highest at the ground since Boxing Day 1938. Such was the interest in the game – Derby would win the Cup that season – that supporters crowded into the bombed Osmaston Stand, putting themselves at considerable risk, as did the hundreds of foundry employees who clambered on to the roof of the Popular Side. There had been at least one football-related fatality due to enemy action near the Baseball Ground. In July 1942, a lone Dornier bomber, flying almost at rooftop height over the town, had attacked the Rolls-Royce works. Over twenty people lost their lives, including Arthur 'Rasher' Bacon, a peripheral player with Derby in the 1920s before becoming a prolific scorer with Reading and Coventry City. Bacon was serving as a special policeman when he was killed during the bombing.

The two Nottingham clubs were affected during the heavy bombing on that city. Despite a machine-gun emplacement on its open Kop, Notts County's ground at Meadow Lane received a direct hit in June 1941, when a bomb fell on the pitch, destroying the north wing of the Main Stand. It meant that Notts had to withdraw from the League South for 1941–2. When they returned in 1942–3, it was to the northern section. On the other side of the River Trent, Nottingham Forest's pitch at the City Ground was damaged in May 1941, but £75 sorted out the repairs and Forest continued uninterrupted throughout wartime football.

Leicester City's Filbert Street ground was hit by a German bomb on the frosty, moonlit night of 14 November 1940, when many

British towns and cities were targeted in a massive attack by the Luftwaffe, during which the centre of Coventry, only 27 miles away, was almost destroyed. Over Leicester, two bombers dropped twenty bombs in a line from Hinckley Road to Aylestone Road; the bomb that hit the football ground was only fifty yards from an electricity power station. The damage to Filbert Street was mainly to the Main Stand, affecting the roof, seats, boardroom, gymnasium, kitchen and toilets. Leicester, in dire financial straits even before the war started, were left with a repair bill estimated to be in the region of £15,000. A request for an FA loan to tide them over was met with a firm refusal. In June 1942, a further disaster hit Leicester when the Main Stand was again badly damaged, this time by a fire which destroyed the dressing rooms, gymnasium and much of the seating. And in putting out the blaze, the local brigade caused extensive water damage to the boardroom and offices. At least City fared better than Leicestershire County Cricket Club, whose Aylestone Road ground was loaned to the US Army Pioneer Corps and the National Fire Service. When first-class cricket resumed in 1946, Leicestershire's pre-war home was so badly damaged that they had to find new headquarters and returned to their old Grace Road venue, where they remain to this day. City, meanwhile, had been turning their minds to using Filbert Street for non-footballing activities to generate income. A boxing tournament featuring RAF sergeant Freddie Mills, the future world light-heavyweight champion, was staged there, as were two gymkhanas. On Boxing Day 1943, around 3,000 inquisitive spectators turned up to see a baseball game between two American service teams; a week earlier, less than 5,000 had been tempted by the visit of Aston Villa.

Considering that Coventry was one of the most heavily bombed places in Britain during the Second World War, Highfield Road, the home of Coventry City, escaped remarkably lightly. While the centre of the city was being pulverised by night after night of enemy action, the ground was hit three times but the damage was confined mostly to the pitch. Nevertheless, City's season came to an abrupt end after the heavy raid of 14 November 1940; it was August 1942 before the damage had been repaired sufficiently for the club to resume their activities in the Midland Regional League. St Andrew's, the home of Birmingham, was hit by German bombs on eighteen occasions, when the dressing rooms and some outbuildings were damaged, but the worst damage was self-inflicted. The Main Stand was being used as an auxiliary fire station when, in January 1942, a fireman doused a brazier with what he thought was a bucket of water. It was petrol; the stand was completely destroyed and all the club's playing kit was lost. Birmingham – they did not add 'City' to their title until 1945 – played most of their home games at Leamington Spa and Villa Park before returning to St Andrew's in 1943. In wartime, few supporters travelled to away matches but in the first half of 1939–40, those who arrived at The Hawthorns were in for a surprise. One side of West Brom's ground was in Warwickshire, where the police had not yet lifted their ban on public assemblies. The turnstiles there were closed, so entry had to be gained through the turnstiles situated in Staffordshire, where the police force took a more lenient attitude.

Villa Park was unique in wartime – the only football ground where improvement work was carried out during the hostilities. Just before the war it had been planned to extend the terracing at the Holte Hotel End, thus increasing the standing accommodation to 15,000. Work had begun in the wet summer of 1939 and, although there were now severe restrictions on the building industry, it was allowed to continue and was completed by February 1940. Thereafter, the terracing, along with the rest of Villa Park, stood empty for almost three seasons. Villa played their home games in the Birmingham and District League on the ground of Solihull Town. When, for 1942–3, Villa could return to Villa Park, they also took their place in the Football League North. In the interim, the Trinity Road Stand had been fitted out as an air raid shelter and the home dressing room was used by a rifle company of the 9th Battalion, Royal Warwickshire Regiment, which had been raised as a local Territorial unit at nearby Witton Barracks. Many seats from the Witton Lane Stand had been distributed to air raid shelters in Birmingham; when the war ended, the club hired a lorry, collected them in and reinstalled them.

While Stoke City's Butler Street Stand at the Victoria Ground was used as an army camp, their Potteries neighbours, Port Vale, were busy in wartime making plans to sell one ground and build another. In 1943, the financially struggling club sold the Old Recreation Ground in the middle of Hanley to the local council for £13,000 and leased it back. In November 1944, Vale bought another site near Burslem Park. They continued in Hanley until 1949, when the lease ran out, and then moved into their new home – returning to the area where the club had been founded some seventy years earlier. The remarkable thing was that the Vale board had formulated these plans in the uncertainty of wartime.

Reading's Elm Park ground escaped bomb damage but the club's offices at Arcade Chambers in the town centre did not. On the afternoon of 10 February 1943, a German aircraft unloaded a stick of bombs on Reading. Several people were killed or injured and the club's records destroyed. Besides Reading's wartime games, Elm Park played host to several American 'gridiron' football matches. In October 1943, a crowd of over 16,000 saw the Red Devils beat the Gremlins 14–0, both teams comprising US servicemen. The game was played on a Sunday, so no admission could be charged, but a collection raised £137 for the British War Orphans' Fund. During 1938–9, Wycombe Wanderers, then in the Isthmian League, allowed their Loakes Park ground to be used for gas demonstrations. On 21 June 1939, the local military and the Civil Defence began to make use of the ground, while the stands and dressing rooms were taken over by the Billeting Authority and the police. In 1943, the High Wycombe Civil Defence Authority asked Wanderers if they could use the Main Stand to accommodate homeless people in the event of the town being bombed.

At Southampton, The Dell, only a mile from the docks, was hit several times, perhaps the most spectacular strike coming in November 1940, when a bomb fell on the pitch at the Milton Road End, creating an 18ft-wide crater. A culvert carrying a stream under the pitch was broken and The Dell was soon under three feet of water. It took a month before the culvert was repaired and the water subsided; in the meantime the Saints were forced to play all their matches away from home. The exception was a 'home' cup game against Brentford which went ahead at Portsmouth's Fratton Park. In April 1941, a fire broke out in the middle section of the West Stand and although it was contained to that area, the Saints' return to The Dell was delayed. They began the 1941–2 season at the Pirelli General sports ground in Dew Lane, Eastleigh – where 1,850 spectators saw Cardiff City win 3–1 – before returning home the following week. At Dean Park, Bournemouth, football continued for a couple of wartime seasons before the club were forced to suspend activities until the transitional 1945–6 season. In the meantime their ground was used by British and French troops and also by the local Home Guard.

The Bristol clubs both had their share of wartime misfortune, but for widely differing reasons. At Ashton Gate, the home of Bristol City, the imposing but unimaginatively named No. 1 Grandstand received a direct hit during an 11-hour raid on Bristol and Avonmouth on 16 January 1941. Alas, the Luftwaffe did not rid City of the 'Cow Shed' stand on the opposite side of the ground. Building restrictions meant that it was 1951 before City were granted a licence to replace the grandstand, which had been of 1904 vintage. Bristol Rovers, meanwhile, simply had landlord problems. Way back in 1932, before Hitler came to power, they had granted a 21–year lease to the Bristol Greyhound Racing Association and, at the same time, given the greyhound company first option should they ever decide to sell their Eastville home. That moment came in April 1939 when, with Rovers' finances a cause for grave concern, the club's chairman, Fred Ashmead, ordered the secretary to write to the greyhound people, offering to sell them the ground. When the rest of the Rovers board found out what Ashmead had done, they tried to withdraw the offer but the greyhound company would not allow the football club to back out. Rovers were too strapped for cash to fight; on 3 March 1940 they themselves became tenants of the ground they had once owned, the sale price of £12,000 going some way towards the club's liabilities of £20,000. Saturday afternoon greyhound racing – floodlighting was obviously not allowed in blacked-out Britain – meant no Saturday afternoon football, so at the end of the 1939–40 season, the club's directors decided that they could not continue in wartime football. In 1944, American servicemen played 'gridiron' football there, but soccer did not return to Eastville until August 1945, when 15,000 saw Bristol City win an opening-day fixture 3–0. By then, two members of the greyhound company, Con Stevens and John Hare, had purchased a controlling interest in the football club and were to play a leading role in Rovers' postwar revival.

In September 1940, an oil bomb landed on Twerton Park, the home of the Southern League club Bath City, who many years later were to be Bristol Rovers' landlords. During the 'Baedeker raids' of April 1942, when cultural targets were bombed, a stand was damaged at the ground in High Street, Twerton, when a high-explosive bomb landed in the adjacent recreation ground. Yeovil and Petters United – later Yeovil Town – lost their Huish ground when the military took it over as an ammunition dump. Then the Americans moved in and offered to repair the pitch if they could use it for baseball. Yeovil declined the offer. Newport County were another club affected by greyhound racing during the Second World War. When the Cardiff Arms Park Greyhound Racing Company were forced to switch their Newport dog-racing programmes to afternoons, County played their home games at Lovell's Athletic Ground, and then at the Rodney Parade rugby ground, before giving up for the duration. Newport's Somerton Park soccer ground, meanwhile, was taken over by the Civil Defence.

Newport's Welsh neighbours Swansea Town found themselves without a home for the 1940–1 season when Vetch Field was requisitioned by the military and an anti-aircraft gun sited there. The Swans began immediate discussions with the town's rugby club for a share of their St Helen's ground, but strictly amateur rugby union and professional soccer did not mix. Eventually the rugby club gave up the lease on St Helen's and rugby purists were horrified to see a local newspaper photograph of a groundsman painting soccer markings on the hallowed turf. It was the autumn of 1944 before Swansea Town moved back home and St Helen's could be exorcised. Along the South Wales coast, Cardiff City were able to continue at Ninian Park, their worst disaster having occurred in the years leading up to the war. In the early hours of 18 January 1937, the Main Stand was destroyed by a fire thought to have been caused by thieves who were after the takings from an FA Cup tie against Grimsby Town, played at the ground two days earlier. Ninian Park was the main venue for Welsh international and representative fixtures during the war.

Swindon Town's County Ground had a chequered career during the Second World War, very little of it to do with football, since Town did not play after 1939–40. In May 1940, a board meeting was told that the north end of the recently erected West Stand was being requisitioned by the local council as an air raid shelter. Town decided to ask for £1 a week rent. Under the heading 'Ground Improvements' the same minutes noted, 'It was decided to place sheep on the playing field.' Another meeting, in July, was told that the War Department had taken over the County Ground. Three days later, the Swindon club was virtually wound up for the duration, almost everything at the ground being sold off. Even the minute books prior to 1930 disappeared and the County Ground became a prisoner of war camp. Swindon, meanwhile, decided to ask for £1,250 per annum for use of their ground by the War Department. After all, they were a business and losing income every week. Eventually they had to settle for something under £500. When the Swindon ground was derequisitioned in March 1945, the club put in a claim for £4,750 for damage and depreciation. At the same time, a quote for £1,106 reconditioning work was accepted. Football was about to return to the County Ground.

Plymouth Argyle may rightly be considered one of football's furthest-flung outposts but, thanks to the importance of the city as a naval and military centre, the Pilgrims' Home Park found itself right in the midst of the bombing during the Second World War. Indeed, it was probably the worst-damaged of all Football League grounds. The citizens of Plymouth were awakened by hundreds of air raid alerts during the war and, in February 1941, the count was climbing towards 300 when the Grandstand at Home Park was destroyed by high-explosive bombs. Not only was the stand lost, but furniture stored underneath it by families living near the naval dockyards also went up in flames. Argyle had not played since the 1939–40 season and their pitch was already overgrown through lack of maintenance; now it was also pock-marked by small craters. With little money available to rebuild immediately after the war, Argyle showed plenty of ingenuity instead. Former army huts were converted into dressing rooms, and obsolete trams and buses used as club offices, and where the Grandstand had once stood, railway sleepers were bought in to form terracing.

Exeter City's St James's Park had a complete rest from football between 1939 and 1945 – indeed, the club almost went out of business – but that meant that the pitch was in a terrible state by the time City thought about the transitional peacetime season. The ground had been given over to the War Department and was used mostly by the US Army. Some fifty tons of soil were spread on the pitch by volunteers, and by late 1944 it was ready to stage a few services matches before Exeter entertained Plymouth Argyle in a friendly game on 20 January 1945.

Ipswich Town closed down in September 1939, but Portman Road did stage football during the war, mostly inter-services matches, although Norwich City played at least one game there and an 'Ipswich Town XI' also featured. Some £13,000-worth of damage was caused to the ground, much of it by neglect, and at the first postwar public trial match a collection was taken on behalf of the Ipswich Town Supporters' Association Repair Fund. At least this time Ipswich could have their ground back. After Portman Road was requisitioned by the War Office for an army training camp during the First World War, the authorities refused to relinquish it in 1918; even when they eventually regained control of it, the club found that heavy military equipment had caused considerable damage. Norwich City's Carrow Road ground was always going to be in the front line because of its close proximity to Boulton Paul's Riverside Works, which manufactured, among other things, aircraft gun turrets. This also meant that the football ground was going to enjoy a high degree of protection and two anti-aircraft guns were mounted in the Canaries' car park, manned by the Home Guard.

This probably helped the Carrow Road ground escape serious damage, although a total of 681 high-explosive bombs were dropped within the city boundary, several of them falling on Boulton Paul's. By August 1944, Norwich City, who had continued to play throughout the war – albeit only friendly games for three seasons – began work on levelling their pitch and painting the stands and dressing rooms in readiness for the return of normal football. The pitch may have needed special attention, since one of the wartime attractions at Carrow Road had been a rodeo. At least one other important football venue was bombed during the Second World War. In March 1944, the Football Association's offices in Lancaster Gate were hit by incendiaries. The FA's secretary, Stanley Rous, and his wife helped to put out the fire.

7

BRAVERY IN THE FIELD

During the second raid on Tamet this NCO carried out his task while visible to the enemy and under heavy fire from automatic weapons. He succeeded eventually in shooting his way from a position in which he was apparently hopelessly surrounded.

Recommendation for the award of a Military Medal
to Harold White, West Bromwich Albion

Willie Thornton enjoyed a fine career with Glasgow Rangers, winning medals and international caps before his playing days ended in 1954. During the Second World War, Thornton had another award pinned to his chest. It was the Military Medal. As with people from all walks of life, some wartime footballers found inner strengths when confronted by danger. Perhaps they surprised even themselves. Certainly, Thornton reflected on the matter deeply in the years that followed. Thornton joined Rangers as a £1-a-week 16-year-old in March 1936 and less than three months later made his debut, against Partick Thistle, to become the youngest player ever to appear for the Ibrox club. He was soon a regular and in 1938–9 won the first of his four championship medals. Then war interrupted a blossoming career. Thornton joined the Scottish Horse Regiment, part of the Royal Artillery, and was serving as a wireless operator during the invasion of Sicily in 1943 when he was awarded the MM. The action for which Thornton received his medal came on the night of 31 July–1 August that year, during the battle for the Sferro Hills, the capture of which was imperative if Canadian and American troops were to attack and take Adrano, on the west of Mount Etna. Thornton accompanied his battery commander to an

105

observation point and for eighteen hours passed down communications and fire orders, often himself coming under heavy shelling and mortar fire. Part of his CO's recommendation read, 'By his coolness and devotion to duty, Gunner Thornton gave great assistance to his battery commander in bringing down his fire on the enemy.'

Writing in 1954, Thornton recalled the night before the Victory Cup final between Rangers and Hibernian eight years earlier: 'It reminded me of a day out in a Sicilian vineyard, where my football memories, as I lay meditating, recalling pre-war football scenes, provided one of my few comforts. "Will those happy days ever come back?" I asked myself . . . The contrast between that moment and subsequent events at Hampden has an unreal quality. The night of the attack. The awful suspense before zero hour, then the advance . . . The vehicles and crowds, slowly wending their way, reminded me of the tanks, armoured cars and infantry moving up. But this time, heaven be praised, they were pleasure bent. Gone, however, were the scenes I always associated with such an occasion. Only the raucous-voiced vendors and team colours remained. Gone were the chewing gum and "Chocolate, tuppence a bar!" men. War had certainly left its mark on football . . . our captain, Joe Shaw, led us on to the field. What a change from the roar of the guns!'

One of Willie Thornton's pre-war opponents was Celtic's Willie Lyon, an Englishman from Birkenhead who made around 200 appearances for the Glasgow club. Lyon, Celtic's centre-half and captain in the late 1930s, was awarded the Military Cross in October 1943, when he was a lieutenant in the 61st Anti-Tank Regiment, Royal Artillery, fighting in the Middle East. His CO wrote, 'Lieutenant Lyon has shown the highest qualities of leadership and courage as an Anti-Tank Troop Commander throughout the campaign. His troop has been very well forward in support of the leading infantry in nearly every engagement, and his disregard of danger and his devotion to duty has been an inspiration to his men and admired by the infantry he was supporting.'

Right-back Harold White was a regular in West Bromwich Albion's team in 1938–9 and also played in the early part of the war before being posted overseas. In December 1941, Corporal Harold White of the RASC was with the fledgling SAS in North Africa, where he took part in five raids on German airfields and was himself responsible for the destruction of more than twenty enemy aircraft. He was awarded the Military Medal and, after his wartime deeds, returned to football and played thirteen times for West Brom in the 1945–6 season before being transferred to non-League Worcester City. Gunner Harry Meakin, who had played a few wartime games for Stoke City, was with the 61st Field Regiment, Royal Artillery, when he was awarded the Military Medal for his work in Normandy in the two months after D-Day. As the Allied armies battled to gain a significant foothold following the landings, Meakin was on almost constant duty as a wireless operator in the forward areas. His recommendation read, 'He has at all times and under all conditions displayed a resourcefulness and devotion to duty which have been responsible for keeping wireless communications intact at all stages of the battle. His conduct and example have been of the highest order.' Meakin, a local man, was signed as a full-time professional in November 1945. He went on to make thirty-five League appearances for Stoke.

When Queen's Park Rangers beat Mansfield Town 3–0 in March 1946, one of their goalscorers was a former army footballer, Danny Boxshall. Born in Bradford, Boxshall had signed for QPR the previous January, playing his first game against Watford on 1 January 1946. He enjoyed the excellent scoring record of 17 goals in only thirty-seven appearances in the immediate postwar period before QPR sold him to Bristol City in May 1948. Just over three years earlier, in late March 1945, Acting Sergeant Danny Boxshall of the 53rd Reconnaissance Regiment, Royal Armoured Corps, won the Military Medal while in charge of a Bren-gun crew in north-west Germany. Boxshall was commanding the lead reconnaissance car after his troop had been ordered to seize a bridge over the River Berkel in the town of Vreden. As he approached the bridge, his car was engaged by the enemy, but Boxshall simply ordered his driver to accelerate towards the Germans. The vehicle sped towards the bridge, Boxshall firing his Bren gun, and the remaining defenders threw down their arms and surrendered without destroying the valuable crossing point. The recommendation spoke of his 'boldness and dash . . . without any consideration for his personal safety'.

Bill Jones joined Liverpool from the Derbyshire junior club Hayfield St Matthew's in September 1938. On D-Day plus 4, Jones landed in Normandy as a private in the South Lancashire Regiment. By the end of the war he had risen to the rank of platoon sergeant and been awarded the Military Medal for an act of great courage during the battle to cross the Rhine. On 27 February 1945, Jones was involved in heavy fighting around the German town of Goch, an important cog in the Siegfried Line. 'Having led his section with great determination and skill into a strongly held German position, he received orders to withdraw to conform with the rest of his platoon. His section withdrew under fire, leaving behind one man killed and one wounded. As soon as Corporal Jones had re-established his section, he went forward alone again to recover the wounded man. This he did successfully, although the fire through which he had to pass had now become intense. His steady example and constant enthusiasm, coupled with energetic initiative and great personal courage under fire, have had a very great effect upon the men in his platoon and company and have made of Sergeant Jones a battle-winning factor in the battalion.' In the first postwar season, Bill Jones played in five different positions as Liverpool won the League championship. He was later capped twice by England and played in the 1950 FA Cup final.

A native of Gateshead, Tommy Barkas, a forward, joined Halifax Town from Bradford City in December 1934 and became a great favourite at The Shay, making 168 League appearances for Halifax. He played for Town during the war but refused terms after it and was transferred to Rochdale in September 1946. As an RAF corporal, Barkas was awarded the British Empire Medal for his bravery during the siege of Malta. Along with a colleague, Barkas tackled numerous fires, including those on a petrol bowser and an ammunition lorry, while overhead some fifty enemy aircraft were dropping their bombs on the beleaguered island. Inside-forward Albert Smith, transferred to Queen's Park Rangers from Birmingham in 1939, escaped from Dunkirk and was also awarded the BEM. He later served in the Middle East and Germany, where he played with an Army team which won two trophies; he made sixty-three postwar appearances for Rangers before his career was ended by a broken leg.

On 29 April 1939, Tommy Rowe climbed the steps up to Wembley's royal box to collect his FA Cup winners' medal after Portsmouth's 4–1 victory over Wolverhampton Wanderers. Rowe had signed for Pompey from his native Poole Town in August 1934, but the 1937–8 season was under way before he established himself as the club's first-choice centre-half. Rowe, then 25 years old, could have reasonably expected to remain a First Division regular for the next few years. As with so many of his generation, however, his potential was to be unfulfilled. In November 1943, after a six-month tour of duty as a bomber pilot with 77 Squadron, Acting Flight Lieutenant Tommy Rowe was awarded the Distinguished Flying Cross. Then his luck ran out. On the night of 22–23 March 1944, on an operation to bomb Frankfurt, Rowe's Lancaster was hit and exploded. Only Rowe and his bomb-aimer, 'Mac' Grant, survived. They were taken to the Dulag Luft at Oberursel near Frankfurt am Main, the interrogation centre for all downed airmen, before they were dispersed to POW camps. As an officer, Rowe would normally have gone to Stalag Luft III at Sagan, but his arrival in the Third Reich coincided with the 'Great Escape' from Sagan, so instead he was sent to Stalag Luft 1 at Barth-Vogelsang on the Baltic coast. It was May 1945 before he returned to Fratton Park as an honoured guest, his playing days over.

Ian McPherson, a winger, scored fifteen goals in only eighteen wartime appearances for Glasgow Rangers, winning a Scottish Regional League Western Section championship medal in 1939–40. McPherson joined the RAF and in June 1944 was awarded the DFC as a pilot officer flying Mosquitoes with 105 Squadron. His medal came as a 'tour of operations' award after fifty-seven sorties. In January 1945, McPherson, by now promoted to flying officer and veteran of 102 sorties, was awarded a bar to his DFC. His recommendation read, 'Since the award of his Distinguished Flying

Cross, Flying Officer McPherson has completed numerous sorties. Throughout all his operations he has consistently displayed exemplary courage and tenacity of purpose, which, together with his outstanding skill and fine leadership, are worthy of high praise.' After the war McPherson signed for Arsenal from Notts County – he had guested for both clubs – and in 1947–8 played twenty-nine times as the Gunners won the League championship. In 1954, after a few games for Brentford and Bedford Town, McPherson rejoined the RAF as a flying officer on a short service commission and spent four years in the physical education side of the service, while still playing a season with Cambridge United. Many books have credited Ian McPherson with being the first British airman to fly over Germany following the outbreak of the Second World War. That man, however, was Flying Officer Andrew McPherson, who was also awarded the DFC after crossing the German frontier on a reconnaissance flight on 3 September 1939.

Les Clatworthy was an amateur with Chelsea when the war broke out. Clatworthy played a few games at full-back during the 1940–1 season, making his debut in a 2–1 win at Cardiff in May, and appearing a few more times the following season. As a flight sergeant pilot with 87 Squadron, flying fighter-bombers, he was awarded the Distinguished Flying Medal in June 1945 and later that year was promoted to pilot officer. His days as a top-flight footballer were, however, behind him. The recommendation for his award read, 'This NCO has proved to be a most efficient and dependable pilot. On many occasions he has led formations of fighter-bombers to attack well-defended targets. On one occasion he took part in an attack on a fuel dump which produced flame up to 3,000ft, while on another he assisted in the total destruction of an ammunition dump in the Spezia area. He has shown a high standard of leadership and his daring attacks have been an excellent example to all pilots.'

Flight Sergeant Dennis Love, a player on the books of Bristol City, was awarded the DFM in April 1945. Love was an air gunner with 90 Squadron of Bomber Command, which flew Stirlings; his award came after thirty-five sorties. Three months after Dennis Love's medal, a near-namesake, John Love, who played for Scottish League club Leith Athletic, was awarded the DFC. Like Dennis Love, he had served in Bomber Command, but it was as a glider pilot that he won his medal: 'During the airborne crossing of the Rhine, north of Wesel, Pilot Officer Love was severely wounded by anti-aircraft fire while piloting a Horsa glider. Although suffering intense pain, he insisted on remaining at the controls throughout the approach to the landing zone. On attempting to land it was discovered that the flaps had been seriously damaged by the ground fire. The brakes had also been rendered unserviceable. Undeterred by this hazardous situation, Pilot Officer Love landed the glider successfully, without damaging the load. His skill and fortitude in adverse circumstances were responsible for the success of the flight.' Despite his injuries, John Love enjoyed a career in England after the war with Nottingham Forest and Walsall, and also managed Walsall and Wrexham.

Not every footballer who was decorated for bravery was serving abroad, however. In July 1942, Aston Villa defender Ernest 'Mush' Callaghan was serving in the Birmingham police force when he won the British Empire Medal for his bravery during a heavy air raid on the city. Born in Newtown, Birmingham in July 1907, Callaghan played in local football before Villa signed him as a full-time professional in 1930. In 1937–8 he missed only two games as Villa won the Second Division championship. Back in the top flight, Villa finished in mid-table and Callaghan was an ever-present in the last pre-war season. On the outbreak of war he joined the police reserve, transferring to the regular force in February 1941. Serving as a policeman in Birmingham meant that Callaghan could continue to play for Villa and he was a regular at centre-half for most of the club's wartime seasons. In the early morning of Tuesday 28 July 1942, however, he faced his greatest challenge when a high-explosive bomb fell on the factory of Gabriels Ltd in Coleshill Street, completely destroying the works and starting two fires in the debris, trapping several people in an underground shelter. PC Callaghan and his sergeant, Harold Wood, recovered one body before falling debris blocked the entrance to the shelter. Callaghan and Wood then broke through the shattered front wall of the factory to rescue three people. By this time, a millwright, Jim Hughes, had joined them. It was to be 45 minutes before the fire brigade and rescue squads arrived. In the meantime the three men faced constant danger as the four-storey factory threatened to collapse at any moment, bringing down with it tons of machinery. During their rescue efforts, another bomb fell close by.

In September 1942 it was announced that Callaghan and Hughes had each been awarded the BEM. Wood, already a holder of that medal, was awarded the George Medal. The official citation read, 'The three men acted in the most courageous manner without thought for their own safety. By their prompt action and determined efforts, the lives of three people were saved.' Two months later, Aston Villa gave a dinner for Callaghan at the Farcroft Hotel, where he was presented with an illuminated testimonial. Callaghan, who had played at Wembley for the British Police against the RAF in 1941, appeared ten times for Villa during the first postwar season before retiring to take up a job as maintenance man at Villa Park. Like most wartime heroes, he was a seemingly ordinary man capable of the most extraordinary deeds.

8

FRONT-LINE FOOTBALLERS

We were working on aircraft landing strips when the Germans invaded. We had to move very quickly after that. We marched for three days to get to Dunkirk. I was reported missing, but I got on a boat and made it home. It was a close shave though.

Wilf Mannion, Middlesbrough and England

Dennis Herod was only 17 when he signed for Stoke City in January 1941, but he quickly became the Potters' regular goalkeeper. 'It was more good fortune than ability,' he said. 'Everyone else was in the forces.' Eventually Herod, too, was called-up. He served with the Royal Tank Regiment, joining them in Sicily and fighting through Italy until his unit was recalled to England. His respite was brief, however: he was back in action on D-Day plus I. 'They were terrible times. If you were front-line infantry or in a tank crew, if you didn't get killed today, then you'd get killed tomorrow. If you were really lucky, you just got wounded. I was lucky.' In Normandy, on 7 August 1944, Herod escaped from his blazing tank with only a fractured jawbone. The shock and pain were bad enough but he was more fortunate than many. His war was over. After treatment in a Manchester hospital he was sent to a convalescent centre at Trentham, near his home. Remarkably, by the end of the 1944–5 football season he was Stoke's regular goalkeeper once again.

Dennis Herod was indeed one of the lucky ones. He went on to make over 200 appearances for Stoke, and by the time he was transferred to Stockport County in 1953, there were probably few supporters who remembered, or were even aware in the first place, that he had seen action during the Second World War. That might be said of many players who plied their trade during the 1940s and early 1950s; Dennis Herod's story illustrates that there were plenty of footballers either unwilling, or unable, to take the soft option of a posting on home soil, putting raw recruits through their physical jerks, or playing morale-boosting football matches among themselves. Many chose to fight, shunning the opportunity for a safe billet. Others who would rather have stayed at home had no option anyway. The army needed only so many physical training instructors. If they had not been fortunate enough to land a reserved occupation in a munitions factory, the rest had to go to war. Their stories are many and varied, covering death, serious injury and long imprisonment in almost every theatre of the conflict.

Sunderland's England international Raich Carter was a footballer who braved the nightly blitz in the early part of the war, on one occasion risking his life on what turned out to be a fool's errand. The Binns department store in Sunderland had been hit by an incendiary and Carter was one of dozens of firemen sent to tackle the blaze. When he arrived, flames were shooting from one side of the street to the other. It was dirty, dangerous work and eventually the firemen were ordered to withdraw. First, though, Carter and a colleague were sent back into the building to retrieve a precious length of hose. The two men made their way up several flights of stairs, burning embers falling on them, sheets of flame running up the walls, their lungs choked by smoke. Carter felt they should abandon the hunt for the hose, but his colleague pressed on before being beaten back by the flames. He collapsed and Carter had to bring him down over his shoulder, stair by stair, finally staggering into the cold night air, lungs bursting. Bent over, head between his legs, gasping for breath, Carter was told that the hose had not been left in the building after all. Another fireman had brought it down with him and dumped it in a yard. When Carter had been promoted to the full-time brigade, the local newspaper received a number of letters accusing the council of favouritism in selecting him out of 240 applicants. The criticism irritated the player, who, with his full-time colleagues, was working long and dangerous hours. Over 250 civilians were killed in Sunderland, over 1,000 injured, and Carter reckoned he had done his share of braving burning, collapsing buildings. Stung by the sniping, he did the only thing possible in his eyes: he joined the RAF, which was ironic since it took him out of harm's way; he was to spend the rest of the war as a physical training instructor.

In June 1944, Tim Ward, a pre-war Derby County wing-half and one of Carter's teammates in the postwar side, was serving in Normandy as a nursing orderly in 153rd Field Ambulance of the Royal Army Medical Corps, part of the 15th Scottish Division. He was involved in the battle to take the Odon River, then Caen. The fighting was heavy and bloody and Ward dealt with more than his fair share of badly wounded and dying men. Ironically, his first casualties were German. In the front line at Estry, he himself suffered a shrapnel wound to the scalp when a Bren-carrier exploded. The night he crossed the River Seine, Ward found himself sharing a ditch with an Oxford-educated German officer. The German had thrown away his weapons and was awaiting capture. Ward's only weapon was the football he always carried in his ambulance, ready for any chance of an impromptu kick-about. In May 1945, Ward saw for himself the horrors of Belsen concentration camp. A few months later, he resumed his career with Derby and was capped twice for England in subsequent years. In the late 1940s there was dressing-room unrest at Derby and leading players left the club; Ward let it pass him by: 'I had seen my friends die in the war. Petty football squabbles didn't seem to matter much after that.'

While men like Carter and Ward were risking their lives at home and abroad, many players were suffering unimaginable hardship as prisoners of the enemy. Some recovered, some did not. On 30 October 1943, a Cardiff City guest team including England's Tommy Lawton and Joe Mercer met a Western Command side which had Frank Swift, another England international, in goal. The match was staged at Ninian Park to raise funds for the Royal Artillery Prisoners of War Fund. Hundreds of men from Glamorgan's own artillery regiment were languishing in POW camps in the Far East.

In the Splott district of Cardiff, at 183 Carlisle Street, the parents of Billy James had already been informed that their son, serving in the 77th HAA Regiment, Royal Artillery, was a prisoner. Billy was a particularly exciting prospect as a young footballer with Cardiff City. In June 1941 he had played at centre-forward for Wales against England at Ninian Park. England won 3–2, but James escaped the attention of centre-half Stan Cullis at least once, to score one of the Welsh goals. Three months later, he was selected to play against England again, at St Andrew's, Birmingham. Here was a player with a big future. Three years in a Japanese prisoner of war camp put paid to that. Malnutrition badly affected his eyesight and it was remarkable that, after repatriation, James managed even six more appearances for Cardiff before being forced to call it a day.

Bobby Tobin, a forward who had signed from Cardiff Corinthians during the war, survived but played only twice more before being released into non-League football with Barry Town. Wing-half Billy Baker, from Penrhiwceiber, was the only Cardiff player whose career successfully bridged the war, despite four years in Japanese hands. Baker had made his debut in 1938–9, against Northampton Town. After his return in 1946, he reached almost 300 appearances and played for Wales before retiring in 1955, when he was with Ipswich Town. Former Welsh schoolboy international Albert Hall, a pre-war Tottenham forward recruited from the junior ranks, celebrated his twenty-first birthday on the day war broke out. He, too, was in the Royal Artillery when he was captured at Singapore in February 1942. The following year, Hall survived the sinking of the Japanese prison ship on which he was being transported; by March 1945 he was turning out for Tottenham at Aldershot, having arrived home at the end of the previous year. In July 1947 he signed for Plymouth Argyle.

Reading's Johnny Sherwood was captured at Singapore in February 1942 and spent over three and a half years as a prisoner of war. Sherwood had signed for Reading in June 1938 and appeared in the Third Division South. He continued to play during the early part of the war, when he switched from wing-half to outside-left and scored in the 3–2 win over Brentford in the 1941 War Cup final at

Stamford Bridge. A few weeks later, Sherwood was on his way to the Far East and eventual captivity. He survived working on the notorious 'death railway' in Burma, his prison ship being torpedoed, and the dropping of the atomic bomb on Nagasaki, where he was last imprisoned. After his liberation in 1945, Sherwood returned to Elm Park via Australia. He signed for Aldershot in September 1947.

Johnny Lynas, who had played with Sunderland and Third Lanark in the 1920s and early 1930s, was Blackpool's assistant trainer when war broke out. Captured at Singapore, he later worked at a prisoner of war camp hospital in Thailand but survived to return to Bloomfield Road. When Blackpool won the famous 'Matthews Cup Final' in 1953, Johnny Lynas was their trainer. Running on to the Wembley pitch was something he perhaps dreamed about but never dared believe would happen, during his long days in captivity.

Compared to life in a Japanese POW camp, incarceration in a German camp was not as bad, although bad enough. Len Stansbridge made his League debut in goal for Southampton at Plymouth in May 1938. He joined the RAMC on the outbreak of war and was captured at Dunkirk. After four years as a prisoner, Stansfield returned to Southampton where he spent six years as a reserve. For twenty-two years from 1962 he was the groundsman at The Dell. Leeds United's Stephens twins, Alf and Bill, were both in the Royal Engineers and were both being taken prisoner at the same time. They even managed to see out the war in the same prison camp. The Earl of Harewood, Leeds United's president from 1961, was a captain in the Grenadier Guards when he was wounded and captured shortly after D-Day. He was held in Colditz from November 1944, on the direct orders of Adolf Hitler, who was looking out for VIP prisoners. Alf Rowlands was a north-easterner serving with the Green Howards when he was captured at Gazala during the Libyan campaign in 1942. After three years in a prisoner of war camp, Rowlands returned home and played for Aldershot Reserves in 1945–6. A pre-war winger, he had converted successfully to centre-half and became a part-time professional with Aldershot, with whom he made ninety-three League appearances before a short spell with Cardiff City in 1949.

After spending half a season in Everton's junior ranks, outside-left Harold Roberts signed for Chesterfield only weeks before the outbreak of war. In March 1942 he took part in the commando raid on the French port of St Nazaire, where he was wounded and captured. Roberts spent three and a half years in a POW camp near Bremen but recovered sufficiently to make over 250 appearances for Chesterfield, Birmingham, Shrewsbury and Scunthorpe up to 1954, and then spend several more years in non-League football. George Ephgrave joined Swindon Town in March 1939, from Aston Villa where he had been a junior. A giant of a goalkeeper – he stood over 6ft 4in tall – Ephgrave managed one League appearance for Swindon before the war, in which he was captured in Crete in May 1941. After his repatriation, he signed for Southampton in September 1946, in time to begin the first postwar season as the Saints' first-choice goalkeeper. He later played for Norwich and Watford.

Two Queen's Park Rangers players returned from German POW camps to pick up their careers with varying results. Half-back Johnny Barr, who was captured in the Western Desert and later found himself working for the Germans in a cement factory, had played eight times in wartime. After his repatriation he managed only four senior games in 1946–7 before dropping out of League football. Goalkeeper Reg Allen, meanwhile, had a remarkable story to tell. After playing for the British Army against the French Army in Paris in 1940, just before the German invasion, he served with the fledgling commando force and was captured in North Africa in 1942. Allen escaped but was recaptured and spent three years as a prisoner before being freed by the Americans in Austria. Allen, who had joined QPR from a local works team, made his League debut in November 1938 and was their first choice until the outbreak of war. In 1950 he was transferred to Manchester United for £12,000, then a record for a goalkeeper. His career spanned over 300 senior appearances. Reg Allen died a sad and somewhat lonely figure, badly affected by his wartime experiences, many said.

When inside-forward Albert Mullard scored a hat-trick for Walsall against Northampton Town in the confusingly named Third

ay 1934: All the Derby County players, except goalkeeper Jack Kirby, give the Nazi salute.
otballers were among the few Britons to see at first hand what was happening in Germany
lowing Hitler's rise to power. *(Author's Collection)*

ctober 1939: The Arsenal ARPs pictured at Highbury. Left to right: England winger Cliff Bastin,
iner Tom Whittaker, England full-back George Male and goalkeeper George Marks. *(Getty
ages)*

January 1940: Eddie Hapgood (left), captain of an FA XI, shakes hands with Stan Cullis, ʰ
counterpart in the Army team, before a match at Selhurst Park. The FA side won 4–3 in front
10,057 spectators. *(Getty Images)*

Opposite, above: September 1941: Members of the Home Guard do their physical jerks at
bomb-damaged Baseball Ground. The pitch is in a dreadful state, and Derby County had n
played there since September 1939. *(Author's Collection)*

Opposite, below: October 1941: Tommy Lawton of Everton, the Army and England, poses f
the camera before a representative match. Lawton was a prolific scorer in wartime football wi
almost 350 goals in all matches. *(Getty Images)*

Above: January 1942: Clementine Churchill addresses the Wembley crowd before the England–Scotland international, which was played in support of her Aid to Russia Fund. *(Get. Images)*

Left: 1943: Airmen queuing at the entrance to a football ground that allowed in service personnel and childre[n] for half-price. *(Getty Images)*

Opposite: May 1942: Brentford players Joe James (left) and Dai Hopkins leave t[he] Wembley pitch with James's daughter Beryl, who is carrying the London War Cup that Brentford had just won by beating Portsmouth 2–0. *(Getty Images)*

Above: March 1943: Corporal Stanley Matthews in action for the RAF against the Police
Civil Defence team at Preston. The RAF won 4–2 before a crowd of 12,000. *(Getty Images)*

Right: February 1944: Raich Carter in action for England against Scotland at Wembley. The s
exhorts all football supporters to do their bit for National Savings. *(Getty Images)*

August 1945: Arsenal players en route for their match against the BAOR team in Dusseldorf. Squadron Leader Tom Whittaker MBE is at the rear of the queue. Whittaker took over as Arsenal manager in June 1947. *(Getty Images)*

November 1945: Moscow Dynamo players walk out on to the pitch at Stamford Bridge, carrying bouquets for their Chelsea opponents. *(Getty Images)*

Division South (North) Cup in April 1946 – following up on the two he had scored against the same opponents only two days earlier – he capped a successful return from a prisoner of war camp. Captured in Crete in May 1941, Mullard, a Royal Marine, had spent four years in German captivity. He joined Walsall from Hinckley United in November 1945 and began a good career which also took in Crewe Alexandra, Stoke City and Port Vale and brought him over 300 appearances and more than 50 goals.

Alec Munro joined Blackpool from Hearts in March 1937 for £3,500 and went straight into the first team, holding his place at outside-right until April 1939. Munro was a regular in the first wartime season, but in the summer of 1942 was captured in North Africa and became a prisoner of war in Italy. He returned to the Blackpool first team in 1946 but had to switch wings the following season when the Seasiders signed Stanley Matthews. Despite his wartime incarceration, he went on to make 146 appearances and played in the 1948 FA Cup final before retiring. Alex McIntosh of Wolves was reported as missing in action, believed killed, in April 1945, but turned up in a German prisoner of war camp. He had joined Wolves from non-League football in 1937 and appeared in forty-seven League games at inside-forward before the war. In 1946, recovered from his experiences as a POW, he signed for Birmingham and later played for Coventry City. Cyril Thompson of Southend United was a local schoolboy player, but thanks to the war he did not sign as a professional until he was 27, after he had been released from a prisoner of war camp. He proved a prolific scorer with Southend in the Third Division South, but a move to First Division Derby County in July 1948 proved spectacularly unsuccessful and he returned to the Third Division with Brighton and then Watford.

Ted Platt, a goalkeeper, signed for Arsenal as a 17-year-old in 1938 from Colchester United, then a non-League club. In January 1940 he made his first senior appearance for the Gunners, against Spurs, but after joining the Royal Fusiliers he was captured by the Italians in Tunisia in 1943. After the British re-entered Tunis in May that year, Platt was able to rejoin his regiment and fought on with them in Italy. He joined Portsmouth in September 1953 and also played for Aldershot. Welsh schoolboy international Len Dutton signed for Arsenal in 1940. He joined the army and was reported missing, but eventually resurfaced and by August 1946 had signed for Norwich City, with whom he made over 150 appearances before dropping into non-League football. Oldham Athletic defender Beaumont Ratcliffe had been guesting regularly for Reading before he was taken prisoner in Italy in 1943. Word reached Elm Park that Ratcliffe had suffered a shoulder injury when he was captured. His recovery was so complete, however, that he signed for Reading in May 1946, and two years later Watford were prepared to take him on, a month after his 39th birthday. Alan Steen, who had made his debut for Wolves as a 16-year-old in 1938–9, was reported missing in action after a bombing raid over Germany. In fact, Steen spent the rest of the war in a prison camp. After the war he played for Luton Town, Aldershot, Rochdale and Carlisle United.

John Kirkham, the Bournemouth centre-forward, was captured in North Africa in 1942. Kirkham made several escape attempts from Italian POW camps before succeeding early in 1944. Later the same year he was guesting for Wolves and back in the Bournemouth team in 1945–6. In November 1943, Ernie Bell, a pre-war player with Hull City and Mansfield Town, played for Aldershot against Southampton, shortly after being repatriated from a POW camp. It was a particularly memorable return: Tommy Lawton was one of Bell's teammates and scored 6 goals in Aldershot's 10–1 win. However, perhaps the quickest switch from prison camp to football pitch was achieved by Charlie Sargeant. A POW for three and a half years, on 21 April 1945 he turned out for Chester at Wrexham, only one week after walking through the gates to freedom. It was his first game in a Chester shirt since 1938. A week after his reappearance he scored one of the goals in a 2–1 win over Wrexham at Sealand Road.

Football was often on the minds of prisoners of war. In 1943, Eddie Hapgood received a postcard from one Albert Jennings, who was imprisoned in Stalag XXB near Marienburg in Germany: 'Dear Eddie, I have been asked by the boys of this working party to congratulate you, and we all hope that by the time this arrives in

England you have created a record. So here's wishing you the best of luck.' The card arrived a few days after the Arsenal captain had played in his forty-third international. Hapgood wrote later, 'That tribute from a prisoner of war, who in the midst of his troubles could spare a thought for one who was free to play football in the Old Country, left me a little breathless when it arrived.' The exploits of Ipswich Town's goalkeeper would also have left Hapgood breathless. After signing for Ipswich from the Scottish junior club Lenathon in October 1938, 19-year-old Tom Brown would have been expecting to spend the next few years fighting for a place in the first team, as Ipswich had just been elected to the Football League. Instead, he found himself in the army. Brown was recruited as a commando and spent time in northern China, assisting the guerrillas who were fighting the Japanese. Demobbed after the war, he resumed his career at Portman Road but his League debut came about in unusual circumstances. After playing for the reserve team in their 6–1 win over Crystal Palace on 11 September 1946, he was called up to the first team the following day after regular goalkeeper Mick Burns injured himself falling down the stairs of a trolley bus.

Inevitably, the evacuation of the British Expeditionary Force from the Dunkirk beaches in 1940 saw its fair share of the footballers who had been first to join up. Derby County's Jack Stamps, a burly centre-forward signed from New Brighton just before the war, enlisted in the Royal Artillery and was sent to France. He was wounded as the BEF retreated and found himself near the end of the queue for a ride back to England. Stamps recalled, 'I'd been chest-deep in the water for hours when I finally reached a small boat. It was pretty crowded and when I went to climb on to it, an officer pointed a revolver at me and said: "Soldier, if you attempt to board this boat, I will shoot you. Make no mistake about it." I said: "Well, if you don't, the Germans probably will."' With that, Stamps hauled himself aboard. Six years later he was scoring 2 goals for Derby in the first postwar FA Cup final.

Wilf Mannion also escaped from Dunkirk to enjoy a fine football career. He was already an established First Division player when war broke out, having made his debut for Middlesbrough in 1937, when he was only 17. After serving in the Auxiliary Fire Service, Mannion was called up in January 1940 and was with the BEF when the Germans invaded France and Belgium. Then it was a race back to Dunkirk. Reported missing in action, but escaping on a supply ship and arriving back in England on the weekend of the 1940 War Cup final, Mannion made his way to the Green Howards' headquarters in Richmond. While stationed in the North Yorkshire town, he was selected to play for England against Scotland; by the time he was posted to the Middle East, he had played another three times for his country. The war, and with it bouts of jaundice and malaria, robbed Mannion of the chance to play international football at his peak. He still became one of the greatest of all postwar inside-forwards, however, with twenty-six full England caps, an appearance for Great Britain, and 110 goals in 368 senior games for Middlesbrough alone.

Like Stoke's Dennis Herod, several players recovered from wounds and severe illness to enjoy good careers after the war. Bill Shorthouse was one of several promising local youngsters taken on the staff of Wolverhampton Wanderers just before the war. Shorthouse joined the Royal Engineers, his wartime appearances for Wolves restricted to a handful of matches, and on 6 June 1944 he was wading ashore in Normandy. Within an hour of scrambling up the beach, he was wounded in the arm. As he lay waiting to be evacuated, Shorthouse felt enormous relief that it was his arm 'and not one of my footballing legs' which had been hit. He wrote later, 'Back in England, it was hospital for me – and I can probably claim to be one of the few soldiers allowed to discard hospital blue for a football strip. The doctor in charge of my case in a hospital near Birmingham thought that football might help me. I contrived to get a ball and do some practice in the hospital grounds. This, too, was probably unheard of – but stranger things than that happened during the war.' Shorthouse signed as a full-time professional for Wolves in April 1946, just before his 24th birthday, and shared in some of their greatest triumphs before leaving Molineux in 1956, after 344 League games for the club.

Another player to be wounded on D-Day but who recovered to enjoy a long career in the Football League was Doug Wright, who had been capped by England in 1938, playing against Norway at his club ground, St James's Park, Newcastle. Wright's wounds were serious enough for him to be told that he would never play football again, but he resumed with Newcastle after the war, and later made 250 appearances for Lincoln City. Roy White was wounded as he escaped from Dunkirk but recovered to play over 150 times at wing-half in wartime matches for Tottenham Hotspur. After the war, White joined Bradford Park Avenue and played in another 150 games for them. Wilf Chitty, a player with Chelsea before the war, was in a reserved occupation and therefore exempt from military service. Nevertheless he finished up in hospital after being injured during an air raid when a bomb fell near his Caversham home. Chitty recovered and was well enough to continue his Reading career in the first two seasons after normal football resumed.

The war brought Tom Cheadle to Port Vale, thanks to a faulty hand grenade. Cheadle, who was lucky enough to have Matt Busby as his PTI, joined the North Staffordshire Regiment in 1939. In Holland in 1944 – Cheadle was apparently now with the Monmouthshire Regiment – the grenade he was throwing exploded almost as soon as it had left his hand. In hospital he met another PTI, Ken Fish, the trainer of Port Vale. On his demob, Cheadle called Fish and arranged a trial with the Potteries club; in May 1946, at the age of 26, Cheadle began a professional career which saw him total over 400 appearances with Vale and Crewe.

Eddie Kilshaw joined Bury from Prescot Cables in October 1937 and made his League debut for the Shakers before the war ended normal football. He joined the RAF and was serving in Coastal Command when the flying boat he was piloting crashed into a hillside on a Scottish island in appalling visibility. Some of the crew were killed but Kilshaw and the other survivors were eventually rescued by the Royal Navy. Ironically, it was a dislocated knee suffered whilst playing with Sheffield Wednesday in April 1949, that ended his career. Kilshaw had joined the Owls for £20,000, then a record for a winger and only a few pounds short of the overall British record, but the injury restricted him to only nineteen appearances. He became a schoolteacher and in 1971 managed the Huyton Boys team which won the FA Schools trophy. His assistant was Alan Bleasdale, who won fame as a playwright; one of the boys in his team was Peter Reid, later of Everton and England.

Stan Mortensen was just beginning to make an impression with Blackpool when his life was almost ended in an air crash. He was serving in the RAF as a wireless operator/air gunner when the Wellington bomber in which he was on an operational training flight caught fire and crash-landed in a fir tree plantation. The pilot and the bomb-aimer were killed and the navigator lost a leg, but the worst of Mortensen's injuries was a cut head that required a dozen stitches. He wrote later, 'The doctors decided that my injuries were such that I would never again be fit for operational duties, and naturally enough I wondered about my football career. Should I ever be able to head a ball again?' As it turned out, Stan Mortensen went on to score 222 goals in 354 appearances for Blackpool, and win an FA Cup winners' medal, as well as score 23 goals in twenty-five full international appearances for England.

George Hardwick had played in a handful of games at left-back for Middlesbrough before the war, marking his debut with a first-minute own-goal. Hardwick was wounded in both legs when the Luftwaffe attacked his RAF base on the Isle of Sheppey, but he was fit enough to play in three wartime cup finals for Chelsea and appear in seventeen wartime internationals, and he captained England in every one of his thirteen peacetime appearances as well as skippering Great Britain against the Rest of Europe in 1947. After almost 400 games for Middlesbrough and Oldham Athletic, Hardwick went into coaching and management, one of his charges being the US Seventh Army's soccer team in Stuttgart.

Paratrooper Don Dorman was an amateur with Birmingham when he took part in the ill-fated Operation Market Garden and was wounded at Arnhem. After the war he made sixty-five appearances for Birmingham before joining Coventry, whose goalkeeper, Alf Wood, had made his League debut in 1937–8. Wood guested for Northampton Town after he was called up to the RASC, and also played for the army. Towards the end of the war he contracted spinal meningitis and was told that he would never play again. So much for medical opinion: Wood made the last of his 246 appearances for Coventry in 1958–9 when, at the age of 43, he came out of retirement after regular goalkeeper Jim Sanders had suffered a broken leg. Sanders himself had taken part in over 200 sorties as an RAF air gunner before being badly wounded and invalided out of the service. At the time he was an amateur on Charlton Athletic's books. By November 1945, however, he had recovered sufficiently for West Brom to sign him. He went on to win an FA Cup winners' medal with Albion in the 1954 final and into the 1960s was happily pulling pints as landlord of a pub in the centre of Derby. Arthur Turner, an amateur with Charlton Athletic who would later sign professional forms and play against Derby County in the first postwar FA Cup final, was the only survivor when the Coastal Command aircraft in which he was an air gunner crashed in the Bay of Biscay. Turner spent several hours floating in the sea before he was picked up. Charlton half-back Freddie Ford lost his right index finger when taking part in the Allied crossing of the Rhine with the Royal Engineers in 1945.

Inside-forward George Smith was signed for Manchester City in the 1938 close season. After a handful of wartime appearances for City, and a spell as a guest with Hearts, he was posted abroad in the army. It was while Smith was serving in South Africa that he suffered a serious gunshot wound to his left lower arm. Nevertheless, the injury did not prevent him from picking up his career in 1946, when he scored 5 goals against Manchester United. The following year, Smith scored another 5 against Newport County, and had netted 80 goals in 179 appearances by the time he was transferred to Chesterfield in October 1951.

Brentford's Tommy Cheetham had already seen military service before he re-enlisted during the war. Cheetham was a professional soldier in India before he joined Queen's Park Rangers in 1935. He made his League debut in September that year; in his first season he set a club record by scoring in nine consecutive matches at Loftus Road. In March 1939, with the impressive record of 92 goals in only 128 matches, Cheetham joined Brentford for £5,000. After the first two games of the 1939–40 season, however, he was recalled for military service and thereafter played only occasionally for Brentford, as well as guesting once for West Ham – and scoring twice. Cheetham was wounded in Normandy, but not badly enough to halt a football career which continued until he retired from Lincoln City in 1948.

Howard Girling, an outside-left who joined Crystal Palace from amateur football in 1942, recovered from wounds received in 1945, as the Allies pushed on towards Germany, and scored 6 goals in twenty-seven games for Palace before being transferred to Brentford for £3,000 in February 1947. He played over ninety times for Brentford before ending his career with Bournemouth in 1951. Exeter City's versatile half-back Steve Walker, who played for the Grecians either side of the war, running up 153 senior appearances in total, joined the Royal Navy and served in HMS *Worcester*, the destroyer that was badly hit with the loss of sixty of her crew during the ill-fated Operation Cerberus of February 1942, when the *Scharnhorst* and the *Gneisenau* broke out of Brest. Walker's ship managed to limp back to Harwich.

Two wounded soldiers had such remarkable recoveries from serious injuries that they were playing international football within a matter of weeks. Arsenal winger Horace Cumner joined the Royal Marines and early in the war suffered severe burns following an accident at a military base. Six weeks later, in October 1942, Cumner scored both Welsh goals in their 2–1 victory over England at Molineux. Bob Thyne, a Darlington centre-half who had signed from Clydebank during the war, was on convalescent leave in London in October 1944, recovering from shock and wounds sustained when his trench took a direct hit on D-Day plus 6. When Bill Shankly reported to the Scotland camp with an injury, Thyne was the only available replacement and became the first Darlington footballer to appear at international level when, with a shell splinter still in his thigh, he played against England at Wembley. Thyne marked Tommy Lawton that day, but the England centre-forward showed no mercy with a hat-trick in his side's 6–2 win. Bob Davies of Nottingham Forest joined the RAF at the outbreak of the war and made nearly 300 parachute jumps before an accident which saw both his legs encased in plaster. Davies, who played five times for Wales during the war, recovered to play again.

Many others survived the war unscathed, despite seeing plenty of action. Liverpool-born Eddie Spicer signed professional forms for the Anfield club as soon as he was 17, in October 1939, but there were no opportunities for him as the war took him away from Merseyside. Late in 1944, however, the game of football re-entered his life in a most unexpected way. By then a Royal Marine commando, Spicer was about to accept the surrender of a sergeant in the German medical corps when his enemy called out, 'Don't shoot. I'm a German football international.' The man, who spoke perfect English, said that he had played against Aston Villa's Ernie Callaghan in 1938 and that they had corresponded for a while. Spicer wrote to his own mother, 'We had an interesting chat while he was being patched up. You'd have thought we were the best of friends.' Spicer was back in England for his first-team debut for Liverpool in the 1945–6 season and went on to make 168 appearances for them, despite twice suffering a broken leg.

One of Spicer's Anfield teammates, Berry Nieuwenhuys, a winger recruited by Liverpool from South African football in 1933, had scored 79 goals in 260 games before war broke out. He joined the RAF and in 1944 was awarded the Czech Medal of Honour in recognition of his service as an instructor with a Czech fighter squadron. Nieuwenhuys appeared in the Liverpool side that won the first postwar League championship before he returned to South Africa in 1949.

As a Partick Thistle player, Peter 'Ma Ba' McKennan would have been delighted with a hat-trick against Rangers. When it came, however, it was not for Thistle but for the BAOR team that beat Rangers 6–1 in Hanover in October 1945. Just over a year earlier, McKennan had been involved in the battle for Caen in July 1944, when he was serving as a sergeant major in the Royal Welch Fusiliers. In August 1945, it was recorded that he had been mentioned in despatches. McKennan had signed for Partick in 1935 and after the war joined West Brom for £10,650, then not far short of the British record transfer fee. His colourful career eventually encompassed the Irish League as well.

Tommy Briggs was one of postwar football's most prolific goalscorers, his career with Grimsby, Coventry, Birmingham and Blackburn bringing him 265 goals in 407 games. Yet the war had taken him to Plymouth and it was there that his professional career began. Briggs played amateur football in the Doncaster area before being called up to the Royal Navy. After serving on landing craft in the Mediterranean, at the war's end he found himself in Plymouth and joined the local Argyle club. Briggs, though, was far from home and in June 1947 asked for a transfer and moved to Grimsby Town to begin his career in earnest. Since Ernie Taylor stood only 5ft 4in tall, it was no surprise that he chose the submarine service during the Second World War. Sunderland-born but on Newcastle United's books when he joined up in 1942, Taylor made a big name for himself after the war. He was part of the famous Blackpool team of the Matthews–Mortensen era in the 1950s, and then signed for Manchester United to help them after the Munich air disaster of 1958. Alf Fitzgerald, a high scorer with QPR before the war, was also a submariner. Fitzgerald made an impressive start to 1944–5 after being unable to play for QPR for the best part of two years: he scored 4 goals in the first three games of that season.

Jackie Bray cost Manchester City £1,000 when he joined them from Manchester Central in October 1929. A clever wing-half, he appeared in two FA Cup finals for City, as well as winning a League championship medal with them and gaining six England caps. After 280 peacetime appearances, he made 177 in wartime, despite joining the RAF in the early stages of the conflict. In late 1945, Flight Sergeant John Bray was awarded the BEM for his work in helping to rehabilitate wounded airmen.

Eric Westwood was a rarity, a Manchester man who played for both United and City, although he was only an amateur at Old Trafford before moving across the city in November 1937. He was a regular at full-back when war intervened but then guested mostly for Chelsea, playing for them in the 1944 War Cup final. Then he went to Normandy, where he fought with distinction before returning to Maine Road in 1946. Westwood ended his career there in 1953 after 263 appearances.

Ken Chisholm, one of football's most colourful characters, served as an RAF bomber pilot when he was playing for the famous Glasgow amateur club, Queen's Park. Chisholm guested for Manchester City, Bradford Park Avenue, Chelsea and Leicester, and won a Scottish 'victory' cap, before signing as a professional for Partick Thistle in June 1946. His career then took him to Leeds United, to an FA Cup Final with Leicester, and to Coventry, Cardiff, Sunderland and Workington. He was renowned as a dressing-room comedian but presumably was not smiling when he became one of several Sunderland players suspended after an illegal-payments scandal in the 1950s.

Sheffield Wednesday outside-left Dennis Woodhead had joined the club as an amateur in June 1942, when he was serving in the RAF. As a flight engineer he flew more than thirty operational missions and on his demob signed for the Owls as a full-time professional. He was involved in two promotions with Wednesday and also helped Derby County back to the Second Division in 1956–7.

Alf Barratt joined Northampton Town in September 1938, appearing in one League game before war broke out. He made one wartime appearance for Northampton, but was busier with 47 Royal Marine Commando, with whom he went ashore on D-Day; in November 1944 he took part in the battle to gain control of Walcheren Island, the one great obstacle to the use of the port of Antwerp. He signed for Leicester City in September 1946 and spent four years captaining their reserve team before moving to Grimsby and then to Southport, where he at last gained a regular place to make over 200 League appearances.

West Ham United centre-half Dick Walker had made over 100 senior appearances before the war. Walker first joined the War Reserve Police before enlisting in the army. He made nearly 100 jumps as a paratrooper and also played for the British Army in the Middle East. Walker also managed 100 wartime appearances for the Hammers, including the 1940 War Cup final. After the war he became the Hammers' captain, making over 300 appearances for the first team and then another 200 for the reserves.

Billy Elliott was a 16-year-old local amateur when he made his debut for Bradford Park Avenue in a 5–1 win at home to Rotherham in May 1941. Elliott managed forty-eight appearances before he joined the Royal Navy. He served on a frigate engaged in hunting for U-boats, but he also found time to play for naval representative teams abroad. The early exposure to senior football certainly helped Elliott's career: after the war he made over 500 appearances for Bradford, Burnley and Sunderland, and won five caps for England at outside-left.

Walthamstow Avenue goalkeeper Larry Gage, a paratrooper, played in the Fulham team in 1944–5 and, according to one report, 'looked good on his return to football'. Gage later went to Aldershot and to Canada before returning to Craven Cottage as fourth-choice goalkeeper, but at Easter 1949 an injury crisis saw him play three games which yielded two wins and a draw and gained Fulham the Second Division championship.

Fulham outside-left Ernie Shepherd made his League debut in a 1–1 draw against Luton Town in the last game before war was declared, then guested for Bradford City and Huddersfield Town in his native Yorkshire. Shepherd enlisted in the RAF and survived the heavy bombing on Malta to play in three postwar promotion teams: Fulham, West Brom and Hull City. Len Quested played for Folkestone Town in the Southern League before joining Fulham as an amateur in 1940–1. After naval service, he became a professional in 1946 and went on to play in 188 games, winning one England 'B' cap, before a controversial transfer to Huddersfield, for whom he played 220 League games. In the early 1980s he was a director of a football club in Australia, where he had enjoyed some of his wartime naval service. When Derby and former Arsenal goalkeeper Frank Boulton made his first wartime appearance for the Rams, in May 1943, he looked 'a shadow of his former self', having lost two stones while serving with the RAF in West Africa. Peter Kippax played for Burnley as an amateur during the war, in which he served as a fighter pilot. Kippax, who had business interests which prevented him from becoming a professional player, nonetheless appeared in the 1947 FA Cup final for Burnley against Charlton, and in 1948 represented Great Britain in the Olympic Games in London. Bill Slater, who later played as an amateur for Blackpool in an FA Cup final before turning professional and playing for Wolves and England, was all kitted out for the Far East when the atomic bombs were dropped on Japan. Instead he was posted to the army of occupation on the Rhine.

Several members of Yeovil Town's famous Southern League team that sensationally beat First Division 'Bank of England' club, Sunderland, in the FA Cup in 1949 had seen active service. Bob Keeton was Derbyshire-born but made his way to the South West for a career in the Football League, making his debut at right-back for Torquay United against Swindon Town in February 1938, when he was 19. During the war he served as a paratrooper in Italy before returning to Plainmoor to pick up his League career in 1946. Nick Collins was another member of that famous Yeovil team. Collins joined Crystal Palace from Canterbury Wanderers in 1934 and made 151 appearances for them before the war. More remarkable was the fact that he had been almost an ever-present at wing-half for the first three wartime seasons; he missed only four matches out of a possible 118 in those turbulent times. Working at a local munitions factory obviously helped him to play regularly, but even so it was an enviable record. From 1942–3, however, his name is missing from Palace's line-ups. By then he was a Royal Naval anti-aircraft gunner serving on merchant ships. In 1946, aged 35, he too signed for Yeovil. Alec Stock, the player-manager of Yeovil on that epic day when Sunderland were beaten, was a captain with the Northamptonshire Yeomanry when he was wounded at Caen in 1944 while commanding a tank. Before the war, Stock had played for Queen's Park Rangers; during the conflict he guested for several clubs including Clapton Orient. His guiding of Yeovil to Cup glory brought his management skills to a wider audience and he later took charge of a number of clubs, including QPR, Fulham and AS Roma. Arthur Hickman, a wartime guest with Aston Villa, was at right-back in the Yeovil team. He was one of the first British troops to enter Belsen concentration camp.

Not all were fortunate enough to survive the war and have football careers ahead of them. Jimmy Blakeney was still 18 when he made a name for himself with 11 goals in only twenty appearances for Accrington Stanley in the Third Division North in 1937–8. The following close season, Arsenal paid £500 for his signature but the war ended his dreams of playing for what was then arguably the most famous club in the world. After serving as a machine-gunner on a merchant vessel, Blakeney suffered a serious accident in 1942. Despite having a metal plate inserted into his leg, he did play in North East junior football after the war, but top-class football was out of the question. Harry Colley, who played a few games at outside-right for Arsenal in 1942–3, was badly injured when a lorry in which he was travelling during the North African campaign hit a mine. A sergeant serving in the Eighth Army, Colley was another footballer whose dreams of a top-class career were ended by the war. Tom Jones entered League football with Accrington Stanley before being transferred to Oldham Athletic in January 1939. During the war, Jones, a tall and creative centre-half, guested for Rochdale and made his final appearance for them in December 1944 before his army posting to Europe. In April 1945, Jones was seriously wounded and had to have both his feet amputated. Five months later he was able to attend two benefit matches held for him, when Accrington met Rochdale home and away.

Tommy Lumley, a postwar player with Charlton Athletic, Barnsley and Darlington, might have started his football career much earlier. Instead he endured a most uncomfortable and often hazardous war. Lumley had trials with Newcastle United and Sunderland before joining the Royal Navy in December 1942, when he was 18. On D-Day, as a wireman on a landing craft with Combined Operations, he was in continuous transit back and forth across the Channel, landing Bren-gun carriers, flail tanks and track layers. Throughout his naval career, Lumley had suffered from violent seasickness and in December 1944 was transferred to

Hayling Island. He was there long enough for a naval dentist to give him nine fillings without anaesthetic before Lumley was posted to India. At last Lumley found happiness. He was put in charge of the sports store and played in the Navy team that won the camp cup. They also played regular fixtures against Italian POWs on an island in the bay. The pitch was shale 'except in the monsoon, when it was a mudheap'. Demobbed in March 1946, Lumley returned home to play for Consett before Charlton gave him his chance in the Football League. It seemed the least he deserved after such a miserable war.

Perhaps the most famous bunch of wartime footballers were the Bolton Wanderers team who, in April 1939, descended on the town's Territorial Recruitment Office to sign on for the 53rd Field Regiment of the Bolton Artillery, in which many of them would spend the entire war. Among them was Stan Hanson, who, fourteen years later, was to keep goal for Bolton in probably the most famous FA Cup final of them all, the so-called 'Matthews Final'. The Bolton unit were at El Alamein, then in Iraq and in Italy, where they lost their great captain, Harry Goslin, killed in action. Goslin was one of several footballers who would make the ultimate sacrifice in war.

9

IT IS WITH DEEP REGRET . . .

The danger and loss of life was constantly with you. You sensed it and feared it . . . It was a real eye-opener. The heartache of listening to grown men, hard men, sitting up in bed crying at night; the empty feeling when a death was announced.

Tom Finney, Preston North End and England

Jackie Pritchard was a goalkeeper of real promise when he won a regular place with Cardiff City in 1940–1. He was also a local lad, which, even allowing for the haphazard nature of wartime football, made his transition to the Cardiff first team particularly pleasing. At the end of that season, however, Pritchard disappeared from the Cardiff line-up. He had enlisted in the local Territorial 77th (Welsh) Heavy Artillery Anti-Aircraft Regiment, and on a grey December day in 1941, along with three City teammates, found himself on a troopship slipping down the Clyde. They were bound for the Middle East but, within twenty-four hours, the Japanese had attacked the American naval base at Pearl Harbor and simultaneously invaded British Malaya. Half the convoy in which the Cardiff boys were sailing was diverted to the Far East. The fate of Gunner Jackie Pritchard was sealed.

As Britain's disaster in South East Asia unfolded, he was involved in weeks of heavy fighting before being taken prisoner in Java. Two years later, Pritchard's mother answered the door at her home in Greenhill Street, Splott, to be confronted by a telegram boy. Her 24-year-old son had lost his life at sea. Grief stricken, she wanted to know how this could have happened; after all, he had been in a prison camp. There were no immediate answers. Indeed, it would be several years before the truth emerged about one of the most shameful episodes of the Second World War. On 29 November 1943, Cardiff City's goalkeeper was one of 548 slave-labour prisoners of war being moved aboard the unmarked Japanese prison ship *Suez Maru* when it was torpedoed by the American submarine USS *Bonefish* north of Bali. The POWs, who had been put to work building airfields, were all in desperate physical condition. Even young men as fit as Jackie Pritchard had been worked almost to death. They were of no further use to the Japanese. When the *Suez Maru* sank, the crew were rescued by a minesweeper. Then the minesweeper's captain ordered its machine guns to be turned on the Allied prisoners in the water. None survived; Jackie Pritchard's name would never again feature on a Cardiff team-sheet.

So the game of professional football, like all other walks of civilian life, suffered its tragedies. Of all the clubs to be affected by the war, Arsenal were probably the worst hit. They had already lost their ground for the duration but the fates that overtook their playing staff were devastating. No less than nine Arsenal footballers died while serving in the forces during the Second World War, on land, at sea and in the air. Sid Pugh was one of them. He hailed from Dartford and joined the Gunners straight from school in April 1936. In the days before apprentice footballers, he was put to work as a telephonist at Highbury and farmed out to Arsenal's nursery club, Margate. Signed as a full-time professional in May 1938, Pugh, a promising half-back, was given his League debut at Birmingham the following April but sustained a severe kidney injury. After war was declared, he joined the RAFVR but in September 1940 managed a guest appearance for Bradford City in their derby game against Bradford Park Avenue. After that he became a regular guest for Northampton Town, but on 15 April 1944, 24-year-old Flying Officer Sidney Pugh was killed on active service.

Cyril Tooze was another member of Arsenal's Margate nursery, where he played under manager Jack Lambert, the former Gunners centre-forward. After the war started, Tooze guested for Brighton.

On 22 January 1944, aged 25, Fusilier Cyril Tooze of the 9th Battalion, Royal Fusiliers was killed by a sniper's bullet during the battle to breach the Gustav Line in Italy.

After he had made his debut against Southend United in October 1940 – a game which attracted only 1,410 spectators to White Hart Lane – goalkeeper Bill Dean, a local footballer more used to playing for his works' team, declared, 'Well at least I can say I played for Arsenal.' Dean appeared twice more before going to sea. On 11 March 1942, he was serving as a stoker 2nd class aboard the light cruiser HMS *Naiad* when she was torpedoed by a U-boat in the eastern Mediterranean.

Swansea-born Bobby Daniel was tipped to have a bright future at Highbury and during the early part of the war he appeared in representative matches for a 'Welsh XI'. Against Western Command at Rhyl in May 1942, he scored twice in his side's 4–1 win. In the return match at Wrexham a month later, he was on target again, in a 2–0 victory. On Christmas Eve 1943, 21-year-old Flight Sergeant Bobby Daniel, RAFVR, was killed on a mission to Prague while flying as an air-gunner with 156 Squadron of the Pathfinder Force. After the war, his younger brother, Ray, starred for both Arsenal and Wales.

Outside-right William Parr was an England amateur international who played eighteen times for Blackpool from his League debut in 1935. Leaving the north to work in Wembley, he assisted Dulwich Hamlet before joining Arsenal in May 1939. Parr made his Arsenal debut in a 5–0 win at Southend in April 1940. A sergeant pilot in the RAFVR, he was killed while serving with the U-boat-hunting 233 Squadron on 8 March 1942, aged 26. Just over a year later, another Arsenal footballer serving in the RAFVR also lost his life in the air.

On 18 March 1943, Sergeant Leslie Lack, aged 22, was reported missing while flying a Spitfire over Holland with 118 Squadron. Lack, an amateur player with Tufnell Park and whose parents lived at Clerkenwell, had been on Arsenal's books without ever having the opportunity to make an impression.

Hugh Glass joined the Gunners from Bonnyrigg Rose, a Scottish junior club, in September 1938 and although he never made the first team, he played in Arsenal's Southern League side throughout 1938–9, in one match partnering Denis Compton on the left wing. On the outbreak of war, Glass joined the Merchant Navy. He was lost at sea on 26 November 1942 when SS *Ocean Crusader*, on which he was serving as a greaser, was sunk by a U-boat north of Newfoundland.

Albert Woolcock, an England amateur international goalkeeper who played for Cambridge University and the famous Corinthians, had two games for Arsenal's reserves in the London Combination League in 1938. A flying officer in the RAFVR, he was killed on board the SS *Abukir* while being evacuated from Dunkirk on 28 May 1940, aged 25.

Harry Cook, an amateur on the books in 1942–3, was killed in a flying accident on 26 February 1943. A sub-lieutenant in the RNVR, he was serving at HMS *Landrail*, the Royal Naval Air Station Machrihanish deck-landing school near Campbeltown.

On 17 June 1944, Arsenal lost one of their great pre-war players when Lieutenant Herbie Roberts of the Royal Fusiliers, centre-half in the Gunners' golden era of the 1930s, died suddenly in Middlesex Hospital after contracting the skin disease erysipelas. Roberts had trained as a gunsmith in his native Oswestry and played for the local team before Arsenal signed him in December 1926, for £200. In October 1937, after well over 300 appearances for the Gunners, he suffered a knee injury which ended his career, and then became trainer to one of the junior sides before enlisting.

Jack Lambert, the prolific centre-forward of the late 1920s and early 1930s, was killed in a car crash in December 1940. Such was his fame that even the *Nevada State Journal* carried the story.

Big clubs or small, it did not matter – all saw sadness. The war did not differentiate between the high flyers and those striving to join them. In 1939, Barnsley had just won a place in the Second Division when their success was interrupted. In the years leading up to the war, outside-right George Bullock was one of the Oakwell club's brighter prospects. Born in Wolverhampton during the First World War, Bullock had been on Birmingham's books before joining Barnsley from Stafford Rangers in 1936. Twelve goals in seventy-one League appearances augured well for the future, and when he guested for Portsmouth in 1942–3 he finished the season as their leading scorer, with 20 goals, including 4 in a game at Fulham in February. Three months later, on 31 May 1943, Naval Airman 1st Class Bullock of the Royal Naval Air Station HMS *Blackcap* was killed in a road accident.

Arthur Baxter was another Barnsley forward killed on active service. A Scotsman, Baxter had done the rounds with Portsmouth, Falkirk and his home-town club, Dundee, but had never appeared in Football League football until Barnsley took him on. He made half a dozen appearances at inside-forward during their Third Division North championship-winning season of 1938–9, when he was 28. On 5 September 1944, Baxter, a private in the Gordon Highlanders, was killed in Italy during the advance on the Gothic Line.

Sheffield United lost two players: Joe Carr, a locally born full-back, was killed at Dunkirk on 31 May 1940, while serving as a gunner in the Royal Artillery; Harry Hampson, scorer of 14 goals in forty-one League games in peacetime, had been the first Sheffield United player to enlist in 1939. A corporal in the Royal Armoured Corps, Hampson died from septicaemia on 24 June 1942.

Most Midlands clubs were affected. Ray Harris, a player in Birmingham's reserves, was a flying officer with Bomber Command's 51 Squadron when he was killed over Holland on 30 March 1943. Tom Farrage scored 3 goals in ten games as an outside-left with Birmingham before the war and then played as a guest for Leeds United, Luton Town and Middlesbrough. A private in the Parachute Regiment, he was killed near Arnhem on 23 September 1944. Bill Darby was on West Brom's books when war was declared. A guardsman in the 3rd Battalion, Coldstream Guards, he was killed in Italy on 27 January 1944. George Handley, a West Brom reserve in the 1930s, died in Italy on 9 July 1943. He was a lance corporal in the South Staffordshire Regiment. Three months after he had played in the 1941–2 War Cup final, Wolves right-half Eric Robinson, who had also guested for York City, was dead. A 23-year-old sergeant in the East Lancashire Regiment, he drowned on 20 August 1942, while on a military exercise. The following year Wolves also lost reserve-teamer Joe Rooney, reportedly killed in Italy, aged 24.

Nottingham Forest saw five of their players killed. Grenville Roberts, an inside-forward from local football, joined Forest in March 1937 and managed half a dozen games in the last two seasons before the war. A private in the West Yorkshire Regiment, he was killed at Dunkirk on 3 June 1940, aged 21. Outside-right Colin Perry was an Aston Villa player before joining Forest in the 1939 close season, along with outside-left Jack Maund. Perry played in all three games of the aborted 1939–40 season, scoring in the 2–0 home win over Newcastle United. A driver in the RASC, he was killed at Tobruk on 28 November 1942. Alf Moult was 19 when he died in France on 11 July 1944, while serving as a private in the 10th Battalion, Durham Light Infantry. Forest full-back Joe Croft and wing-half Frank Johnson, both reserves, also perished.

The former Derby and England captain Tom Cooper, who had been transferred to Liverpool in December 1934, was serving as a regimental policeman in the King's Regiment when he died following a motorcycle accident in Suffolk on 25 June 1940. Derby lost one player: Donald Marriott was one of several local amateurs who turned out for the Rams during the war. He came from the Derbyshire village of Ticknall and was a wireless operator/air gunner in the RAFVR when he was killed on 2 June 1943, aged 22.

Albert Clarke played for Torquay United and Birmingham before being transferred to Blackburn Rovers in 1938. He was an instant success at Ewood Park, scoring 2 goals on his debut and finishing as Blackburn's leading scorer in the last peacetime season, when they won the Second Division title. After 1939–40, he made no further appearances for them, although he guested for Torquay, Newport County and Cardiff City. On 16 June 1944, a private in the Devonshire Regiment, he was killed near Ranville in France.

Left-half Frank Chivers was the driving force behind Blackburn's championship success in 1938–9, although when Rovers signed him from Huddersfield Town in March 1938, it was as a centre-forward.

Chivers had worked down the pit in South Yorkshire when he was playing as an amateur with Barnsley in the late 1920s. On the outbreak of war he returned to the mines and guested for his old club, Huddersfield, but in April 1942 he was killed in a mining accident in the Don Valley.

Lieutenant Harry Goslin, who was fighting with the famous Bolton Wanderers unit, the 53rd Field Regiment, Royal Artillery, was killed on 18 December 1943. His unit was under ferocious German attack in the Apennine Mountains when a shell exploded in a tree directly above him. His death came as a great shock to the people of Bolton, for whose club he had made 334 peacetime appearances, many of them as an inspirational captain. During the war he had played for England and guested for Norwich City and Chelsea. His last appearance for Bolton had come in March 1942 when, on a short leave, he played for them at York.

The Rosenthal brothers of Tranmere Rovers both suffered tragic ends, albeit forty-four years apart. Reserve player Gordon Rosenthal was 22 when he was killed on 10 August 1942 while serving as a sergeant pilot in the RAF. He was flying a Spitfire when it came down in the River Dee. Gordon was an excellent swimmer who had represented Liverpool, but when the aircraft landed in the water he was concussed after hitting his head on the cockpit canopy and was drowned. Gordon's brother, Abe, made one appearance for Tranmere before the outbreak of the war, in which he served as a glider pilot. During the war, Abe guested for St Mirren, Bath City and Swindon Town before enjoying a good career with Bradford City and Tranmere. At Bradford, he was a part-time player who owned a lollipop and ice-cream making business behind a stand at Valley Parade. Abe had survived the war but in February 1986, after disturbing an intruder at his Liverpool home, he suffered a heart attack from which he did not recover.

Inside-forward Stan Docking made a decent enough start to his football career with local club Newcastle United but, still unable to hold down a regular place, he was transferred to Tranmere for £1,000 in 1938. Docking scored 7 goals in thirty-one League games during the last peacetime season, but in the summer of 1939 returned to the North East to sign for Hartlepool United. Aircraftman 2nd Class Docking was serving in the RAFVR when he died on 27 May 1940.

Ernie Davies was signed by Tranmere from Cheshire amateur football in November 1936 and made forty-seven League appearances for them before signing for York City in 1939. The outbreak of war meant that Davies did not play for his new club but instead continued to guest for Tranmere in the early wartime seasons. In August 1942, a corporal in the 1st Battalion, King's Own Royal Regiment (Lancaster), he was killed in North Africa, aged 26.

Former England schoolboy international Stan Duff had a spell with Tranmere too, and was also on the books of Leicester City and Chester before joining New Brighton in 1939. Leading Aircraftman Duff was serving as a wireless operator/air gunner when he was killed in September 1941. Keith Haimes, whose middle names were Armistice Theobold, signed for Tranmere as an amateur in October 1940. He was killed in Holland in October 1944, serving as a lance sergeant in the 5th Battalion, the Wiltshire Regiment. Across the Mersey from Tranmere, bad news eventually filtered through to Goodison Park. Leading Aircraftman Brian Atkins, a Liverpool man who had been signed by Everton, was 22 when he died in Italy on 22 April 1944. Bill Sumner played two games for Everton in each of the first two seasons of regional football before he also became a casualty of war. Liverpool reserve George Collister was a sub-lieutenant in the RNVR when he lost his life in a road accident in Holland on 13 May 1945, aged 23.

Leeds United lost several of their playing staff, the most well-known of whom was England international inside-forward Eric Stephenson, who had been capped against Scotland and Northern Ireland before the war. Stephenson played for Leeds in the first two wartime seasons, when he was serving as a PTI, but it was as a major in the 2nd King Edward VII's Own Gurkha Rifles (The Sirmoor Rifles) that he was killed in Burma on 8 September 1944. In the 1946–7 season, Leeds played Celtic in a benefit match for Stephenson's widow.

Robert Montgomery, who had signed for Leeds from the Irish club Portadown, was one of the first players from Elland Road to enlist. He joined the RAF, and was killed in the early part of 1944. Former England schoolboy international, Les Thompson, who came from the Dearne Valley, was killed in Burma in July 1945 while serving as a private in the 2nd Battalion, Welch Regiment. Alan Fowler was yet another England schoolboy star who signed for Leeds, but despite a decent return of 8 goals in fifteen League appearances he found his chances limited at Elland Road. In 1934 he moved to Swindon Town and was their leading scorer for three seasons up to the war. Fowler was 37 when he was killed while serving as a sergeant in the 4th Battalion, Dorsetshire Regiment, in France on 10 July 1944. A plaque was dedicated to him at Swindon's ground. Swindon Town listed two other players among their wartime losses: Bill Imrie, the former Scottish international, and Jim Olney, both half-backs.

In September 1939, Alf Keeling appeared to have the football world at his feet. Born in Bradford in 1920, Keeling had been a phenomenal success at almost every sport he tried as a schoolboy: football, cricket, athletics and tennis all came naturally to him. He made one League appearance for Bradford Park Avenue before Portsmouth signed him in April 1938. Before Pompey could give him a game, however, Manchester City stepped in to take him to Maine Road. Then war was declared and Keeling found himself guesting for both Bradford clubs while awaiting his call-up. In May 1941, Keeling joined the RAF and learned to fly in Calgary under the Empire Training Scheme. Posted to 235 Squadron, he was piloting a Bristol Beaufighter when it shot down a Junkers 88 over the Bay of Biscay in October 1942. He told the *Morley Observer*: 'We saw it first and thought it was another Beaufighter. Then, as we closed and opened up, the Junkers tried to turn away but one of its engines gave out black smoke and it went straight down into the sea on one wing tip.' On the way home, the Beaufighter's compass began to behave erratically and Sergeant Keeling brought the aircraft down on the French coast. German anti-aircraft fire damaged the plane's hydraulics and undercarriage but Keeling eventually got the aircraft back home, although he had to perform a belly-landing. On 1 December 1942, Keeling was again flying over the Bay of Biscay when his aircraft was shot down. No trace of the aircraft, Alf Keeling or his navigator, Sergeant Jack Brook, was found.

Luton Town goalkeeper Joe Coen was signed from Bournemouth in 1932, although he was a Glaswegian. He made 145 peacetime League appearances for Luton but on 15 October 1941, three days before he was due to play for the Hatters at Leicester, Leading Aircraftman Coen, a pilot under training, was killed in a flying accident. Charlie Ladd, also on Luton's books, was a stoker 2nd class when he was one of 1,418 sailors lost when HMS *Hood*, the symbolic flagship of the British fleet, was sunk by the German battleship *Bismarck* during the Battle of the Denmark Strait on 24 May 1941. Three years earlier, the *Hood*'s football team had defeated a team from the German pocket battleship *Deutchsland*. Luton also lost Charlie Clark, a pre-war reserve, to the war. He was a lance sergeant in the Hampshire Regiment when he died of his wounds in Tunisia in January 1943.

Albert Bonass, the former York, Darlington, Hartlepools United and Chesterfield outside-left, was already quite a veteran when he left Third Division North football to sign for Queen's Park Rangers of the Southern Section in the summer of 1939. Bonass played in all three games of the aborted 1939–40 season before returning north to join the RAF. A native of York, Sergeant Bonass, a wireless operator, guested for his former club and had been named in their team to meet Halifax Town at The Shay when, on 9 October 1945, he was killed in a flying accident near York. He was 34.

Thus, the business of football and the tragedy of war sometimes seemed to go hand in hand. Jack Wilkinson, an army motorcyclist, was named as goalkeeper for the Eastern Command team to meet a Football League XI at Ipswich in February 1943. A few days later, Wilkinson, who was on Sheffield Wednesday's books, was killed in a motoring accident. Corporal Tommy Taylor of the Durham Light Infantry was on the books of Preston North End when he played as a guest for Middlesbrough against Bradford (PA) in a League North match at Ayresome Park on 4 April 1942. Taylor scored a hat-trick, including a penalty, in Boro's 3–2 win. Six days later he was killed in a motorcycle accident near his army camp. Preston's David Willacy was a 25-year-old sergeant pilot in the RAFVR when he died on 1 September 1941. Another player on Sheffield Wednesday's books to die was Ordinary Seaman Albert Stanton, who was 21 when he was killed on 20 August 1942, serving in a landing craft.

York-born Les Milner played a single game for his local club before being transferred to Hull City, but failed to make his mark there and returned to York City, making another ten appearances and scoring 4 goals before the war. A sergeant in the Seaforth Highlanders, he was killed near Bayeux on 25 June 1944, aged 26. Lance Corporal of Horse Geoff Reynolds of the Life Guards was also attached to York City when he was killed on 4 August 1944. Local boy Gordon Addy was a brilliant teenage footballer when Norwich City signed him. Addy continued to impress during wartime football for the Canaries. As a private in the 1st Battalion, Royal Norfolk Regiment, he was killed in March 1945, during the crossing of the Rhine. Another Norwich player to die was full-back Alex Johnson, who played five times in 1938–9. A corporal in the RAFVR, he lost his life in the Middle East on 31 July 1944. Private Peter Monaghan of the Highland Light Infantry (City of Glasgow Regiment) was 27 when he died in Holland on 27 January 1945. Before the war, Monaghan had appeared in sixty-seven League games for Bournemouth in the Third Division South. He was in the Bournemouth team that had humiliated Northampton Town 10–0 on the last Saturday of peace. In May 1946, Bournemouth staged a benefit match for his wife and daughter, against Southampton.

Allan Thorney of Crystal Palace, a 19-year-old guardsman with the Irish Guards, died on 7 June 1943. In October 1944, his brother John, also a guardsman in the same regiment, was killed in Holland. Harry Strike, who was with Halifax Town, was serving as a corporal in the 7th Battalion, Seaforth Highlanders when he was killed in France on 30 June 1944. Hubert Redwood, Manchester United's pre-war right-back, was a corporal in the South Lancashire

Regiment when he died on 28 October 1943, shortly before being discharged from the army.

Wally Sidebottom played one game for Bolton Wanderers during peacetime, at outside-left against Huddersfield in 1938–9. He was a regular for the first two wartime seasons and also guested for Rochdale, for whom he scored 5 goals against Southport in November 1940. On 23 October 1943, Sidebottom perished in the biggest British naval disaster in the English Channel during the Second World War. An able seaman, he was serving on the light cruiser HMS *Charybdis* when she was sunk by German E-boats. Altogether, 460 men from Sidebottom's ship died during the failed attempt to intercept the German blockade runner *Munsterland*.

George Salvidge made four League appearances at outside-right for Hull City before the war. He was killed at Tobruk on 23 November 1941, a lance corporal in the 2nd Battalion, York and Lancaster Regiment. Wilf Shaw was a long-serving full-back with Doncaster Rovers: 184 League games between 1930 and 1939. A private in the 2nd Battalion, Argyll and Sutherland Highlanders, Shaw died on the Dutch–German border on 20 February 1945, aged 32.

Fulham lost several players. Jimmy Tompkins, the Cottagers' outstanding left-half of the 1930s, started the war as a private in the Territorial Army, but by D-Day he was a major in the Royal Fusiliers. He had been seconded to the Hampshire Regiment when he died in France on 10 July 1944. A few weeks later, his wife was killed by a flying bomb in London. In the 1950s their son, Neil, who was briefly on Fulham's books, was a National Serviceman when he also lost his life. By 1939, Dennis Higgins had established himself at outside-right in Fulham's first team; in January of that year he scored a hat-trick at Bradford. He was a private in the Durham Light Infantry when he was killed in North Africa on 25 September 1942. Neither George Fairbairn nor Ernie Tuckett – who had previously played for Arsenal and Bradford City – had managed to break into Fulham's first team by the time war was declared. Guardsman Fairbairn of the 2nd Battalion, Coldstream Guards was killed in Tunisia on 21 February 1943; Corporal Tuckett of the

RAFVR died on 27 May 1945, following an accident at a Yorkshire airfield. That Tuckett's death should have come after the end of the European war was especially sad because his naval lieutenant father, next to whom he was buried, had died in the final month of the First World War, when Ernie was just 4 years old.

Fred Fisher signed for Millwall from Chesterfield in 1938–9 and ended the season with 6 goals from thirteen games at outside-right. The former Barnsley winger continued to play regularly in the first three seasons of wartime football, but on 10 July 1944, while serving as an air gunner with 166 Squadron RAFVR, Sergeant Fisher was killed over France. Frank Ibbotson, a young outside-left, joined Reading from Portsmouth in May 1939. Two months later he was called up for military training and it is quite likely that he never even trained with Reading, never mind played a game for them. Wounded in the Normandy invasion, Lance Corporal Ibbotson of the RASC died in France on 15 July 1944, aged 25. Inside-forward Bill Isaac, whose family lived in East Cramlington, Northumberland, began his career with Second Division Newcastle United but never made their first team and in 1938 tried his luck with Brighton in the Third Division South. He made three appearances in the 1939–40 season before the Football League closed down. A bombardier in the Royal Artillery, he died on 14 April 1941, aged 21.

Percy Saunders joined Brentford from Sunderland just before the start of the 1939–40 season and scored his new club's first goal of the campaign, a seventieth-minute effort which earned them a 1–1 draw at Everton. One week later, Saunders's goal had been scrubbed from the records when the Football League closed down. In February 1942, Sergeant Saunders arrived in Singapore with the 18th Divisional Workshop, RAOC; three weeks later that 'impregnable' bastion fell to the Japanese. Percy Saunders died in early March, aged 25, lost at sea while trying to escape.

Charlie Sillett was a defender whose sons, John and Peter, were both to make a name for themselves in postwar football. Charlie was a veteran of 175 League games for Southampton before he signed for non-League Guildford City in 1938. Sillett had joined the

Saints from Tidworth, where he was an army PTI, but it was as a leading seaman in the Merchant Navy that he was to lose his life aboard SS *Corvus* on 27 February 1945, when the ship was torpedoed and sunk by U-1018 off the Lizard; two hours later, the U-boat itself was sunk by depth-charges from the frigate HMS *Loch Fada*.

Bury lost three of their amateur players from the early days of the war. Flight Sergeant Frank Pollard was an air gunner in a Halifax bomber when it crashed on houses in the hamlet of Pont de Tasset, near the Swiss border, on 15 August 1943, whilst on a mission to help the French Resistance. Incredibly the pilot was thrown clear but Pollard and two colleagues had moved into crash position in the 'safer' rear part of the plane. Pollard had appeared in Bury's forward line in 1940–1 and 1941–2. News also came through of the deaths of Bill Poole, who had kept goal in two games in 1941–2, and Jackie Wood, a forward who played in the first wartime season.

Club officials were just as likely to die as players. Ipswich Town's chairman Lieutenant Colonel John Murray Cobbold of the Welsh Guards died on 18 June 1944, when a V1 flying bomb hit the Guards Chapel at Wellington Barracks, London, killing 119 military and civilian worshippers. The Cobbold family had a tragic war. Only a few days earlier, Lieutenant Colonel Cobbold's nephew, Major Robert Cobbold of the Welsh Guards, had been killed in Italy. The V1 which hit the Guards Chapel caused the war's greatest single loss of life due to a flying bomb, but one man who escaped was Stanley Rous, the FA secretary, who had been invited to attend but, at the last minute, was reminded of an engagement at his local Rotary Club and so was not at the fateful service.

Flying Officer Colin Seymour, son of Newcastle United chairman and former player Stan Seymour, was killed in a flying accident near Perth on 9 October 1943. He was a wireless operator/air gunner. Lieutenant David Bearman, younger son of Tottenham Hotspur's chairman, Fred Bearman, died on 19 November 1944. Although a Royal Fusilier, he was seconded to the Somerset Light Infantry when he was killed during the static fighting before the Allied advance in Italy was renewed the following spring. In 1939, Thomas Smith, a former Leeds City player then farming in the Northamptonshire village of Ravensthorpe, was called out of football retirement to manage Northampton Town as they began their first wartime season. For a friendly match against Sheffield Wednesday, he called up his son, Colin, who played in the Cobblers' 7–2 defeat. On 21 August 1942, Sergeant Colin Smith, a wireless operator/air gunner with 218 Squadron, was killed on a bombing raid over Kiel.

10

WARTIME WEMBLEY

There was nothing like walking out at Wembley, even in wartime. When we played Scotland there in 1944 the atmosphere was just like the pre-war days, even better, really, because the war was going our way and everyone in the crowd was in good spirits.

Raich Carter, Sunderland and England

In May 1945, tens of thousands of Londoners poured into the Empire Stadium. Together with a choir conducted by the familiar figure of T. P. Ratcliffe, the FA Cup final's famous 'man in white', they took part in a thanksgiving service to mark the end of the war in Europe. Over 5,000 miles away, however, the war in the Far East was far from over and in the stadium office lay a letter from a group of soldiers serving in Burma: 'As we sit here in the jungle, we are thinking of dear old Wembley.' Their sentiment was unsurprising. Throughout six years of war, Wembley had continued in its role as the home of English football. The stadium had staged cup finals and international matches as the game struggled to keep its shape, ready for the return of men like the soldiers in Burma, who dreamed of the day they would once again cheer on their favourites. For every supporter, football at Wembley meant business as normal, or as normal as it could be under the circumstances. The stadium was also the perfect stage for demonstrating soccer's value to the war effort. If anyone had questioned the importance of football during the early months of the Second World War, when internationals resumed at Wembley there could be no doubting how seriously the Government took the game as a means of boosting morale – and raising money for charity. At one match no less than seven members of the

Cabinet, including Clement Attlee, the future Labour prime minister, were among the crowd. Even Winston Churchill, certainly no natural supporter of the working man's sport in peacetime, was happy to press the flesh of the nation's footballers in time of war.

Many games raised money for war charities and so enjoyed even greater patronage. England's Eddie Hapgood recalled that the royal box was always full for international matches at Wembley, and not just with British royalty. The exiled kings and queens of several European countries occupied by the Nazis were wheeled out to pump the hands of players at international matches and to present trophies at cup finals. So, too, were high-ranking military personnel. Field Marshal Montgomery, and even General Eisenhower, were ready to tread the Wembley turf. Monty was a Portsmouth supporter, the Rt. Hon. A.V. Alexander, First Lord of the Admiralty, was known to shout for Chelsea. The fickle Eisenhower, however, switched his allegiance from Chelsea to Charlton midway through a cup final. After presenting Charlton with the League South Cup at Wembley in April 1944, Ike told reporters, 'I started cheering for the blues, but when I saw the reds were winning, well I had to go on cheering for them.'

If a future US president showed little appreciation of the tribal nature of soccer, almost everyone else felt they were privileged to obtain a Wembley ticket. The home of the FA Cup final since 1923 remained the flagship ground of English football throughout the war, happily escaping the worst of the London Blitz. In 1944, an incendiary bomb which landed on the pitch caused quite a mess but no significant damage; and in August that year, a V1 flying bomb exploded outside the stadium, killing two greyhounds from the nearby kennels and releasing several others into surrounding streets. Sadly, more dogs had perished on the outbreak of war, put down when racing was suspended and no homes could be found for the animals. Many greyhounds were evacuated, however, soon to be returned when a single weekly daylight meeting was allowed from late September 1939. Football returned to the stadium on 13 April 1940, when Wales celebrated their first-ever visit to Wembley by beating England 1–0 before a crowd restricted to 40,000. The Welsh goal came from Bryn Jones, Arsenal's record £14,000 signing from Wolves in 1938. Tottenham's Willie Hall missed a penalty for England; three years later, Hall was to have both his legs amputated following illness. The atmosphere at Wembley was muted, however, not least because four days earlier, Germany had invaded Denmark and Norway. The war was coming closer to home.

By the time of the second big wartime game at Wembley – the cup final between West Ham United and Blackburn Rovers on 8 June 1940 – the stadium was temporary home to hundreds of bewildered French and Belgian refugees who had fled Hitler's blitzkrieg into their countries. Civilians and soldiery alike had choked the roads leading to the Channel ports, and as Blackburn and West Ham were making sure of their Wembley places with semi-final victories over Newcastle and Fulham respectively, the remnants of the BEF were straggling along the beach at Dunkirk, desperate to find space on the last of the small boats sent to rescue them. Although the first cup final of the war lacked the status of a peacetime FA Cup final, there was still plenty of pomp and ceremony as the band of the Irish Guards played the national anthems of Britain and France. At half-time it was announced that there were 'six Dunkirk heroes' in the crowd. They sat in a special section with many of their wounded comrades, who were dressed in hospital uniform of blue jacket, white shirt and red tie. The crowd rose as one to give the soldiers a mighty roar of welcome. It was a far greater cheer even than that which had greeted the only goal of the game, scored by Sam Small of West Ham in the thirty-fourth minute. The Hammers' manager, Ted Fenton, later recalled the game as being about 'as hilarious as a wet Sunday in Cardiff'. Fenton, of course, could never have known that one day cup finals would indeed be staged in Cardiff, albeit with a roof over the stadium to protect spectators from Welsh rain.

Wembley staged six major wartime cup finals, nine wartime international matches involving England, a makeshift international between Belgian and Dutch refugees, and five other prestigious representative games as well as minor matches. In May 1941, Arsenal and Preston North End drew 1–1 in the second League War Cup final, which featured one of those oddities thrown up by the guest system: between appearing against Arsenal in both the Wembley cup final and the replay at Blackburn, Andy Beattie, Preston's left-back, played for the Gunners in a League game at Millwall. At Wembley, Arsenal's Leslie Compton missed a penalty after only 3 minutes, his effort booming back off the woodwork almost to the halfway line. Then Tom Finney, Preston's young outside-right, whipped in a knee-high centre from which Andy McLaren volleyed the Lancashire club in front. Late in the game a breakaway goal by Denis Compton took the teams to Ewood Park, where Preston won 2–1.

Reporting on the 1942 London War Cup final between Portsmouth and Brentford at Wembley, the *Daily Express* said, 'With the last kick of the game the ball was sent into the crowd and a souvenir hunter, although chased by a policeman, escaped with it. The latest bulletin is that the ball has not been recovered.' Brentford won the game 2–0, both goals coming from England winger Leslie Smith. The match programme asked spectators to 'make their way quietly' to the appropriate areas should the warning sirens sound. The following year, the usual Wembley ceremony prevailed before the League South Cup final between Arsenal and Charlton Athletic. Before kick-off, the crowd was entertained by the band of the Coldstream Guards and the teams presented to the Duke of Gloucester. At half-time, a combined American military band took over. In the event of a draw after extra time, the game was to be decided by the next goal or corner, but by the time the musicians of the US 102nd Engineers and the 156th Infantry bands were tuning up, Arsenal were already 4–1 ahead; they scored 3 more goals in the second half to win 7–1. Charlton returned to Wembley for the 1944 League South Cup final, enjoying much better fortune with a 3–1 victory over Chelsea, during which General Eisenhower famously switched sides.

In April 1945, the *Sunday Times* reported increased police activity before the South Cup final between Chelsea and Millwall at Wembley, when uniformed and plain-clothes officers carried out an extensive petrol check. Particular attention was paid to vehicles coming from south-London garages, which were just outside the

10-mile limit for Hackney carriages. Whatever underhand means supporters were using to reach Wembley when only essential journeys were allowed, this was the Wembley final which had so irked Frank Butler of the *Sunday Express*, with its undignified scramble for star guest players and its poor football for all that. Chelsea won 2–0, in front of 90,000 spectators.

Attendances had grown steadily since the 1940 final with its 42,000 crowd, but the capacity was of only academic interest to many supporters, especially in the early years of the war when one of the Wembley cup finalists was guaranteed to be from the north, and even later when the north v. south final was always staged in London. The principle adopted by the Government for transport in wartime was very simple: the needs of the war must come first. That meant absolute priority first for service personnel, then for vital workers and materials. By 1943, hundreds more trains each day were needed. Drastic travel restrictions, including the withdrawal of cheap day tickets and tickets for various kinds of pleasure travel, became effective from September 1942. Jolly days out to Wembley were not easy to arrange. When the poster campaign asked, 'Is Your Journey Really Necessary?' football fans might have argued that it was; the Government did not agree. So supporters from northern clubs mostly tuned in to the wireless instead of descending on the capital, while the crowds for international matches at Wembley were also drawn largely from the London area.

Scotland were the second international visitors of the war, in October 1941 when goals from Jimmy Hagan and Don Welsh gave England a 2–0 victory. The Scots played there twice in 1942. In January, the wife of the Prime Minister was present when England beat Scotland 3–2 on a snow-covered Wembley pitch which bore blue markings instead of the usual white lines. Mrs Churchill had a vested interest: the match was being played in support of her Aid to Russia Fund. After being introduced to the teams, she took a microphone and announced that her husband had that morning returned from signing the Atlantic Charter, the so-called United Nations Agreement. The crowd cheered enthusiastically but the drama of the moment was spoiled somewhat by a sailor who vaulted over the barriers to join Scotland's Jerry Dawson in goal for the pre-match kick-in. Within 60 seconds of the kick-off there was drama of a different kind. Hagan took a pass from Wilf Mannion and left the Scottish defence flat-footed as he skated through to put England ahead. Lawton's two goals completed the scoring, but there was an unhappy ending for his Everton colleague, Torry Gillick: the Scot was carried off on a stretcher after colliding with goalkeeper George Marks. In October, the Scots held England to a draw as Spitfires constantly circled over the 75,000 crowd, a wartime record attendance for an international match in England. King George II of Greece and King Haakon VII of Norway were unlucky enough to witness the first goalless game between the two nations since the original international fixture in 1872.

At half-time in the England–Wales game at Wembley in February 1943, an RAF plane flying at 500ft released six containers on parachutes. Each container held a pigeon belonging to the Royal Signals. Once the containers had fallen to the ground, Signalman Taylor of the Canadian Army released the birds, which carried messages supporting the Wings for Victory campaign. Six months earlier, Signalman Taylor had released two carrier pigeons with news of the ill-fated Dieppe raid in which over 900 of his countrymen lost their lives and many more were wounded or captured. For Wales it was an unhappy return to the stadium where they had recorded a win in the first Wembley international of the war: this time they lost 5–3. The following September, the Welsh again lost heavily at Wembley, this time 8–3 before an 80,000 crowd. There was a similar attendance for England's 6–2 win against Scotland in February 1944, and 90,000 when England repeated that scoreline against the Scots only eight months later. Lawton scored a hat-trick that October afternoon, and when France played at Wembley in May 1945, the Everton centre-forward captained his country for the first time. The game ended in a 2–2 draw, with Lawton and Raich Carter scoring for England, while the Arsenal right-back, Laurie Scott, missed a penalty. The result was a surprise – the French had been expected to lose heavily – but it was the make-up of Wembley's first foreign visitors that said so much about the times.

Goalkeeper Julien Da Rui, who played for Lille OSC, had been taken prisoner at Dunkirk but escaped after three weeks of captivity and made his way back home. Like Ladlislas Siklo, the inside-left from RC Lens, left-back Jean Swiatek was born in Poland. Swiatek moved to France with his family when he was only eighteen months old; he was just making his way in senior football when the Nazis invaded. Swiatek was sent to a labour camp in Germany but in May 1943 escaped and made his way to Bordeaux where, remarkably, he was able to play for the amateur team of Gironde, which won the French championship. Right-back Maurice Dupuis had won club honours with Racing Club of Paris before the war. After the fall of France he became a policeman and played wartime football for Toulouse. He also joined the underground movement and fought in the battle for Paris in 1944. Two other Racing Club players, wing-halves Lucien Jasseron and Jean Samuel, had served in the Free French Air Force. The last 'wartime' visitors to Wembley were the Belgians, who lost 2–0 in January 1946. By then the war was over, but it would be September before official internationals resumed.

From May 1943, the Empire Stadium also played host to several prestigious charity matches between sides representing the RAF, Combined Services, National and Metropolitan Police, and Civil Defence. All the teams were packed with top-class footballers. In April 1946, the Army Physical Training Corps beat an FA XI 5–3 in front of 90,000 spectators. The APTC included Tommy Lawton, Jimmy Hagan, Joe Mercer, Billy Wright and Denis Compton. Despite the titles of the two teams, the game was effectively an international trial match.

Wembley contributed much throughout the war. In 1942 a 'pageant of youth' was staged in the arena. The Fitness for Service movement had encouraged reservists and civilians to take part in physical training and organised sport. American troops had played baseball on the hallowed turf, both teams comprising professional players. When 5,000 members of the Civil Defence were stood down at the war's end, Wembley staged the show. In 1946, the Empire Stadium was still being used as a demob centre for servicemen, some of whom had been released ahead of schedule to help rebuild bomb-damaged London. Indeed, servicemen had been associated with the stadium ever since the Dunkirk evacuation. In 1943 the doors of the restaurant had been thrown open to any member of the armed forces who could get there to enjoy a Christmas party. And in the Burmese jungle, soldiers of the so-called 'Forgotten Army' thought about dear old Wembley and prayed that, one day, they would see her again.

11

THE CAPS THAT DIDN'T COUNT

As we slipped into our plain white shirts – this was not a full international, therefore the FA badge was not on the left breast – the confidence which had been with me for so many days suddenly passed, and instead I felt as nervous as a kitten.

Billy Wright, Wolves and England

It was always a bone of contention with Raich Carter. 'Just think,' he'd complain, sitting in the kitchen of his home at Willerby on the outskirts of Hull, 'you play seventeen times for your country during the war, in some of the best teams ever put out, and you don't have even one cap to show for it.' As it happened, Carter did not even have enough caps to show for his thirteen appearances in peacetime. During a bombing raid on Sunderland in 1943, the Carters' house was hit and his pre-war caps destroyed. Yet if Raich Carter accepted their loss as just one of the misfortunes of war, he was always rankled by the fact that he never had anything to show in the first place for those wartime internationals. The former Sunderland and Derby County inside-right had every reason to feel peeved. Although some of England's early wartime teams may have had a makeshift look about them – at that stage they were not even thought of as unofficial internationals, simply representative matches – by the end of 1941, the England side was looking as strong as many of those fielded before the war. Statistics alone tell part of the story. During the war, England played thirty-six unofficial internationals, fielding almost eighty different players. Thirty of those players had been used in the first three internationals alone; thereafter the side was much more settled. Moreover, players

159

of the calibre of Stanley Matthews, Joe Mercer, Tommy Lawton and Stan Cullis played in the majority of wartime internationals. England lost only eight matches – Carter was on the losing side only once – and won twenty-two. This was certainly a golden era for the national side.

The last peacetime international had been against Romania in May 1939. The first wartime game was against Wales at Ninian Park the following November. The team against the Welsh contained only three players – goalkeeper Vic Woodley and forwards Len Goulden and Leslie Smith – who had appeared in Bucharest six months earlier, although Eddie Hapgood had simply been rested against the Romanians. Four members of England's first wartime side had never won a cap in peacetime, while Walthamstow Avenue's James Lewis, who came on as a substitute, was an amateur international. In contrast, for Wales only Ronnie Burgess had not been capped before, and he would become a great name for them in postwar football. One week later, England and Wales met again, at Wrexham, where the teams were unrecognisable from the sides which had drawn 1–1 only seven days earlier. England fielded eleven different players, Wales five. Despite being 2–0 down at half-time, the English won 3–2. When Scotland were beaten 2–1 at St James's Park, Newcastle, in December 1939, eight more players made their wartime debuts for England. Two of them were from the local club; one of them was a Scot. The Manchester City pair of Sam Barkas and Eric Brook were involved in a motoring accident on their way to the match and England had to call up Newcastle United's Joe Richardson and Edinburgh-born Tommy Pearson, who was to be capped for Scotland in 1947. Brook was so badly injured in the accident that he never played football again.

The first England–Scotland game of the war provided an entirely unexpected international debut for the hard man of the Barnsley defence, Bernard Harper, who was enlisted when Stan Cullis was unable to make the trip north. When Harper, a local lad, was captaining Second Division Barnsley in the last pre-war season, he could never have imagined stepping out for England. He did quite well, as it turned out, but that was the end of his dreams. By 1946, he was considered too old even for Barnsley, despite having kept fit as an RAF PT instructor throughout the war. England's goals came from Lawton and Harry Clifton, another Newcastle player. Blackpool's Jock Dodds scored for the Scots, while Raich Carter missed a late penalty. Carter was to miss another penalty for England later in the war, but still ended it by scoring one more goal than the number of games he had played in.

Thus by the first Christmas of the war, international football had been quickly re-established, although the turnaround of players was bewildering. By the end of the season, England had played twice more, a 1–0 defeat by Wales in April in the first Wembley international of the war, and a 1–1 draw with Scotland at Hampden Park. The Hampden match was staged against the background of the Dunkirk evacuation and a German propaganda broadcast threatening a Luftwaffe attack on the ground before half-time. It was not surprising that Scotland's national football stadium was only half full – that still meant an attendance of around 70,000 – and the barrage balloons hovering silently over Clydebank provided those who still needed it with a grim reminder of the times. There was some doubt as to whether the army had granted leave to Cullis, Mercer, Bert Sproston and Don Welsh, but all four arrived on the same train. However, a few hours before kick-off, Sam Bartram of Charlton Athletic had his RAF leave cancelled, leaving England without a goalkeeper. Chelsea's Vic Woodley, who had kept goal in each of England's last nineteen internationals before the war, jumped on a train north, arriving just in time to spare full-back Eddie Hapgood the ordeal of guarding England's net. Aston Villa's Frank Broome, who played centre-forward that day, recalled, 'Eddie didn't let on, but he was in a real state when he thought he might have to keep goal. They had big Dave McCulloch of Derby at centre-forward and I don't think Eddie fancied it.'

Broome, who was himself a talented all-rounder – he had played in all five forward positions for England before the war and in 1947, as an emergency goalkeeper at Derby, he would keep Tommy Lawton's Chelsea at bay for almost 90 minutes – remembered the strange atmosphere of those early wartime internationals. 'I think the first games were just billed as an England XI. We certainly didn't feel that we were playing for England in the same way that we had done before the war. I'm not sure the spectators took it all that seriously, either. It was just a lift, a bit of a tonic to help forget all the bad news for a while. There wasn't the passion you got in pre-war internationals. I'd never been to Hampden before, but Tommy Lawton said that when he played there a year earlier, and there was a crowd of 150,000, the wall of noise nearly knocked him over when he walked out.' Nevertheless, if the point of playing international football in the earliest days of the war escaped some people, three of the four national associations were anxious to continue in 1940–1, when England met Scotland and Wales twice each. In the first Scotland game, Lawton made his only England appearance of the season in between getting married and being posted to Aldershot, where he would join the growing number of footballers-turned-PTIs. The newly-wed Lawtons enjoyed a brief honeymoon in Scotland, where England's centre-forward managed two games for Greenock Morton, scoring for them in a 3–3 draw with Hamilton. Lawton was also on target when the Scots arrived at Newcastle in February, but it was Scotland who won, 3–2 with the help of an own-goal from Fulham's Joe Bacuzzi.

When the Welsh were beaten 4–1 at Nottingham Forest's City Ground in April, Charlton's Don Welsh scored all England's goals. The England team showed nine changes from the previous match, only Bacuzzi and Cullis playing in both games. Indeed, Cullis was one of England's regulars throughout the war, playing in twenty internationals with only Matthews, Mercer and Lawton ahead of him in the list of appearances. The Wolves centre-half was top of the list, however, when it came to selecting the most valuable player of 1941. Frank Butler of the *Sunday Express* was asked to name six players in that category and placed Cullis ahead of everyone else. Stanley Matthews agreed with Butler's assessment: 'Cullis . . . used to be one of my motivations during training . . . the thought of being on the end of a crunching tackle from Stan Cullis focussed my mind totally.' Another man who did well to keep out of Cullis's way was

Clyde's centre-forward, Dougie Wallace, who had scored twice in the Scots' victory at St James's Park in February 1941. When the sides met at Hampden in April 1943, England won 4–0 in front of 105,000 spectators who witnessed a remarkable incident. As the players jockeyed for position at a Scotland free kick, Wallace grabbed Cullis by a tender part of his anatomy. A brawl quickly developed and Cullis spent the last ten minutes of the match chasing Wallace all over the pitch, admitting later, 'I tried to kick him – but I couldn't catch him.' It was Cullis's only chance for revenge; as punishment for his transgression Wallace was never again selected to represent his country. Even in wartime there were standards to observe.

Along with the Everton wing-halves Cliff Britton and Joe Mercer, Cullis was becoming part of a legendary England half-back line, one which most of the game's contemporary commentators considered probably the best, not just during the war but of all time. In September 1944, Mercer would replace Cullis as England's captain, but four years earlier he was innocently involved in an unseemly 'club or country' row which made plenty of headlines. In April 1940, Mercer had been selected for the England–Wales match at Wembley, but Everton considered they had a prior claim and named him for their Lancashire Senior Cup semi-final against Liverpool scheduled for the same afternoon. Requests for the services of footballers in the armed forces had to be made through their CO, and there was some doubt as to whether the FA had gone through the proper channels. Everton had certainly done so, and stuck to their guns. In reality, the red tape had become tangled but sports editors rubbed their hands together: 'Everton Declare War On The FA', screamed one headline. 'Next Step In The Mercer Sensation', ran another. 'Behind The Scenes Crisis', read a third. There was a war on; it was unusual for football to steal headlines, even on the back pages. It was the Saturday lunchtime before Mercer was released from duty at his army camp near Chester. He could get to Goodison Park but not to Wembley. Everton's supporters were pleased to see him, but two of the club's directors were later suspended over the affair.

In May 1941, one week after his 4 goals against Wales, Don Welsh scored 2 against Scotland at Hampden Park, where 78,000 saw England win 3–1. One month later, Welsh was on the scoresheet for his country yet again, in a 3–2 victory at Ninian Park. Also playing against Wales that day was Lester Finch, a pre-war amateur international who had been hovering on the edge of selection after being included in several strong FA teams. Finch is still a legendary figure in the history of Barnet, for whom he played 476 times between 1928 and 1953, scoring 226 goals, and his inclusion in a wartime England team, when he was serving in the RAF, is still a source of pride for that club. In October 1941, Scotland paid their first wartime visit to Wembley, where England fielded their sixth goalkeeper in ten internationals. Vic Woodley (Chelsea), Frank Swift (Manchester City), Tom Swinburne (Newcastle United), Sam Bartram (Charlton Athletic) and Johnny Mapson (Sunderland) had preceded Arsenal's George Marks, who marked the first of eight consecutive England appearances by keeping a clean sheet against the Scots. Yet again Don Welsh found the back of the net for England; Sheffield United's Jimmy Hagan scored the other goal.

The choice of Birmingham's bomb-damaged ground for the game against Wales later the same month was surprising, not just because St Andrew's had been considered too dangerous even for run-of-the-mill league games in the early wartime seasons, but also because the Birmingham club was not competing in any major competitions in 1941–2. The attendance was restricted to an all-ticket crowd of 25,000, but if Birmingham's Don Dearson had been looking forward to playing in front of his home supporters, he was soon wearing an embarrassed look after missing a penalty for Wales, who lost 2–1. Given the limited number of wartime opponents, England's policy of taking international matches around the country was probably a good idea, but in 1942, when Scotland were met three times in ten months, two of the matches were at Wembley: England's 3–0 win in January and the goalless draw in October. In April 1942, England and Scotland met at Hampden in a thrilling match, one of the most evenly contested and entertaining of any wartime international. The game ended 5–4 to Scotland, with both Lawton and Jock Dodds scoring hat-tricks, although the winning goal came from Bill Shankly, who, according to Eddie Hapgood, 'nearly went crazy when he scored'.

Lawton, meanwhile, recalled the way in which the Football Association left players to make their own way to international games. The FA notice told them to report to the Central Hotel in Glasgow not later than 10 p.m. on the eve of the Hampden match, adding, 'Members of the party are advised to obtain a meal prior to travelling.' 'However,' wrote Lawton later, 'what was the discomfort entailed in a wartime train compared with the feeling you were playing for England?' That was at odds with how Stan Cullis apparently saw it. Bill Slater, who played for Wolves when Cullis was manager at Molineux, said, 'He always told us the story about going to Glasgow and back in the war, standing on the train all the way to Scotland and all the way back again.' After their 4 goals at Hampden – albeit they lost the game – England failed to score in their next two matches, a 1–0 defeat in Cardiff after which goalkeeper Marks was taken to hospital suffering from internal injuries, and the dull goalless draw against the Scots at Wembley, when the Britton–Cullis–Mercer half-back line played for England for the first time. Two weeks later England played Wales again, this time at Molineux, the home of Stan Cullis's Wolverhampton Wanderers. It was not a happy homecoming for Cullis, who was on the losing side, 2–1. Nine cameramen were at work at Molineux, recording the entire game for one of a series of Ministry of Information films showing wartime life in Britain and intended for distribution in the USSR.

Russian cinema-goers would have seen the legendary half-back line of Britton, Cullis and Mercer again in place against the Welsh. Mercer had been with Everton since September 1932, forcing his way into their first team on a regular basis in 1935. Three years later he became England's left-half and, on the brink of a long international career when war broke out, it was only natural that he should become a regular throughout the war. Mercer's early life had also been touched by war. His wife, Norah, told how Joe's father's own career had been interrupted by the start of the First World War: 'He was captaining Nottingham Forest and then the war came and that was it. His dad was unfortunately taken prisoner and didn't come home again until 1918. Joe was only two or three when his dad went away and the first thing he remembered about him was him walking in, taking a football out of his kitbag and throwing it to Joe. And from that day, it was football, football, football . . . his whole life was football.' While Joe Mercer was ruing the fact that his football career had been interrupted by the war, just as his father's had before him, Cliff Britton was enjoying something of a renaissance to his own international career. After establishing himself in the Everton team in 1932, Britton made his England debut in 1934 and went on to win nine caps before the war. He appeared only once, however, in Everton's 1938–9 championship-winning team, instead guiding the reserve team at Goodison Park. Then the war saw his playing career revived and Britton won twelve caps in that famous middle line.

Cullis had joined Wolves in 1934 after being on Bolton's books as an amateur, and was their captain by the time he was 19. The first of twelve peacetime caps came at centre-half against Northern Ireland in 1937 and he took over the England captaincy for the fiery game in Bucharest in May 1939, the last international before the war. Although only 22 years old when he led England for the first time, Cullis had displayed a maturity well beyond his years. In the face of severe provocation from the Romanians he had looked after Mercer, his boyhood pal from Ellesmere Port, whose normally placid nature had been stretched too far by some thuggish tactics. 'One of the Romanians took the sole of Joe's boot, and I saw Joe threatening him, so I had to tell him: "If you do anything I'll send you off, never mind the referee. We're going to finish with eleven men – and win."' And, of course, they did.

Despite its legendary status, the Britton–Cullis–Mercer combination would represent England only eight times, although Cullis and Mercer had appeared alongside each other earlier in the war when the right-half position was usually taken by the stylish Huddersfield Town player, Ken Willingham, who had also played in the last eleven pre-war internationals. The last appearance by England's fabled trio came at Cardiff in May 1944, in a 2–0 victory over Wales. By then England had established themselves as the truly dominant force in wartime international football, scoring a hatful of goals along the way. Wales were beaten 5–3 at Wembley in February 1943, and Scotland 4–0 at Hampden in April that year; the Scots used a set of jerseys loaned to them by Tommy Walker of Hearts, who provided his souvenirs of past internationals when the Scottish FA's supply of clothing coupons ran out. The Welsh game saw the international debut of referee George Reader, who had made three appearances at full-back for Southampton just after the First World War. So far as anyone knows the first ex-professional footballer to take charge of an international match, Reader went on to referee the 1950 World Cup final in Brazil and, in 1963, became the Saints' much-respected chairman.

A 1–1 draw against Wales at Ninian Park followed, and then England's forwards went on the rampage, scoring 22 goals in their next three matches. They began in September 1943 with an 8–3 win over Wales at Wembley, after which the London newspapers heaped much criticism on Cullis for his tactics in deliberately 'starving' Stanley Matthews on the right wing. England's captain defended himself: 'I heard before the game that Wales would put two men on Stanley Matthews. As a result, I decided we would attack on the left, through Denis Compton . . . We won handsomely but the papers gave me a right rollicking . . . They insisted the spectators had gone to watch Matthews, not me, and demanded I be forced to give up the captaincy.' Whether or not it was right to ignore the supreme talent of Stanley Matthews, the scoreline spoke for itself. Cullis received a letter from the FA secretary, Stanley Rous: 'You will remain as captain.' The game in which Matthews was isolated also saw the international debut of one of his Blackpool teammates, a man who was to become one of England's postwar stars. Stan Mortensen, though, stepped on to the Wembley stage in a red shirt. A few minutes after the start, Ivor Powell, the Queen's Park Rangers wing-half, suffered a fractured collar-bone. The Welsh had no twelfth man, so all eyes fell on Mortensen, England's only reserve. 'I was so excited that I stood up on the touchline and started to pull off my RAF tunic in full view of the huge crowd,' he said later. Led away to get changed in a less public place, Mortenson returned to lay on 2 goals which reduced the Welsh deficit to 4–3 before England came again.

In February 1944, England beat the Scots 6–2 at Wembley. Before that, in October, came an 8–0 Scottish humiliation at Maine Road, Manchester, a game which Cullis described as 'the finest football match I have ever seen'. Stanley Matthews called it 'the most memorable wartime international, a day when England were irresistible'. Joe Mercer reckoned it was 'the greatest game I can remember'. England's goalkeeper, Frank Swift, said that this was 'the finest team I ever played in . . . taking into consideration that it was a wartime game, with both sets of players affected by wartime conditions . . . I've yet to see such performance of movement, unselfishness, or team spirit as England showed . . . Or the courage to equal that of the Scots.' Although he missed a penalty that afternoon, Raich Carter found it hard to recall playing in a better match. Tommy Lawton, scorer of four of the goals, also agreed. According to Lawton, 'it was the greatest game I ever played in'. Bill Shankly said, 'When I heard the teams announced, I said two prayers – one of thanks for the Scottish selectors for leaving me out, and one on behalf of Adam Little, who they had selected to replace me.' Lawton also recalled the lengths to which some people went to be part of the 60,000 crowd at Maine Road that afternoon. 'There were plenty of dodgy tickets around, I'm sure, but the funniest thing was seeing three small boys trying to get into the reporters' entrance with forged press tickets.' The game also saw the local authority open up a large communal air raid shelter, left empty since the end of the blitz on Manchester, to accommodate many of the servicemen who had hitch-hiked to see the game. Lawton was relieved to hear this: 'It meant that all the service lads got a bed for the night.'

By now, almost all England teams were themselves 'all service' – every member of the side was in the armed forces – and selected pretty well fifty-fifty between Army and RAF players. Carter noticed that this was having a beneficial effect on the England team. 'The

RAF team was fairly settled, and so was the Army side, so it was like picking an international team from only two clubs. Each bunch of players were so used to playing with each other that it was then just a matter of merging the two halves together instead of lots of individuals. The result was that, in my opinion, the England team of the later war period was one of the best-ever.' He could have added that it was a pity, then, that proper caps were not awarded.

Nine weeks after losing 6–2 at Wembley, the Scots put up a better show at Hampden, where a crowd of 133,000 saw them lose 3–2, with the RAF's Carter scoring one of England's goals and the Army's Lawton the other two. At Cardiff, a month later, England won 2–0 in a game where Cullis found himself protesting about leeks in his team's goalmouth. Wally Barnes, the Arsenal full-back who was making his debut for Wales that day, recalled, 'Stan Cullis . . . became ruffled when some bright sparks in the crowd began to throw leeks into the English goal whenever we attacked, and Stan complained to the referee.'

'What can we do about these leeks?' demanded England's captain.

'If I was you,' advised Mr A.E. Davies of Aberystwyth confidentially, 'I'd collect them up. They make splendid thickening for a stew.'

England won 2–0, although their victory was made more comfortable by the fact that Barnes was laid out by an accidental blow in the stomach during a goalmouth mêlée and had to spend the rest of the game struggling along on the right wing. When his Arsenal teammate, Leslie Compton, enquired about his health Cullis was furious and ordered England's right-back to 'stop fraternising with the enemy'.

By the time another international season opened, Cullis had been posted overseas and Mercer captained his country for the first time, against Wales at Anfield on a drizzly September day in 1944. Cullis's replacement at centre-half was the Portsmouth stopper, Reg Flewin, who together with Stan Mortensen was making his international debut for England, although of course Mortensen had already sampled the atmosphere as a Welsh substitute. Mercer began as though he wanted to win the game on his own, and with Charlton's

Don Welsh also favouring an attacking wing-half role, poor Flewin was soon exposed. Within 15 minutes Wales were 2–0 ahead: a Don Dearson goal following a corner, and a Billy Lucas effort laid on by Leslie Jones of Arsenal. Lawton had a hand in both England's goals, first distracting goalkeeper Cyril Sidlow for Carter to sidefoot the ball over the line, then heading the second himself from a Matthews centre. At half-time the score stood at 2–2 and there it remained. It had been far from a classic but the Welsh had fought hard and made the most of England's surprising naivety in committing to all-out attack so early in the game. Perhaps they were missing Cullis's grudging approach to football.

In October, at Wembley, Scotland were again heavily defeated, the 6–2 scoreline being a repeat of their previous visit eight months earlier and coming almost exactly a year after their 8–0 drubbing in Manchester. Again Lawton was the scourge of the Scots, his hat-trick bringing his total of goals against them to 10 in the last four meetings. This time, however, the circumstances were different. In the following day's *Sunday Graphic*, Roy Peskett wrote, 'Tommy Lawton beat Scotland. England's dynamic centre-forward, giving the greatest display of his life, pulled back a match which looked well won by Scotland 34 minutes from time.' Scotland had gone in at half-time 1–0 ahead and looking as though they might hold on to their lead, but Lawton levelled the scores 11 minutes into the second half, and then the floodgates opened. Peskett described Lawton's equaliser: '. . . he fastened on to a long pass from Frank Soo, eeled his way past Stephens, beat Baxter in his stride, and with 93,000 throats roaring him home, smashed the ball past the Scottish keeper. The England team stood still and clapped Lawton back to the middle. Even some of the Scots patted him on the back as he made his triumphant way to the centre spot.'

In February 1945, Lawton lined up against Scotland yet again, this time at Villa Park where he failed to score, thanks to the brave efforts of a naval petty officer called Bobby Brown, the goalkeeper from Queen's Park, the Glasgow amateur club. Brown kept at bay several Lawton efforts but he could not stop 2 goals from Mortensen and another from Charlton's 'Sailor' Brown as England squeezed through 3–2. Two months later, at Hampden Park, Bobby Brown was on the receiving end of a more comprehensive England victory, which meant that Scotland had lost their last seven games against the old enemy. Worse even than that, the 6–1 scoreline was the Scots' heaviest-ever defeat in their national stadium. For Tommy Bogan of Hibernian, the day was a particularly miserable experience. His international debut lasted all of 40 seconds before he crashed into Frank Swift and was carried off by the goalkeeper himself. Bogan's place was taken by Les Johnson of Clyde, who scored Scotland's goal. They might have had a second, but Liverpool's Matt Busby missed a penalty against his former Manchester City teammate, Swift, who had faced many a Busby spot-kick during training at Maine Road. Two days earlier, the American president, Franklin D. Roosevelt, had died in Warm Springs, Georgia, and, before the kick-off, the 133,000 Hampden crowd kept an impeccably observed minute's silence. They were still relatively quiet, even after the game got under way.

By the time of Raich Carter's hat-trick against Wales at Ninian Park on 5 May 1945, the war in Europe was all but over. Before the end of the month, hostilities were ended and at last there was new opposition for England when the colourful French side arrived at Wembley to become the first non-British team to avoid defeat on English soil. That was the last international match of the war, although not the end of unofficial internationals. Wartime games were replaced by 'Victory' internationals. In September 1945, with the transitional league season just starting, England played their first game against Northern Ireland since November 1938. A crowd of more than 45,000 packed into Windsor Park, Belfast, where Mortensen scored the only goal of the game. Tommy Lawton remembered the journey across a calm Irish Sea, bathed in early-autumn sunshine: 'For what seemed miles we passed hundreds of dismantled Nazi submarines. Picked out by field glasses, they looked like mammoth sharks, their teeth drawn.' It was all so different from September 1941, when Lawton had been a member of the Army team which sailed across the Irish Sea in a blacked-out ship in the small hours of the morning, wondering whether they had been shelled or torpedoed after a mine was detonated by the ship's gun-crew.

By now, Tom Finney of Preston North End had made his bow on the international stage, although, far from being awarded a cap to commemorate it, he eventually found that the game had been downgraded. It was the middle of a July night in 1945, following a services match in Austria, when Finney got what amounted to his first England call-up. He was roused from his bed and told to report to the captain's office immediately. Finney could not imagine what misdemeanour he had committed to be hauled before an officer in the small hours of the morning. He was handed a telegram. The FA had requested that the army release him for an international tournament in Berne, a series of matches to celebrate the fiftieth anniversary of the Swiss FA. Finney set off immediately. He travelled to the Austro-Italian border, then to Udini and Naples, from where he was flown to Croydon aerodrome. Linking up with the FA party in London, he then flew to Zurich on board a Swiss aircraft. At the last moment the Air Ministry had refused to supply transport for a party of mere footballers and it was the hosts who came to the rescue.

For the first time in several years the England players were wearing civilian clothes. Switzerland had remained neutral throughout the war, and khaki and air-force blue had to be discarded for the visit. The team that faced Switzerland in Berne's Neufeld Stadium on 21 July 1945 was a strong combination – Swift (Manchester City); Scott (Arsenal), Hardwick (Middlesbrough); Soo (Stoke City), Franklin (Stoke City), Mercer (Everton); Finney (Preston North End), Brown (Charlton Athletic), Lawton (Everton), Hunt (Sheffield Wednesday), Smith (Brentford) – but the side was later redesignated an 'FA Services XI'. At the time they were referred to as 'England', the players were all English and they wore England shirts. Finney was in no doubt that this was his international debut.

The game attracted a crowd of 35,000, who saw the Swiss win 3–1 with goals from Fink, Friedlinder and Amado. At left-back for Switzerland was Willi Stefan, a former Swiss air force pilot who was to play for Chelsea in the first postwar season of 1946–7. Brown scored England's goal. Three days later, the English team – with a couple of changes now styled an 'England XI' – beat Switzerland 'B' 3–0 at the Grasshoppers Stadium in Zurich, Finney scoring only 4 minutes into the game. The match had originally been scheduled as a floodlit fixture but the English players did not fancy that novelty, and so the kick-off was brought forward 5 minutes and each half restricted to 40 minutes. This game was also later redesignated, as an FA XI fixture. Defeat by the full Swiss side had been a surprise, but they had spent several weeks preparing for the game at a rural training camp. For all their perks, England's travelling footballers were still military personnel.

In October, Wales beat England 1–0 at The Hawthorns. Three weeks later, the first home international for nearly seven years not to involve England took place at Hampden Park, where Scotland beat Wales 2–0. Then Belgium made a two-match visit, losing 2–0 at Wembley and drawing 2–2 at Hampden where a last-minute penalty from Manchester United's Jimmy Delaney preserved Scotland's unbeaten home record against non-British opposition. In February 1946, the Scots made the boat trip from Stranraer to Larne before winning 3–2 at Windsor Park. Delaney scored the last-minute goal that beat England at Hampden in April, and Paddy Sloan of Tranmere Rovers gave the Irish a 1–0 win at Ninian Park in May. That month Switzerland were beaten 4–1 by England at Stamford Bridge, and 3–1 by Scotland at Hampden. The international stage was broadening all the time. At the Colombes Stadium in Paris on 19 May 1946, goals from Ernest Vaast of Racing Club of Paris, and Jean Prouff of Stade Rennais, beat England, whose reply came from Jimmy Hagan. Raich Carter played in the match but again had nothing to show for it as the curtain came down on the international games for which there were no caps.

Only Lawton, Matthews and Carter enjoyed international careers either side of the war. Lawton would win another fifteen caps after signing for Chelsea and then sensationally moving to Third Division South club, Notts County. Stanley Matthews would just carry on and on, playing for England as late as 1957 – his first cap had come in 1934 – and continuing in League football until he was 50. For

Carter, who had formed a devastating right-wing partnership with Matthews in both the RAF and England teams, there were to be another seven caps. Stan Mortensen, whose international career had begun in such strange circumstances, would be an England regular after the war with twenty-five appearances (and 23 goals). George Hardwick, the classy Middlesbrough full-back who played seventeen times in wartime internationals, would go on to win thirteen caps in peacetime, every one of them as captain.

Wolves' 22-year-old half-back Billy Wright, who appeared in the 1946 Victory internationals, would also go on to skipper his country and furthermore become the first man to play 100 times for England. Jimmy Hagan, the Sheffield United inside-forward, who played fifteen times during the war, would win only one cap after it, and he would have to wait until 1948 for that. Hagan was unlucky to play at a time when Carter, Mortensen and Wilf Mannion were also around. Middlesbrough's Mannion, who had also emerged in wartime with four England appearances, would win twenty-six caps between 1946 and 1951. Goalkeeper Frank Swift was ever-present for Manchester City for four seasons before the war and missed only one game in 1938–9, yet he could not get into the England team because of the fine form of Chelsea's Vic Woodley. Woodley, though, played only twice in wartime internationals, Swift eventually becoming the regular goalkeeper, with Bert Williams of Walsall making the occasional appearance as wartime football drew to a close. Then Swift took over the job and won nineteen caps in peacetime. Ironically, Woodley was called out of non-League football with Bath City to win an FA Cup winners' medal with Derby in the first postwar final, an honour which had eluded him in all his years with Chelsea.

Scotland had a poor war as far as international football was concerned. Between 2 December 1939 and 14 April 1945, the Scots won only three and drew two of sixteen games against England. In the transitional season of 1945–6, things went much better and Scotland were unbeaten in five games, including the 1–0 win over the English at Hampden. As the final whistle neared, a goalless draw seemed the most likely outcome, but when Jackie

Husband sent over a free-kick, every Scot in the crowd seemed to jump for it. Luckily for them, Willie Waddell got there first and knocked it on for Delaney to score the only goal of the game. It was some consolation for the run of seven defeats by England and the 36 goals the Scots had conceded in that time. Scotland's excuse was that, unlike England, they could never field a settled side. England always seemed to have that Britton–Cullis–Mercer half-back line, and Carter, Matthews and Lawton always seemed to play up front. What team could have matched such a force? For Scotland, goalkeeper Jerry Dawson, full-back Jimmy Carabine and forwards Tommy Walker and Jimmy Caskie each played in at least half the matches, but otherwise it was a very irregular team. Two mainstays of the postwar Scotland team to emerge were the Rangers pair of Waddell and George Young. Outside-right Waddell made five appearances in wartime and seventeen afterwards. Young became a colossal presence at the centre of Scotland's postwar defence. He played only twice during the war but won fifty-three caps in peacetime, setting records for the number of consecutive appearances and the number of times he captained Scotland.

Wales, who began the war with a reasonably experienced team, fared better overall than Scotland, although there were those two heavy defeats – 8–3 and 5–2 – by England in 1942 and 1943. Nevertheless they had a few successes against the English, as well as an occasional draw, and players like Wally Barnes, Trevor Ford, Ronnie Burgess and Alf Sherwood emerged from wartime football to play a key role in Wales's postwar fortunes. Northern Ireland, who resumed international football only in the autumn of 1945, had one great player still available to them. Peter Doherty had been capped six times before the war, when he was with Manchester City; although his representative football had largely been restricted to the RAF team, he was still good enough to play in a full international in 1946, by which time he was a cup-winner with Derby County. Although the Irish did not play against other national sides until the war was over, the Irish FA XI that did play during the war was a very strong team. Doherty skippered what was practically a full international side:

In 1942 we beat a British Army side that contained six English and four Scottish internationals. A year later we beat them again, then in 1944 we met the Combined Services and that was an unbelievable game. They had Frank Swift in goal, Matt Busby at centre-half, and a forward line of Matthews, Carter, Lawton, Mortensen and Mullen. The crowd was about 50,000, which I think was a record for Irish football, and with about a quarter of an hour to play, the score was 4–4. Then an injury to Jack Vernon upset our rhythm and they scored four times in the last ten minutes. Raich Carter scored four and I also managed to get four. I think all three of those games against the services sides were a great boost to Irish football. And for me, it was great to play for Ireland again.

Yet even Doherty's appearances for the 'full' RAF team were sometimes not far short of international status. In April 1944, for instance, the RAF met the Army in Edinburgh, where a 50,000 crowd turned out to see players like Doherty, Ted Ditchburn, Laurie Scott, George Hardwick, Ronnie Burgess, Stanley Matthews, Ted Drake and Leslie Smith, all current or future internationals. The RAF could also call upon Raich Carter, Stan Mortensen and Bert Williams. The Army side was even stronger (they won 4–0 that day) and included Frank Swift, Leslie Compton, Stan Cullis, Joe Mercer, Jimmy Hagan, Tommy Lawton and Jack Rowley. Like Stan Mortensen's appearance for Wales when he was England's twelfth man, Reg Lewis, the Arsenal forward, found himself playing for the RAF after being selected as travelling reserve for the Army. Lewis, a brilliant ball-player who was making his mark in wartime football after coming into the Arsenal side in 1939, was called up at Ayr in January 1942 after the RAF arrived with only ten men.

Even teams representing the various army commands and districts, as well as the police, civil defence and fire services, were made up of some of the best professional footballers in the land. When Northern Command met Anti-Aircraft Command at Mansfield Town's ground in February 1945, the opposing goalkeepers were Cyril Sidlow of Wolves and Wales, and George

Swindin, who had won a pre-war League championship medal with Arsenal and who would gain another with the Gunners after the war. Others on display were Jimmy Mullen of Wolves and England, Spurs left-back Bill Nicholson, Trevor Ford of Swansea Town, and Archie Macaulay of West Ham and Scotland. The Free French and Polish forces and the Belgian, Czech and Norwegian army teams all fielded good-class players, some of whom stayed on to play for British clubs after the war. More significantly, there also emerged several touring sides. As the fighting in Europe receded, they visited liberated cities to boost the morale of troops and civilians alike. So, too, did various club teams. Indeed, football had been on tour for much of the war.

12

FOOTBALL'S VERA LYNNS

Those games for the troops were interesting. Playing football behind the front line was very odd. So was sailing across the Channel and back. It was certainly a new experience, going to a football match and worrying about U-boats.

Bert Sproston, Manchester City and England

At the beginning of February 1940, Western Europe remained largely unaffected by the air and land war. Germany was still preoccupied with Poland and, apart from the U-boat threat, which had meant the introduction of food rationing the previous month, probably the nearest most Britons came to feeling that war had arrived on their doorstep was when a Heinkel was shot down near Whitby. Excursions by the Luftwaffe over the United Kingdom were comparatively rare, however; overall, life seemed just one long grind of petty restrictions and great inconvenience. Even across the Channel there was little to report as 160,000 Regular and Territorial soldiers of the British Expeditionary Force dug in and waited during one of the worst winters on record. They needed entertaining and football was about to do its bit. Against this background of the Phoney War, an eighteen-strong party of footballers sailed from Dover in the first few weeks of 1940, bound for France. Suddenly the British Army found itself with probably the best soccer team it had ever fielded. The party was on its way to Paris, then Lille and Reims, to play matches against the French Army. The Germans were largely inactive in the west, the British and French content to watch and wait. It seemed the perfect time to rally spirits with a few football matches. It was time for the game's Vera Lynns.

On the moonless night of 9 February 1940, the squad of army footballers came ashore at Calais. The French port had been blacked-out since the first day of the war and the disembarking players bumped into each other, tripped over and cursed as they were guided to their transport. They were Reg Allen (QPR), Arthur Riley, Matt Busby and Willie Fagan (Liverpool), Andy Beattie (Preston North End), Bert Sproston (Manchester City), Harry Goslin and Albert Geldard (Bolton Wanderers), Stan Cullis (Wolves), Joe Mercer, Tommy Lawton and Billy Cook (Everton), Maurice Edleston (Reading), Don Welsh (Charlton Athletic), Denis Compton (Arsenal), Wilf Copping and Eric Stephenson (Leeds United) and Arthur Cunliffe (Hull City). After an overnight billet on the edge of the town, the men climbed into two army lorries for the journey to Paris. To their astonishment, and in sharp contrast to Calais, the French capital was ablaze with lights, just like the 'Gay Paree' of old. Through its streets thousands of British and French soldiers on leave wandered from bar to bar, or took in the sights before returning to the boredom of manning gun emplacements, sitting in trenches or guarding aerodromes. On the afternoon of 11 February, most of them made their way to the Stade Olympique de Colombes, scene of the 1938 World Cup final, to renew acquaintance with some of Britain's finest footballers.

The British Army fielded eight full internationals and when, early in the game, outside-left Emile Veinante, who had represented France in the 1938 World Cup, was injured, it seemed likely that the British would romp home against only ten fit men, most of whom had just returned from serving on the Maginot Line. But goalkeeper Rudi Hiden, by 1938 one of sixty-two Austrian professionals playing for French clubs, performed wonders and restricted the British team to a single goal from Edleston. Indeed, it was another excellent display of goalkeeping by the Army's Allen, which saved British blushes and earned them a 1–1 draw; and even then it took a last-minute goal-line clearance from Mercer to save the day. Hiden might not have been available to the French but for the Ministry of Labour, who had refused him permission to work in Britain when Arsenal wanted to sign him for a £2,500 transfer fee in 1930. Two of the home team, Gusti Jordan – another Austrian – and Oscar Heisserer, would play in the French side that shocked England at Wembley five years later. Heisserer, who scored the equaliser at Wembley, had first been capped for France in 1936 and was later to claim, 'The war stole my best years.' He was modest enough not to mention that during the conflict he had continually risked his life by helping many Jewish people cross the border from France into Switzerland. His death, at the age of 90 in October 2004, was widely reported in the French media.

From Paris the British party moved on to Lille where Eric Stephenson, later to be killed on active service in Burma, scored the only goal of the game. In Reims, Stephenson was on the mark again and together with Mercer earned the British a 2–1 victory. Attendances at the three matches had been varied. A crowd of 35,000 had seen the game in Paris, followed by 13,000 in Lille and 15,000 in Reims. Three months after the British Army team returned to England, the Nazis swept into France through Belgium. Thousands of the troops who had been present at the matches in Paris, Lille and Reims were now hurled into the reality of war. There was no time to think about football now. It would be more than four years before top-class British footballers returned to France in anything but a fighting capacity, but as the tide of war in North Africa and the Middle East began to turn the Allies' way, so too there was time for football again in those theatres.

In December 1942, Trooper Tom Finney of the Royal Armoured Corps joined the converted liner *Queen Mary* and, along with 7,000 other servicemen, set sail for Egypt. The young Preston North End outside-right soon discovered that there was little time for football amid the daily grind of supply work and manoeuvres, all carried out in unbearable heat. Then came a surprise posting, to the Wanderers football team which had been formed to play matches for the entertainment of the troops. For the next few months Finney travelled with the Wanderers, playing matches against national teams and service elevens across Egypt, Syria and Palestine as well as taking part in depot matches. Most of the service teams bore the names of famous clubs back home: Glasgow Rangers, Arsenal,

Manchester City, Millwall. Finney's own depot team was less glamorous: Bovington United. One tour with the Wanderers involved thirteen matches in just over three weeks and took him to Jerusalem, Tel Aviv, Haifa and Beirut. The team included Ted Duckhouse, Birmingham's centre-half, Dominic Kelly, a defender on Newcastle United's books, Albert Cox, the Sheffield United full-back, Dick Bell, who had played in West Ham's forward line in the last pre-war season, Mickey Fenton, Middlesbrough's England forward, Ted Swinburne, the Newcastle goalkeeper who had played for England in December 1939, Willie Redpath, who was later capped for Scotland while with Motherwell, and Glasgow Rangers player John Galloway, a captain in the Royal Signals who had been guesting for Chelsea.

Finney eventually found a familiar face partnering him at inside-right when Preston North End colleague, Andy McLaren, who was serving in the RAF, was posted to the area. They celebrated by beating the Egyptian FA. In another game against an Egyptian side, one of the opposition's reserves was Omar Sharif, later to earn international fame as a film star. Finney recalled the Egyptian spectators: 'They were absolutely amazing. The din they made whenever their side scored would have put Hampden Park to shame. But when we scored, they all dropped down on their knees and prayed to Allah. Whenever they had a corner, they'd try to interfere with our goalkeeper and the police would have to intervene with whips.' Through all this, however, Finney was troubled by the fact that he had been pulled out of the front line to play football: 'It bothered me a lot. It seemed unfair that I was talented enough to get in the side, but other people were left to get on with the fighting. Eventually I told the CO of my concerns, but he brushed them aside. We were playing a vital role in maintaining morale. That was his view, anyway.'

Ironically, the Preston winger's next posting took him right into the fighting, and he was admonished for suggesting that football would be a morale-booster: 'I was posted to Foggia, in southern Italy, and since the Wanderers had proved so popular in Egypt, I thought that a similar team would do the same job there.

Unfortunately, the captain wasn't a football fan. He told me that all footballers were dodgers. I tried to tell him that I was as ready as the next man to do my bit and he took me at my word. The following day I was in action with the Queen's Royal Lancers, with a squadron of Honey tanks.' For the next few months Finney worked as a driver or a mechanic, often taking the place of a soldier who had been killed the previous day. Month after month, Finney's unit took part in the heavy slog up the boot of Italy. The weather was terrible – cold, rain and mud through the autumn, winter and early spring of 1943–4. Only after the Allies broke out of Cassino and Anzio, took Rome and went slowly on to Florence and the Apennines did the troops enjoy the glorious summer of 1944. Eventually Finney's unit came to rest on the banks of the River Po, where comfort parcels arrived containing football boots and other kit. It was time to start playing again.

The war in Italy all but won, the Preston man found himself in a strong Eighth Army team, managed by none other than Andy Beattie, captain of Preston and Scotland. Beattie's Scottish teammates Willie Thornton of Rangers and George Hamilton of Aberdeen were in the side, although Finney had no idea that Thornton had won the Military Medal in Sicily. Other teammates included goalkeeper Jack Wheeler of Birmingham, Charlie Adam of Leicester City, Frank Squires of Swansea Town, and York City's Sam Earl. Adam, another Scot, had come into the armed forces by way of the Building Trades Flying Squad, formed to repair bombed houses, shops and factories; he would play for Leicester in the 1949 FA Cup final. Squires had come up through Swansea's youth ranks before the war and would enjoy a decent career in League football after it. Earl's career had begun with Bury and after the war he would continue in League football with Stockport County. It was a good team, and Jack Wheeler, who was serving in the RASC as a water-carrier driver, was particularly impressed with Beattie: 'Andy Beattie was a brilliant tactician, the best manager I ever played under. We started training at 6am and travelled around in three-ton trucks. We were all promoted to sergeant, so that we could enjoy the privileges of the sergeants' mess. I also trained with the Italian club, Udinese.

It was a remarkable footballing experience, one I wouldn't have had but for the war.' As the war neared its end, the Eighth Army team travelled around Italy and went into Austria, playing against other service teams. Finney regarded the highlight of his time in Italy as the game he played for the Central Mediterranean Forces against the touring Army XI in the Vomero Stadium, Naples. The CMF side were twice in the lead, but a late goal from Aston Villa's John Martin preserved the tourists' unbeaten record.

By this time, morale-raising football had also resumed elsewhere. As long ago as September 1944, as the Allied invasion of North West Europe gained momentum, an FA Services XI had been sent to play in Paris and Brussels. Again, this was a strong squad and included the captains of England, Scotland and Wales. Each player was insured for £20,000 and the BBC flew over their star football man, Raymond Glendenning, to send back commentaries on the games. The 30,000 crowd at the Parc des Princes was composed of liberated French civilians and Allied troops, including several American GIs, who saw the FA team beat a French XI 5–0. Raich Carter, who scored 3 goals that afternoon, recalled, 'It was the first big football match there since the country had been liberated and we received a fantastic welcome. The whole city had a carnival atmosphere and one thing that struck me was that the average Frenchman didn't look nearly as bad as I'd feared. They weren't particularly shabby or hungry looking. The worst thing was the high barbed-wire fences around the stadium, which had apparently been used as a holding camp by the Germans before people were sent to the concentration camps. That I found difficult to get out of my mind.'

After the final whistle, the players were left with barely an hour to board their aircraft for Brussels; non-operational flying had been banned after darkness had fallen. The following day, in the Daring club's stadium which only a month earlier had been in German hands, the Services team were apprehensive as they ran out to face a Belgian XI. Two hours earlier, soldiers had been busy clearing the terraces of mines. Overhead the RAF provided air cover and, barely 30 miles away, heavy fighting continued as the Germans put up considerable resistance to being pushed back over the lower Rhine. It was an unnerving backdrop to a football match, but the FA Services emerged victorious with a 3–0 win. Their only problem after that was how to decline the thoroughbred whippet presented to their captain, Matt Busby. It seemed that the Belgians did not understand the concept of quarantine, but a diplomatic incident was avoided and the footballers continued on their way.

Six months later, in March 1945, a strong FA XI was flown by Dakota to play two games in Belgium, against the national side and against the Diables Rouge, the Belgian 'Red Devils' or parachute brigade. The party was: Bert Williams (Walsall), Laurie Scott (Arsenal), Bert Sproston (Manchester City), George Hardwick (Middlesbrough), Matt Busby (Liverpool), George Smith and 'Sailor' Brown (Charlton Athletic), Stanley Matthews and Neil Franklin (Stoke City), Tommy Lawton and Joe Mercer (Everton), Stan Mortensen (Blackpool), Leslie Smith (Brentford) and Maurice Edelston (Reading). In Bruges, the FA team received a rapturous welcome from thousands of British troops – some of whom had torn down a wooden fence to gain admission – and went on to win 8–1. Four of their goals came from Lawton; the following day the Everton centre-forward added another 3 to his huge tally of wartime goals as the FA XI beat Belgium 3–2 at the Stade du Daring in Brussels. Two weeks later, the FA XI returned to Belgium. This time the FA relied on several players already based in Europe and flew only a small number over from England, ferrying them in aboard a number of Ansons, the little training aircraft known as the 'Flying Greenhouse'. The aircraft in which Sproston, Hardwick and the two Smiths were flying came into land, only to find a Liberator bomber broken-down across the runway. The four footballers left their stomachs behind as their pilot took evasive action, climbing steeply out of harm's way. After enduring an onward journey aboard an abandoned German bus, which broke down on the way, the FA team – it was just as much a Combined Services side – drew 1–1 and 0–0 with their Belgian opposition. In Brussels they found the pitch at the Heysel Stadium as hard as iron after being used as a tank park by the Germans.

The war was now going well; the touring footballers were spreading their wings. On the evening of Saturday 5 May 1945, eighteen soldiers assembled at the Great Western Railway Hotel in Paddington in time for dinner. Everyone was in good heart. The previous day all German forces in North West Germany, Holland and Denmark had surrendered unconditionally. The lights were going on again in Europe and the army's footballers were ready to tour once more. The invitation – or rather instruction – to play in Italy had come from the War Office with an official reference number: AFA/17a/7/44-45. Uniform would be worn by all ranks, baggage limited to 55lb, and players would have to bring their own towels, soap, razor blades, toothpaste – and their own football boots. Anyone selected to play for England against France at Wembley on 26 May would be flown back for the match.

It was a wonderful weekend, the last weekend of the war in Europe. Heavy rain on the way down to Swindon dampened no-one's spirits, and when the players awoke on Monday morning, they found it was a perfect day. At 11 a.m. their Vickers Warwick transport laboured into the skies over the Wiltshire countryside. The players' last glimpse of England was the sea front at Bournemouth, where early bathers were reserving the best spots in anticipation of the glorious day ahead. Down the Channel, across the Bay of Biscay, then over Corsica and Elba. The Italian coast came into sight, Rome, the Anzio beachhead and the Bay of Naples. After five and a half hours' flying in the noisy, uncomfortable Warwick, the players climbed out stiff-legged at Pomigliano airfield before being driven to a nearby camp and a night under canvas. An early visitor was Stan Cullis, who had been posted to Italy in 1944. Not long after had arrived, Cullis had been ordered to raise a team to play the Yugoslavian Partizan army eleven which had been sweeping aside every British service team it met. The Wolves and England centre-half was allowed to select from the entire Central Mediterranean Forces and he gathered together a formidable team. The Yugoslavs were duly hammered 7–2 before 45,000 delighted servicemen in the Bari stadium.

The day after Cullis had visited them, the army footballers took in some of the sights – Pompeii, the Church of the Madonna – and then an ENSA show starring Cicely Courtneidge. By then, the players knew that it was VE Day: the war in Europe, which six years earlier had interrupted their careers, was finally over. Strangely, the celebrations were muted. Indeed, Jack Rowley, the Manchester United forward, was already regretting the trip. Doubled up with dysentery, he was taken to hospital the next day and played little part in the rest of the tour. Frank Swift was also distracted: he had left his football boots in England. Eventually the NAAFI came to the rescue, providing the Manchester City goalkeeper with a brand new pair. That afternoon the Army team played their first match, at the Vomero Stadium against No. 3 Army District, a team selected from units stationed between Bari and Gibraltar. On a bone-hard pitch and in scorching conditions, the tourists won easily, 6–0, despite the district team enjoying the services of Swift, after their own goalkeeper, Bert Hoyle, injured his hand with 30 minutes to play. Swift, resplendent in his new boots, army-issue khaki shorts and Hoyle's jersey, several sizes too small, was beaten only once, by a penalty.

A 150-mile trip to Rome aboard an army lorry provided the footballing soldiers with ample reminders of the war just ended. They were still some miles from Monte Cassino when they saw the ruins of the monastery, destroyed by Allied bombing during the battle for the Italian capital. Monte Cassino itself was utterly devastated, the airport littered with burnt-out German and Allied tanks. As the players were driven through the town of Valmontone, they saw people living in caves and in the shells of ruined houses. The following day's audience with the pope and a night at the opera to hear *La Boheme* sat uneasily with what they had witnessed only a few hours earlier. Then back to business. On Saturday 12 May, the tourists beat an 'Army in Italy' team 10–2; Lawton scored 5. Another long road trip followed, this time to Ancona and the 7–1 defeat of a District Services XI, which included Wolves goalkeeper George Hepple and Jesse Pye, a Sheffield United forward soon to be transferred to Notts County and play for England. In Rimini, the Army team faced sterner opposition in the shape of the Naples Area XI, champions of the Central Mediterranean Forces. The Naples team included Bryn Jones, Arsenal's record signing of 1938, and Bob

Pryde, the veteran Blackburn Rovers centre-half; the tourists had to work hard for their 2–0 win.

In the magnificent municipal stadium in Florence, on a beautiful pitch far removed from the baked earth of previous grounds, the opposition was much easier: the Fifth Army XI, which included several members of the Brazilian Army who were on secondment, were beaten 10–0. It might have been an easy victory but it was here that the army's footballing tourists came to realise that they were not always going to be treated as heroes. Many of the khaki-clad crowd resented the pre-war professionals who had been drafted into the PT corps and seemed to do nothing but play football. 'Come on the D-Day dodgers,' was one of the more polite catcalls. Tommy Lawton understood their feelings but countered, 'We'd all joined the army and went where we were told. I felt we were still doing our bit. Being criticised by men who'd seen real action hurt, of course. But I wasn't ashamed. We did a good job back home, entertaining people who had been through hell in the Blitz. It was a relief for them and you felt as if you were doing something worthwhile. Now we wanted to do the same for the troops who'd been in the thick of the action.'

In late May, Lawton, together with his clubmate Joe Mercer, left the party to return to England for the international against France. The rest of the side returned to Naples and the game against the Central Mediterranean Forces team, a contest which was the result of a challenge from Andy Beattie, who was running the Eighth Army side which was also playing around Italy. It was a needle match, so important that a neutral referee was called up, one Corporal Rosner of the American army. Considering his country's lack of soccer tradition, Rosner did a good job in front of a crowd of 30,000, who had their first glimpse of Tom Finney in the CMF side, which eventually had to settle for a 2–2 draw. The touring team rounded off their matches with a short visit to Greece, where all but Frank Swift went down with something called 'sandfly fever', a viral disease characterised by fever, eye pain and headache among other symptoms. No wonder some of the games had to be cancelled; and poor Jack Rowley was only just getting over his dysentery. For all that, it had been an enjoyable trip. Joe Mercer had distinguished himself both on and off the field. His non-footballing duties were those of messing officer, or 'scrounger-in-chief', as Matt Busby, the team's player-manager, called him. Together with Willie Watson, the Huddersfield Town outside-left and Yorkshire cricketer, Mercer's job was simply to cadge food. Cliff Britton was the transport officer; in other words he was in charge of the lorry which took the players from game to game. Lawton and Swift had responsibility for all the baggage except the football kit. That duty fell to Bert Sproston. In times of war, even international footballers had to muck in.

While Matt Busby's footballing equivalent of an ENSA concert party were showing off their skills in Italy, in North West Europe the British Army of the Rhine (BAOR) had been formally established following the defeat of Germany. Its first commander was Field Marshal Montgomery, the Portsmouth supporter who had taken the surrender of German forces at Luneburg Heath. With a football fan in charge, the BAOR naturally needed a soccer team and one was eventually gathered together in the autumn of 1945. Their aim was to entertain the troops by playing games against British clubs flown over in midweek. Glasgow Rangers, Birmingham, Brentford, Manchester United, Portsmouth, Sheffield United and Nottingham Forest were soon lining up against a BAOR team which included players like Leslie Compton and Reg Lewis (Arsenal), Dennis Westcott (Wolves), Billy Steel (Greenock Morton), Tim Ward (Derby County) and Eddie Baily (Tottenham Hotspur). The idea was a huge success. A crowd of 35,000 – all in military uniform – squeezed into the stadium in Cologne for the visit of Notts County. There was defeat by an FA XI, and then Birmingham, one of the best club sides of the time, were beaten 2–0. Before the game against Everton, both sets of players were taken by coach to see the damage to the Mohne and Eder dams as a result of the famous 'Dambusters' raid.

Every match played to packed audiences but, despite the big attendances, the trips did nothing for visiting clubs' finances. They paid their own expenses and spectators were admitted free of charge. But then as well as providing some relief for the occupying forces, the players could also see the terrible poverty being suffered by the German people. After Glasgow Rangers had been beaten 6–1 in

Hanover, hundreds of local civilians moved into the emptying stadium to pick up the cigarette ends discarded by a crowd of 30,000 servicemen. The matches were taken around Germany – Berlin, Hamburg, Munster, Dusseldorf – and some visiting clubs had trouble getting back home. Forest were due to land at RAF Syerston, near Newark, but there were gale-force conditions over England and their aircraft was forced to divert to Margate. The Birmingham party was delayed by fog, which worried the club's three Welsh internationals – Don Dearson, George Edwards and Billy Hughes – who feared they would miss that weekend's international match against Scotland at Hampden Park; they eventually made it. Fog also held up Queen's Park, so badly that their reserves had to fulfil a Scottish League match against Queen of the South that Saturday. Portsmouth, still holders of the FA Cup they had won in 1939, could probably claim the prize for the worst trip home. Conditions were so bad that all air traffic was grounded and the Pompey players set off for England aboard an army lorry. For seventeen hours they were bounced over bomb-damaged roads in bitterly cold weather. Then they endured a 16-hour train journey. And even then they had got only as far as Calais and still faced a boat trip across the Channel. To cap it all, they had been beaten 3–1 by the Army side.

At weekends the BAOR team faced international elevens. Two matches were played against Scotland, in the tiny town of Celle, where the army players lost 4–2, and in Hamburg the following day, when the game ended in a 1–1 draw in front of a 40,000 crowd. Field Marshal Montgomery appeared in the dressing room after the final whistle. 'Put on a good show . . . win all your games . . . I'll expect a daily report on your progress,' he told the BAOR players. A trip to play two games against Polish opposition, in Krakow and Katowice, began with a visit to the Warsaw ghetto where thousands of Jewish people had been killed. In Krakow, the Poles won 3–2. The match in Katowice was drawn, but the British players spent much of the time dodging knee-high tackles and avoiding lumps of rock thrown by the crowd over a tall wire fence. It was a strange welcome for an allied nation to receive. The visit to Poland was in stark contrast to the BAOR's next port of call: Switzerland. After the deprivations they had seen on their earlier travels, the army players were overwhelmed by conditions in this neutral nation. The tourists defeated the Swiss national side 2–1 in Lausanne, survived their bus skidding on a narrow mountain road on the way to Arau, and beat the local police team 4–0 in Basle, for which they each received a wristwatch. In Berne they had the novelty of playing under floodlights.

After a short break, the BAOR team reassembled in Germany for an international tournament. Their first opponents, the Russians, scratched, and then Denmark (in Hamburg) and Norway (in Dusseldorf) were eliminated before the BAOR side faced Holland in Lyons. That game was won easily and the team moved on to Berlin for the final against Czechoslovakia in the Olympic Stadium where, a decade earlier, the black American athlete Jesse Owens had infuriated Hitler by winning a clutch of gold medals. Britain's army footballers also sprinted to the finish, winning 6–3. One member of that championship-winning BAOR team, the little Greenock Morton inside-forward, Billy Steel, had been spotted while playing section games with the Royal Corps of Signals, with whom he had landed in France soon after D-Day. At the beginning of 1945, Steel and his section were resting at Amiens when a game was arranged against a local side. To the astonishment of Steel and his teammates, the opposition favoured each section of the crowd with a solemn bow before the game got under way. Later that year, on a sand-covered pitch in Hamburg, Steel found himself playing against a team of displaced Italians. Then the BAOR team came calling. Within two years, Steel was a Scottish international, played for Great Britain against the Rest of Europe and moved to Derby County for a British-record transfer fee of £15,500.

Derby were one of several clubs making trips to play sides other than the BAOR team. In August 1945, a party of Rams players and officials took off in two RAF Halifax aircraft for Germany, for matches against 83rd Group and 8th Corps. The first game was won 10–4, the second lost 1–0. The latter fixture was played at Kiel, one of the most heavily bombed cities of the war. The only usable ground was the Kilia Stadium, made ready only after hundreds of soldiers had toiled to fill in a bomb-crater near one corner flag.

Eventually around 5,000 spectators, all of them in uniform, saw the 'home' side's victory. The Forgotten Army was not forgotten so far as football was concerned. In 1945, an RAF team of professionals, who included Queen's Park Rangers players Ivor Powell and Billy McEwan, played seventy-five games in only four months as they entertained troops in India and Burma. Then the Allies dropped atomic bombs on Hiroshima and Nagasaki. Suddenly Kiel did not look so bad and, anyway, the war was over. For football's Vera Lynns, the job was done.

13

OUT OF THE ASHES

What a lovely time to play football. Families were being reunited, the blackout had ended, and there was a great feeling of comradeship. For all the horrors of the war – and there were plenty – it also changed many people's lives for the better, mine included.

Dennis Herod, Stoke City

The final football season of the Second World War kicked off on 25 August 1945. Officially the war still had a few days to run because the Japanese would not surrender with a signed document until 2 September, but the dropping of two atomic bombs on their country had signalled the end. Ten days before football again rang up the curtain, the Allies celebrated VJ Day; as with VE Day in May, there were celebration matches between a handful of clubs, but now competitive football was back. The country also had a new prime minister. In July, Labour had been swept to power with an overwhelming majority for the first time in the party's history. The nation which had revered Winston Churchill as its wartime leader rejected him for its peacetime prosperity. Many of the country's professional footballers, in dispute with their employers, had voted for Clement Attlee. On the eve of the new season they read of Attlee's warning to the country: peace had heralded not days of plenty but even greater austerity. The abrupt ending of Lease–Lend by the US government meant major cuts in imports, while goods meant for home consumption would now have to be exported. There were hard times ahead. On a brighter note, after more than 2,000 nights of blackout, the lights had been switched on again, although midwinter football matches would still have to kick off early: floodlighting was still some years away. It was announced that in December one million servicemen would be demobbed; a million people would also be released from munitions work. Some of them would be footballers, back in the only full-time employment they had ever wanted.

As football strived for normality, everyone knew that it would not be easy to shake off the effects of the war. Writing in the *Athletic News Football Annual*, Ivan Sharpe, a famous amateur international of the pre-First World War era, had warned as much: 'This is the seventh season of emergency football – a period more protracted than expected and teeming with problems for clubs and players. The only advances on last season are that the full list of international matches is resumed and that the FA Cup competition returns, though the Cup change is a gain more in name than in fact to the main body of competitors – the professional clubs – whose Football League War Cups have been highly popular.'

As they were prone to do throughout wartime, when plans for the 1945–6 season were put forward by the Football League, many clubs had objected. The League wanted to revert to the set-up which had been abandoned in 1939: First, Second and Third Divisions North and South. The only concession was that there would be no promotion and relegation. Clubs would have a full season in which to settle down before the serious business resumed. Led by Arsenal, the full member clubs – those in the First and Second Divisions – disagreed, albeit only by a small majority. They wanted to divide themselves into two groups, north and south, although they were prepared to let their lesser brethren, the associate members who made up the Third Divisions, return to their pre-war format immediately. The minnows also railed against this, and so the northern and southern sections were each further divided into two sections, resulting in the confusing Third Division South (South) and Third Division South (North), and the Third Division North (West) and Third Division North (East). The new Third Division sections were agreed barely a month before the beginning of the season and the fixtures had to be hurriedly rearranged. The only absentees were Hull City and New Brighton, both of whom were in the midst of reorganisation and moving grounds. Guest players would be restricted to six per team with the hope that this could be reduced as soon as possible.

Clubs, both big and small, argued that the shortage of players and the difficulties of travel and finding hotel accommodation had not been sufficiently eased. Their case was underlined as early as 12 September 1945, when, under the headline 'It's A Nightmare For Soccer Managers', the *Daily Mail* reported, 'There has been a lot of head scratching by harassed football club managers over the heavy League programme . . . Almost every manager has a story to tell of borrowing and making-do . . . They have had to beg to secure the release of their men in the forces . . . Then there is the travel problem. The luxury motor-coaches in which teams travelled the country in 1939 have gone; trains are fewer. It is a good thing that there is no trip like the 480 miles Derby County had to cover last week to play Plymouth . . . 480 miles these days, when it is impossible to reserve train accommodation, and even the corridors are packed, is no joke for any team.'

Ipswich Town did manage to hire a motor coach, although much good it did them. In October, the vehicle taking Ipswich to London to play Clapton Orient in the Third Division South (North) managed only 11 miles before it broke down at Stratford St Mary, in the heart of Constable country. A relief coach struggled on for another 17 miles, as far as Kelvedon in Essex, and then the players had to bribe the driver of a delivery van to take them the rest of the way; they received some strange looks as they climbed down from the van at Brisbane Road. The Ipswich team contained six pre-war regulars who also played a significant number of games in 1945–6; they included Jimmy McLuckie. In 1938 the Scot had helped Ipswich from the Southern League into the Football League, but he was now 38 years old and on the brink of retirement. The war had robbed him of a proper swansong.

Clubs were affected in different ways – Preston, for instance, still had fifteen players serving abroad and another twenty-two in the services in Britain – but Ipswich's situation was typical of many. When Aston Villa drew 1–1 at Luton Town on the opening day of the season, they fielded six players who had appeared in the fixture in September 1937. Mush Callaghan, George Cummings, Alex Massie, Bob Iverson, Frank Broome and Ronnie Starling had all survived the war and were able to pick up more or less where they had left off. On the second Saturday of the season, Villa beat Luton 7–1 at home, following which Massie retired to become their manager after 500 appearances as a player for the club. Massie enjoyed a remarkable start to his managerial career. From 20 October to Christmas Day, Villa won eleven games in succession. George Edwards, a pre-war signing from Norwich City, scored in every one of those matches and ended the season as Villa's top scorer with 43 goals in as many games. Only Trevor Ford, with 44 goals for Swansea Town, scored more that season. Twelve months later, Ford was leading the Villa attack, with Edwards supplying him from the wing.

Yet for all Villa's potency in 1945–6, it was their neighbours, Birmingham City – the 'City' tag had been added on 1 July 1945 – who were the leading club in the League South. From 3 September to 9 March they won eighteen consecutive home matches. Inevitably, the games between the two clubs played to packed houses: over 63,000 at Villa Park on 12 January, 40,000 at St Andrew's a week later. Birmingham had a new manager, the former Derby County, Burnley and England footballer and Derbyshire cricketer, Harry Storer, who had previously managed Coventry City. Storer was well known as a disciplinarian who called the proverbial spade a spade. More sensitive footballers regarded him as simply uncouth but, whatever their view, his uncompromising approach took Birmingham to the championship and to the semi-finals of the FA Cup in 1945–6. The battle for the League South title boiled down to an all-Birmingham affair which ran right to the season's end. Although Villa needed to win their last two matches to pip City for the championship, they could not quite manage it, beating Millwall but only drawing at Coventry. It left Storer's team with the title by virtue of a superior goal-average. They could look back on several big victories, but one that stuck in the memory was the 8–0 defeat of Tottenham Hotspur in

October, when the Birmingham centre-half, Ted Duckhouse, had scored a goal from the halfway line, no mean feat with the heavy, waterlogged footballs in use at the time. Like Villa, Birmingham had been able to rely on several pre-war players. Harold Bodle, Don Dearson, Duckhouse, Fred Harris, Dennis Jennings, Charlie Jones and Arthur Turner, all regulars in 1945–6, had also appeared in the 1938–9 season. Provided their legs had not 'gone', it was obviously helpful still to have the services of such experienced footballers.

In the League North, Sheffield United began in disastrous fashion, losing 6–0 at Newcastle after a four-hour journey to Tyneside on a crowded train. Early in the season United lost the two Sheffield derbies against Wednesday, but they eventually put their bad start behind them and climbed rapidly up the table. A fast-flowing attacking style brought them a rich harvest of goals. Blessed with two nippy wingers in George Jones and Bobby Reid, pre-war players who both liked to shoot hard and often, and with Jimmy Hagan a much stronger, more developed player after wartime football in top-class service teams, United collected 38 out of a possible 42 points. They ran up eight consecutive victories in that period and took the title 5 points ahead of Everton. The war had given Hagan an early opportunity for international football and he now made an inspiring captain for his club. Pre-war centre-forward Charlie Thompson was another significant factor in Sheffield United's success; he made only fifteen appearances but scored 9 goals. Leading scorer Albert Nightingale (with 22 goals) had been discovered playing wartime football in the Rotherham area, while Walter Rickett (15 goals) and Colin Collindridge (13) were both local players who had been signed in 1939 and had developed throughout the war.

Accrington Stanley, Rotherham United, Stockport County and Doncaster Rovers had all prospered in the various Third Division North competitions, and Stockport and Doncaster had been involved in a remarkable game. In March 1946, they played a Third Division North Cup match for 203 minutes without settling the tie. The game was eventually abandoned at 6.43 p.m. because of bad light. The first match had ended 2–2 and so did the second, after 90 minutes plus two periods of 10 minutes' extra time, plus another 93 minutes of stalemate; Doncaster won the replay 4–0. In the Third Division South's subdivided leagues, Queen's Park Rangers and Crystal Palace had both won championships, but the cup success of Bournemouth & Boscombe Athletic was particularly pleasing. Because of their geographical position, Bournemouth had been forced to drop out of the wartime leagues in 1942. They resumed in 1945–6 with guest players, including the former Manchester City, Liverpool and Scotland star Matt Busby, who played two games before he was appointed manager of Manchester United in October. There was an embarrassing FA Cup exit at the hands of Welsh League club Lovell's Athletic, but Bournemouth prospered in the Third Division South Cup. After a marathon semi-final replay against Queen's Park Rangers at Loftus Road – Jack Kirkham scored the only goal of the game after 136 minutes – they beat Walsall 1–0 in the final at Stamford Bridge before a crowd of 19,000.

The Second World War changed many things, but in Scotland it could hardly be said to have altered the pattern of football. Rangers were the reigning champions when war was declared. They won the regional league titles throughout the war, were champions in the transitional season of 1945–6, and retained the title proper in 1946–7. In 1940 they were champions of the hastily arranged Regional League and then, for six years in succession, won the Southern League, which was as near as anyone could get to a proper First Division. Indeed, the make-up of this division in 1945–6 was retained for the first postwar season. Willie Thornton had been away and was decorated for gallantry in Sicily, but many of Rangers' regular pre-war players were still available, working in reserved occupations and thus free on Saturday afternoons. One aspect of Scottish football was changed because of the war: the League Cup, first staged in 1940, was retained for peacetime football. It would be 1960 before English football followed suit and introduced a third senior competition for League clubs.

The FA Cup had enjoyed a lucky escape during the war. It had been stored in a Portsmouth bank – Pompey being the last pre-war winners – but on the night the bank received a direct hit during an air raid on the town, the club's manager, Jack Tinn, was sheltering under his stairs at home with the trophy clutched between his legs. In 1945, Portsmouth at last had to defend the Cup on the football pitch. The competition resumed, on a two-legged basis up to and including the quarter-finals, and Pompey released their grip on the trophy immediately, losing to the only goal – which Reg Flewin put in his own net – of the two-game tie against Birmingham City in the third round. In the same round, Derby County beat Luton Town 9–0 on aggregate, and Charlton Athletic were 4–3 aggregate victors over Fulham. Four months later, Derby and Charlton met in the first postwar FA Cup final, Charlton earning a unique place in the history of the trophy by becoming the first club to lose a match in an early round but still proceed to the final: they lost 2–1 to Fulham but still emerged winners of the overall tie.

Indeed, the 1945–6 FA Cup contained even more twists and turns than are usually reserved for football's favourite competition. When Derby's run started in January, their pre-war full-back, Jack Howe, was boarding a troopship in India, homeward bound after army service. Yet Howe still collected a cup-winners' medal. Full-back Jack Parr, a local player recruited as a junior before the war, played right through the Cup campaign, every match up to and including the semi-final. Then, three weeks before the Wembley game, he broke his left arm in a match at Luton, and Howe stepped into his place. Derby's veteran outside-right, Sammy Crooks, was also unlucky. Between the wars only Arsenal's Eddie Hapgood had played more games for England than Crooks, who by 1946 was chairman of the Players' Union. Crooks was injured during the second leg of the quarter-final against Aston Villa. His place went to one of Parr's pre-war junior teammates, Reg Harrison, of whom Crooks said after the final, 'Little Reg didn't let me down.' Vic Woodley, England's regular pre-war goalkeeper, had been dragged out of semi-retirement to play, following an injury crisis at the Baseball Ground. The former Chelsea man began the season with Bath City in the calm waters of the Southern League; he ended it in front of 98,000 spectators in the most important match in the football calendar. It is called the romance of the Cup, and the aftermath of war was throwing up plenty. Derby also had the wartime guest system to thank for the fact that they could field what would become the greatest inside-forward pairing in the club's history. Raich Carter and Peter Doherty were both stationed nearby and, as happens in times of war, a number of circumstances had conspired to bring them together at Derby.

When Carter joined the RAF, he was posted to Innsworth Lane, near Gloucester. At the same time the Carters' house in Sunderland had been rendered uninhabitable after a German air raid. Rose Carter had gone to live with her parents in Derby, so Raich sought permission to guest for Derby County, in order to see his wife at weekends. While playing for Derby, he met the CO of an RAF rehabilitation centre at Loughborough. Each week the football club set aside seats for two coachloads of patients from the centre to attend matches at the Baseball Ground. Carter thought that helping wounded airmen back to full health would be a worthwhile occupation. And Loughborough was only 17 miles from his wife in Derby. He duly got his posting. Peter Doherty was also stationed at Loughborough and soon the two men were forging a brief but unforgettable era in the history of the Rams.

They began as guest players but, to Derby's good fortune, both had fallen out with their respective clubs. The war over, Carter felt justified in asking Sunderland for a new ten-year contract, which meant that he would enjoy two more testimonials. Sunderland responded by placing him on the transfer list. After a midnight taxi-dash from York to Sunderland to complete the forms – Carter and the Derby secretary, Jack Catterall, found the platform so packed they could not get anywhere near their connecting train – the player signed for Derby officially. Doherty, meanwhile, had fallen out with Manchester City after being dogged by them in his attempts to guest for other clubs when he could not reach Manchester. At one point City came up with the absurd suggestion that on the days that he could not travel to play for them, he could guest for Manchester United. 'It was ridiculous,' Doherty said. 'Obviously, if I could fit in games with one Manchester club, I could do the same for the other.' He, too, went on the transfer list but City made life as difficult as possible before he could sign for Derby permanently.

Derby had only four of their pre-war team on duty at Wembley – their captain, Jack Nicholas, Howe, Dunkirk veteran Jack Stamps, and Dally Duncan – while Charlton Athletic could call up six: Sam Bartram, who had been stationed at Derby in the RAF when war broke out, John Shreeve, Bert Turner, John Oakes, 'Sailor' Brown and Don Welsh. On Charlton's left wing was a player called Chris Duffy, a 27-year-old Scot who had been discharged from army service after D-Day, suffering from shock. In the Cup run, Duffy became a regular scorer, including a hat-trick against Preston North End at The Valley on a gloomy Wednesday afternoon in February. It was only in the semi-final, however, that he finally caught the attention of the national newspapers. Against Bolton Wanderers at neutral Villa Park, Duffy had put Charlton ahead 10 minutes before half-time, but it was his second goal, 5 minutes into the second half, which made the occupants of the press box sit up. It came at the end of a thirty-yard run in which he skipped over or round the tackles of at least five opponents before shooting past goalkeeper Stan Hanson, one of thirteen Bolton players to be involved in the retreat from Dunkirk. In the press room after the game, reporters wanted to know all about Duffy, starting, remarkably enough, with his forename; he was that unknown. The Charlton manager, Jimmy Seed, himself the veteran of a German gas attack in the First World War, was happy to fill in the details, including the fact that Duffy was recovering from a cartilage operation on his right knee, which meant that, all through that mazy run, he had been trying to manoeuvre the ball on to his left foot. It was the stuff of headlines and Duffy was the subject of plenty of those on the following day's back pages.

On the Saturday before the final, Derby, without either Carter or Doherty, lost 2–1 to Charlton at The Valley in a League South game watched by 50,000 spectators. Then an enterprising journalist with an eye for a good story took the Derby skipper to a gypsy encampment on the outskirts of London. In 1895, so the story went, Derby County had removed some gypsies from land which was to become the Baseball Ground, the club's home for the next 100 years. The gypsies had cursed Derby never to win a major football honour and, indeed, they had subsequently failed in three FA Cup finals – one by a record defeat – and had never won the League championship. Palms were crossed with silver, the curse was lifted, and the reporter had his story. But would Derby soon have the FA Cup?

First there was a threatened players' strike to overcome. The Derby players were furious that their wives had been given cheaper stand tickets than those allocated to directors' wives. Led by senior players, Doherty, Carter and Nicholas, they told the club chairman, Ben Robshaw, 'No decent tickets, no game.' Until the day he died, Carter was adamant that the 1946 FA Cup final would not have gone ahead if the Derby directors had not relented: 'It was an insult, the directors' wives sitting under cover right near the Royal Box and our wives out in the open.' Doherty, ever ready to fight an injustice, agreed: 'There had been problems with tickets right from the start. Instead of getting reserved seats for friends, we were given cheap standing tickets. Then, on the Thursday before the final, we each received a half-guinea ticket for our wife or nearest relative. We protested, asking for covered seats. The club said it was nothing to do with them, the FA had allocated the tickets. We stuck to our guns and two hours later, we each received guinea or two-guinea seats. In the end it was a storm in a teacup and was soon resolved. But we wouldn't have played and it showed how petty clubs could be towards their players just after the war.' Whether Ben Robshaw learned anything from the affair is debatable. The following year, driving to Derby's main railway station to catch a train to London for a match against Arsenal, he went straight past full-back Bert Mozley, who was waiting at a bus stop on his way to catch the same train. Mozley said that the chairman did at least favour him with a wave as he sped past.

The issue of the seat tickets resolved, Derby walked out with Charlton before a Wembley crowd of 98,215, who paid a total of £45,000 in entrance money. The atmosphere was charged with emotion, tears rolling down the cheeks of hardened men during the singing of the traditional FA Cup final anthem, 'Abide With Me'. For all that had happened since VE Day and VJ Day, this was the first true indication that things were returning to normal after six years of war: the FA Cup final was about to kick off again. Charlton, no strangers to Wembley after playing there twice in the previous three seasons, waited to be introduced to King George VI. Queen Elizabeth and the two princesses, Elizabeth and Margaret, watched from the stand. First it was Derby's turn, their boots repaired with sticky tape, some of the numbers on their less-than-white shirts fraying at the edges, a sign of the austere postwar days to come. A month earlier there had been a rather mournful appeal in the Charlton match programme: 'We are collecting coupons for kit. Can anybody help us?'

For the first 80 minutes of the 1946 FA Cup final there was no score. 'It was just like a normal First Division match,' said Jack Howe. Then Bert Turner took the first of two actions which would see him become part of football's folklore: he diverted the ball over his own line to give Derby the lead. Two minutes later he ensured his place in FA Cup history by equalising from a free kick: the first man to score for both sides in an FA Cup final. Or was he? Peter Doherty always claimed that he had also scored an own-goal: 'The ball deflected off my right shin. Turner's shot would never have beaten Vic Woodley if I hadn't diverted it.' Whoever's goal it was, the scores were level and the game went into extra time. Five minutes from the end of normal time, however, but for the poor quality of postwar footballs, it could have been settled in Derby's favour. Stamps saw his shot on its way past Bartram and into the net, but before it could travel that far, it burst. 'The bloody thing just went "phut",' said Stamps later. Again the incident entered FA Cup history because the referee, Mr E.D. Smith from Whitehaven, had apparently said in a wireless interview just before the final that the chances of the ball bursting were 'millions to one'. It is hard to understand why he would have laid those odds. Footballs were bursting all over the place. Two of Charlton's recent League South matches had to be resumed with a new ball. The League game between Charlton and Derby on the Wednesday after the final would see another burst ball. And when Charlton returned to Wembley to meet Burnley in the 1947 FA Cup final, the ball burst yet again. Good footballs were simply in short supply at the end of the war.

The replacement ball in the 1946 final was soon nestling in the Charlton net. With 2 minutes of extra time played, Doherty pushed teammate Duncan out of the way to reach a loose ball and restore Derby's lead with a cracking shot. Then Stamps dribbled past two defenders before shooting again; this time the ball did not burst on its way past Bartram. Stamps's splendid solo effort had put the game beyond the reach of the Londoners, and a few seconds after the start of the second period, the burly centre-forward who, six years earlier, had ignored the officer who threatened to shoot him, scored his second goal of the game. It was Derby who emerged victorious, their 4–1 win giving them the FA Cup for the first, and so far only, time in their history. Charlton, though, had played their part. Alex James, the former Arsenal and Scotland star, by then working as a newspaper journalist, summed up: 'The 1946 FA Cup final was a memorable game with a glorious finale.' After all it had been through, the game of football deserved no less.

The seventh season of wartime football gave clubs a taste of what they could expect throughout the 1940s. Most spectator sports prospered in the immediate postwar years: cricket, boxing, greyhound and horse racing, and even ice hockey and speedway, enjoyed hugely increased attendances. So, too, did cinema and theatre. But football was the biggest winner. People flocked to Football League grounds as never before. True, there had been a boom after the First World War, but nothing compared to this. From 35.6 million in 1946–7, seasonal attendances rose to 41.2 million in the following two seasons and were still edging 40 million in 1951–2. By comparison, in 2003–4 attendances in all four divisions totalled only 27.8 million, and that was the highest for thirty years. Social patterns have changed enormously to account for much of the difference, but the circumstances of 1945–6, and the seasons which immediately followed it, were unique. The thirst for a return to normality provided football with the perfect opportunity to cash in. Even the Football League's regional competitions were packing in the crowds. In December 1945, there were 60,926 Merseyside supporters at Goodison Park for the visit of Liverpool. In January 1946, a record crowd for a wartime league fixture, 63,820, saw Aston Villa draw 2–2 with Birmingham City. In April, a crowd of 62,144 watched the Manchester derby at Maine Road.

It was cup football, however, which proved the biggest attraction. The War Cup competitions had been a great success, so much so that in February 1945 the *Manchester Guardian* noted that the problem of football absenteeism, which was affecting industrial output, 'has been particularly serious in Birmingham this week'. Birmingham were in the middle of the League North Cup qualifying competition, and local rivals West Bromwich Albion were their opponents. It was not surprising that there was huge interest in the first postwar FA Cup proper.

Charlton's semi-final at Villa Park had been watched by 70,819 spectators. When Derby played at Villa Park in the first leg of the quarter-final, there was a crowd of 78,588 present, still the record for the ground. Some of them had travelled from Derby on the Friday evening and wandered Birmingham's freezing streets in the small hours. Workers at a foundry which adjoined the Baseball Ground had been given permission to take Saturday morning off so that they could travel to Villa, but a machine moulder at a neighbouring foundry was suspended for taking time off to watch the match. Sixty of his workmates came out on strike. Derby received 100,000 applications for tickets for the return leg – the Baseball Ground held about 37,000 – and their scheme to sell tickets at a reserve match, thereby boosting the attendance for the second-team game, met with cries of outrage. Some fans wrote letters to the local newspaper, signing themselves 'Fair Play' and 'Cup-Tied'.

Derby's semi-final replay against Birmingham City at Maine Road, Manchester, was watched by 80,407, still the record for a midweek match between two English clubs outside Wembley. The

Rams' right-half, Jim Bullions, recalled how the crowd spilled right up to the touchline in scenes reminiscent of the famous 'White Horse' game at Wembley in 1923. 'As we sat in the dressing-room before the kick-off, we heard what we thought at first was thunder. It was the sound of people's feet in the stand over our heads. When we took throw-ins and corners, we had to move people out of the way. It was incredible.'

It was surprising that such a situation had been allowed to develop. Less than three weeks earlier, similar scenes had led to horrific consequences. On 9 March 1946, all roads leading to Burnden Park, Bolton, were packed. Bolton Wanderers were playing host to Stoke City in the second leg of the FA Cup quarter-final, and the visitors had Stanley Matthews in their ranks. Throughout the war, Matthews had played hardly any football for Stoke. An RAF posting to Blackpool meant that he appeared primarily for that club, so Bolton fans had enjoyed plenty of opportunities to see the 'Wizard of the Dribble' as he played most of his club football in the North West. This match, though, was quite different. The FA Cup was back and Bolton held a 2-goal advantage from the first leg. Would they prevail? Could Matthews turn the tie Stoke's way? Over 85,000 people wanted to see at first hand, but the record attendance – and therefore the capacity – for the ground was just under 70,000.

Burnden Park stood on the south side of Bolton, about half a mile from the town centre. Throughout the morning crowds built up in the streets around the ground as supporters arrived early, determined not to miss a moment of the match. Home fans queued up, waiting for the turnstiles to open. They were joined by away fans who had arrived on early trains before making the 10-minute walk from the railway station. There was no segregation of rival supporters, no thought of crowd disorder. Everyone had come to see a football match, not to cause trouble. When the gates opened at 1 p.m., tens of thousands moved forward in orderly fashion into Burnden Park and took up their positions. Yet still the streets were choked as thousands more supporters arrived. Not everyone was prepared to stand around for hours. Many could not anyway. First they had jobs to do, arriving at Burnden breathless after grabbing a cup of tea and a sandwich before jumping aboard a Bolton Corporation bus. They, too, shuffled their way into the ground. Behind them still more fans flocked towards the stadium which, like almost all football grounds in Britain, had grown from small beginnings.

By 2.15 p.m. – still 45 minutes to kick-off – conditions were already becoming uncomfortable both inside and outside the ground. The pressure was now so great around the turnstiles that many would-be spectators were being pushed up against the walls of the stadium. On the terraces there was hardly any room to move. Small boys were being passed over heads to the front; extricating a bag of sweets or an apple from a jacket pocket became a physical impossibility and keeping one's feet became a priority. Yet still the turnstiles clicked and clattered, feeding more people on to the terraces. Those at the front were being pressed further forward but it was now impossible to move in any direction. Outside, the streets surrounding the ground were as packed as the terraces inside. There were no police radios; it was almost impossible for officers in the ground to communicate with those controlling the tens of thousands still hoping to gain admission. A call from a PC Lowe to close the turnstiles reached the head checker too late to make a difference. Discomfort now turned to distress as people began to fall to the ground and others could not avoid standing on them.

With 10 minutes to kick-off, the crush outside the turnstiles was relieved almost at a stroke. A spectator, trying to escape the ground with his young son, had picked the padlock on a large exit gate designed to spill large numbers back into the streets at the final whistle. But people were not leaving Burnden Park; thousands more were pouring in. The pressure on the terraces was now unbearable.

At five minutes to three, a huge roar signalled the appearance of the teams. On the terraces, tens of thousands of people craned their necks to catch a first glimpse of their favourites. The sea of humanity swayed and rolled. Most were held in place by a series of strategically placed crush barriers which prevented the swaying masses from pressing down to the front of the terracing. But there was one area, near the bottom of some steps, where no crush barriers had been erected. Thousands of people were compressed into this gap, funnelling down uncontrollably. Then barriers elsewhere started to buckle under the strain, and down went the crowd, tumbling forward. Bodies began to pile up, two, three, four deep. Twelve minutes into the game, a police sergeant walked on to the pitch and spoke to the referee. Mr Dutton stopped play and took the teams off the field.

The players sat in their dressing rooms for 25 minutes. Word spread that two or three spectators had been killed. Then referee Dutton reappeared, telling the players that, on the advice of the chief constable of Bolton, he was resuming the game. When the teams took the field again, they saw that the pitch had grown smaller. Thousands of spectators were sitting over the original touchline and new markings had been made with sawdust. At half-time the teams turned straight round with no break. The players were unaware that this was English football's worst tragedy: thirty-three people had been killed, over 500 more injured. Best to get the game over with as soon as possible said the officials. It ended goalless; Bolton were through, Stoke were out. That night few people really cared.

A Home Office inquiry, chaired by Ronw Moelwyn Hughes, KC, found that while the Bolton club and the police had taken proper steps, the machinery was lacking. The real trouble lay in the fact that there had been no scientific assessment of the ground's capacity; this was simply regarded as the greatest number of people to have been safely accommodated there on a previous occasion. There was also no means of knowing when the maximum capacity was about to be reached, nor facilities for the immediate closing of the turnstiles. An attempt had been made to open exit doors but the keys could not be found. Matters had been made worse by the fact that several turnstiles had been rendered unusable, which meant that over 28,000 destined for the Railway Embankment end had to enter from the Manchester Road. Also, ticket holders for the Burnden Paddock had also been admitted through turnstiles in this area and then escorted around the pitch to their places, adding to the huge build-up in the north-west corner of the ground. In addition to those fans who had poured in when the exit gate was opened by a panicking spectator, thousands more had simply climbed over turnstiles and walls. Some had walked along the railway line and down the embankment before breaking into the ground through a fence. A thousand people climbed over the entrance to the boys' enclosure. They had free rein: the police were reluctant to release any officers from the Burnden Stand where they were guarding food stockpiled by the Ministry of Supply.

A relief fund for the injured and their families and those of the dead realised £40,000, and a series of government recommendations were made so that in future, football supporters could attend matches in safety. Yet despite the huge amount of money pouring into the game through the turnstiles in the postwar years, when players were still on a maximum wage, little was spent on ground improvements. In January 1971, sixty-six spectators were killed at Ibrox when barriers on a stairway collapsed during the traditional New Year's match between Rangers and Celtic. In May 1985, fifty-six people perished when a stand at Bradford City's Valley Parade was engulfed in flames. And forty-three years after the Bolton disaster, the Hillsborough tragedy saw the death of ninety-six men, women and children, all crushed to death when too many people found their way on to a football ground terracing. Only then was the lesson of Burnden Park fully absorbed.

The huge attendances in the immediate postwar years masked an underlying decline in British football. While hundreds of thousands of supporters flocked to League grounds every week, giving rise to the myth of the so-called 'Golden Era', the game in Britain – the land that invented football – was being left behind by developments on the European mainland. The four British associations had never entered the World Cup, and only in 1946 did they rejoin FIFA, the world governing body from which they had withdrawn in 1928. More significantly, British football ignored the way the game was being coached and played abroad.

When a Great Britain team defeated the Rest of Europe 6–1 at Hampden Park in 1947, it served only to delay the realisation that the balance of power in world football was changing. Not until Hungary won 6–3 at Wembley in 1953 did football's managers and administrators accept that they were probably stuck in a time warp. Yet events in the final wartime season should have alerted them.

In November 1945, the Moscow Dynamo club made a short visit to Britain, ostensibly to cement further the relationship between two allies, in reality to provide another reminder that Stalin's Russia would be a key player in postwar world affairs. They came cloaked in mystery, they played shrouded in fog, and returned home with victories on both the sporting and propaganda fronts. Their game was, in every sense of the expression, political football. Over the next forty years, successive Soviet regimes would use sport for political purposes; Moscow Dynamo's short tour of Britain, as Europe still reeled from the war, was probably the first example. The idea of matches between British and Soviet teams was nothing new. In February 1935, Arsenal had been invited to tour Russia that summer but the trip did not take place. In 1944, Stanley Rous, the FA secretary, had told Ivan Mikhailovich Maisky, the genial and popular Soviet ambassador in London, that he would be happy to arrange for a Soviet side to play in Britain. The idea was raised again in May 1945, when Mrs Churchill, president of the Red Cross Aid to Russia Fund which had benefited so much from football, visited Moscow. Finally, in October that year, although the old wartime alliances were already beginning to crumble, arrangements were in place.

Football had been introduced to tsarist Russia in 1887, when the Charnock brothers from Blackburn ran cotton mills outside Moscow. They formed a factory football team which, long after they had lost control, became a front for anti-tsarist activities. In 1923, Felix Dzerzhinsky, the man who became founder of the Communist secret police, the NKVD, changed the club's name to Dynamo Moscow, affiliating it to the electrical trades' union. After the Second World War, Dynamo became the blueprint for secret police football clubs throughout the Eastern Bloc. When they landed in Britain, Dynamo did so as the current Soviet champions. Both the NKVD and the Dynamo club had been inherited by Dzerzhinsky's successor, Lavrenti Beria. In 1942, Beria had sent players from Dynamo's main rivals, Moscow Torpedo, to the gulag camps on trumped-up charges. This was no ordinary football club, popping over on a goodwill visit.

Dynamo arrived as an unknown quantity, but soon made their needs plain to the Football Association. The Russians presented the FA with a list of fourteen requirements. These included: being able to use their own Russian referee in at least one match; an assurance that their opponents would field only teams selected from a list of names submitted to Dynamo in advance; they would take all their meals at the Russian embassy; they would play only on 'normal' football days, and would play no more than one match in seven days; substitutes would be permitted in their matches; they would definitely play Arsenal; few, if any, social events would be arranged for them. They would also take 50 per cent of all gate receipts after Entertainment Tax and expenses had been deducted; clearly they still understood capitalism. After landing at Croydon aerodrome, the Dynamo party were taken to spend their first night in Britain at Wellington Barracks in central London. Dynamo described their billet as 'feudal'. FA secretary Stanley Rous conceded that they were indeed 'bare and uncomfortable'. An Arsenal director came to the rescue, offering them his family-owned Park Lane Hotel, the first hotel in Europe to boast en-suite bathrooms. That was of little interest to the Dynamo players, who were offered beds in the hotel's billiard room. Eventually the FA got the whole party into the Imperial Hotel in Russell Square.

Dynamo trained at the White City before playing their first match, against Chelsea at Stamford Bridge on 13 November, by which time Britain's national newspapers had done an excellent job of promoting the mysterious Russian footballers; well before midday the Fulham Road was packed with thousands of football fans hurrying towards the Chelsea stadium. The turnstiles were opened at 1 p.m.; little over an hour later they were closed again with perhaps 90,000 people wedged inside, although the official attendance was given as 79,496. Spectators poured on to the greyhound track which surrounded the football pitch, and then right up to the touchlines. Hundreds climbed on to the roof of the East Stand to gain a vantage point; others smashed down gates, and some even broke into nearby flats to view the match from the rooftops. Police and stewards were powerless to stop them. Mikhail Semichastny, the Dynamo captain, later claimed that safety had been sacrificed for profit. However people gained admission, they saw the Russians take the field in blue shirts and voluminous darker-blue shorts with a white stripe around the bottoms. When they kept their legs together, the Russian footballers appeared to be wearing skirts. Each player carried a bouquet of flowers and, at a word of command from their trainer, they each stepped smartly forward to present their floral gift to an opponent. Chelsea's players did not know what to make of it; they quickly handed the flowers on to their trainer, Norman Smith, who left the field 'looking like a harvest festival' according to Tommy Lawton. Before the kick-off, the referee, Lt Commander G. Clark, RN, had to explain the ritual of the coin toss to Semichastny. In Russia the referee would offer two pieces of paper to the captains, one stating 'kick-off', the other 'choice of ends'.

The drama off the field was more than matched by the game itself. At times the Russians moved the ball about with bewildering speed. They seemed to be going faster at the end than at the beginning; they were certainly fit. Chelsea, too, emerged with great credit. Len Goulden and Reg Williams put them 2–0 in front, and when Vic Woodley saved a penalty from Leonid Soloviev it seemed that the Londoners would pull off a famous victory. But Dynamo were soon on level terms. Vasili Kartsev scored from long range and then outside-right Archangelski equalised. With 9 minutes remaining, Chelsea went back in front with a towering header from Lawton, their £11,500 signing from Everton. Four minutes from time, the Russians scored a third, their lanky inside-forward Vsevolod Bobrov – later to become an ice hockey star – putting the ball into the net when about five yards offside. The linesman's flag stayed down and no Chelsea player complained. It had been that sort of afternoon. The Russian wireless commentator remarked, 'We have passed our first examination with honour.' The following day, a London evening newspaper printed another extract from the radio commentary: 'Chelsea played with a strengthened team. Determined to beat Dynamo at all costs, the club has spent thousands of pounds to secure some of Britain's best footballers. For instance, Chelsea paid £14,000 for Tommy Lawton, just so he could play against Dynamo.'

The British press was certainly impressed, and far less biased. The former England forward, Charles Buchan, writing in the *News Chronicle*, was typical: 'No team has ever given a better exhibition of class football and failed to win.' When, a few days later, Dynamo beat Cardiff City 10–1 before a crowd of 31,000 at Ninian Park, the *Western Mail* commented, 'If British football is to compete with this spectacular stuff, we shall have to revise our views on tactics and training.' The Cardiff manager, Cyril Spiers, agreed. After the game he had asked a City player why he felt that his team had played so badly. 'To play well, you have to have the ball – and I hardly had a kick all match,' came the reply. Maybe they were just confused: both sides played in blue shirts. The Cardiff match came after the Dynamo party had visited the docks and a coalmine. That was good propaganda, meeting some of capitalist Britain's downtrodden workers. So too was telling the readers of Soviet newspapers that Cardiff were in front of Chelsea and Arsenal in the First Division, when they were actually playing in the Third Division South. As a memento of their visit, the Russians were each presented with miniature silver miners' lamps; in return the Welsh received a bunch of chrysanthemums each, in place of hammer and sickle insignia which had possibly been stolen.

On 21 November, Dynamo arrived at White Hart Lane for the highlight of their visit, a match against Arsenal. The fixture had assumed greater significance since elements of the British press were calling for a representative team, preferably England, to take on the Russian champions. There was certainly no shortage of takers for club matches: after Dynamo had packed Stamford Bridge, the FA received over thirty requests for games against the tourists. Facing a representative eleven was not in Dynamo's plans, however. They had made that quite clear from the beginning.

Arsenal's problem was that almost all their first-team squad were still serving in the armed forces. Many were stationed abroad, but with the Dynamo match scheduled for a Wednesday afternoon, even those who could normally play with the help of a weekend pass from a British base were not available. The Arsenal manager, George Allison, did what he always did in such circumstances: he called up guest players. This might have gone unchallenged had those guests not included Stanley Matthews and Stan Mortensen. On the eve of the game, Dynamo's captain, Semichastny, put his signature to a statement which ended: ' . . . Because of the composition of this team we consider that the Dynamo team will meet tomorrow one of the representative English teams.' He did not point out that Arsenal included two Welshman. Nor that Dynamo themselves had guest players, notably Bobrov, who scored 24 goals for CDKA Moscow in 1945, and Nikolai Dementiev from Moscow Spartak.

After all the fuss, the match looked unlikely to take place at all when London became enveloped in one of its famous 'pea souper' fogs. But 54,640 people had turned up and they wanted to see something of the mysterious Russians, however fleeting. For this game – as far as Dynamo were concerned the most important of their visit – the Russians produced their own referee, Nikolai Latyshev, who, seventeen years later, would take charge of the World Cup final between Brazil and Czechoslovakia. At Tottenham, Latyshev took a unique approach so far as British football was concerned, patrolling one touchline while leaving the other to be shared by the two English linesmen.

At half-time Arsenal led 3–2 with goals from Mortensen (2) and Ronnie Rooke, the Fulham centre-forward who later joined Arsenal. It was an ill-tempered affair. Rooke complained about the brutality of Semichastny, Matthews spent most of the match fending off shirt-tugging defenders, and Arsenal had to replace their goalkeeper, Wyn Griffiths of Cardiff City, after he was concussed. The Russians levelled the scores and then went ahead, Rooke had what looked like a perfectly good equaliser ruled out by Mr Latyshev, and at one stage Dynamo had twelve men on the pitch. Rooke complained bitterly: 'I fought off two Russians who were trying to use me as a ladder . . . the referee said I had handled it . . . but I had both hands tied behind my back.' George Allison attempted to have the game abandoned because of the swirling fog but the Russians were determined to finish the match now they were in front. A few days later, the Arsenal manager was astonished to hear that Soviet radio had reported that he wanted the game stopped because he had big-money bets on Arsenal to win, and had fainted when his request was refused. It was all propaganda, of course, as were Russian newspaper reports that Dynamo had beaten, not Arsenal but 'England'.

Controversy followed Dynamo to Glasgow, where they met Rangers. Again there was the visit to see local workers, this time at a Clyde shipyard; and with 90,000 tickets sold, Rangers were in no mood to press on with their plans to include new signing Jimmy Caskie, from Everton, after Dynamo flatly refused to turn out if he was in the opposing team. By now the British press were painting a different picture. These exciting, mysterious Russian footballers were now the brooding, silent representatives of Communism. The game at Ibrox also had elements of farce. Dynamo again had twelve men on the pitch at one stage, but, thanks to a controversial penalty award, Rangers managed to draw 2–2 after being 2 goals down. After their four games had been watched by over a quarter of a million people, the FA attempted to arrange a fifth match, against a representative eleven at Villa Park. They even selected a team, which was almost the full England side, and 70,000 tickets were printed. Then the Dynamo party was called home before the game could be played. It was just another twist to a remarkable tale.

Dynamo's success in Britain was soon exploited by the Soviet regime. The players were made Heroes of the Soviet Union. A film of the trip was shown in cinemas across the country. The weekly sports newspaper, *Krasnyi sport*, commented that the tour had been 'a triumph for our school of football, which is based on collectivism, organisation and the unbending will for victory, the characteristic qualities of the Soviet man'. Mikhail Semichastny told a Moscow radio audience that he had been impressed with British stadiums, at least so far as they protected spectators in bad weather, but he added, 'As is well known, British football is on a money basis. Everything is done at the stadiums to accommodate as many people as possible and consequently make more money.' It was a theme picked up by the Moscow theatre. In 1947, a musical comedy entitled *19–9* (the goals for and against) depicted the Dynamo team as incorruptible socialist heroes bravely battling against corrupt capitalists. By then football was being played over the new battleground of the Cold War.

The success of Moscow Dynamo should have alerted British football to how quickly the game was developing elsewhere. In the *Sunday Chronicle Football Annual*, Ivan Sharpe commented, 'Surprise of the tour was not so much the results – the British teams were not yet in full training – as the impressively high standard of the Russians' attacking play. In positional work, and crisp ground combination, they were captivating . . . in goal they had the spectacular strength common to Continental countries . . . But their defensive play as a whole was by no means up to the standard reached in other sections of the side.' Sharpe could also have mentioned several other features of the Dynamo approach, for instance their 20-minute pre-match warm-up, after which they returned to the dressing room; British footballers did not take to the field for the first time until 5 minutes before kick-off. Then there was the fluidity of the Russians, where players were not hidebound by strict positional play. Even as late as the 1956 FA Cup final, Don Revie of Manchester City was astonishing everyone by playing slightly behind the forward line even though he wore the number-nine shirt, traditionally the centre-forward's jersey. The press marvelled at this 'deep-lying centre-forward' tactic, but all Revie had done was switch positions; he had just kept the same shirt. Dynamo did not wear numbered shirts in 1945, but if they had done, then the numbers would not have mattered other than to identify their players. British football had pursued a policy of isolationism between the wars; in 1945 its rulers were certainly not ready to open their minds on the strength of a visit from some strange Russian footballers. As the postwar game unfolded, Moscow Dynamo were largely forgotten.

For some, of course, there was an unusual opportunity to sample foreign football at first hand in the immediate aftermath of war. Stepney-born Vic Barney was expecting to join Arsenal's junior ranks when war broke out. Instead he was invited to join the British Army, and although there were plenty of opportunities to play football – sometimes as many as four games a week – eventually he was posted abroad. Barney served in North Africa, Sicily and Italy before football re-entered his life in the most unusual circumstances. In 1945–6, he found himself playing in Italian league football. Barney had been put in charge of the Vomero Stadium in Naples. The ground was in a dreadful state. The Germans had used it as a transit camp for prisoners before, in September 1943, the citizens of Naples turned on their former allies, fighting from street to street, door to door. After four days of German reprisals – they were ordered to turn the city into 'mud and ashes' – the bodies of hundreds of dead civilians were dumped at the Vomero ground. With their own Ascarelli Stadium destroyed by Allied bombing in 1944, the Napoli club arrived at the Vomero to start again. They found the pitch littered with spent bullets and scorched by petrol.

With a staff of twenty German prisoners of war, who lived in the ground with him, Barney was charged with the job of helping to make the stadium playable again. He did more than that: he turned out for Napoli, who won the championship of a group of central and southern clubs. Napoli wanted him to sign on when he left the army. 'It was an adventure. I still have the photograph of me, a lone Englishman, among a team of Italians. I shall never forget it,' he said. After being demobbed, Barney played for Reading, Bristol City, Grimsby Town and Headington United (now Oxford United) before retiring at the age of 35. When he returned to Naples in the 1990s, they remembered him. 'When I went back, the club president invited me and my wife to dinner and we were wined and dined before a game against Milan. It was nice that they remembered after all those years.' Unlike the British, the Italians had continued with their normal football competitions until the end of 1942–3. Then followed two seasons of regional competitions until 1945–6, when an attempt was made to resurrect a form of national championship. The top four clubs from Napoli's group and the top four from a group of northern clubs began the *Campionato* in April 1946. Napoli and Bari were the only two Serie B clubs involved and it was no surprise when Torino, the 1943 champions, again lifted the title in this transitional Italian season. As in Britain, by 1946–7 the Italians were back to their normal structure.

It was a different picture in Germany, although in June 1944, less than two weeks after the Normandy landings, the Germans had pressed on with their national play-off final in Berlin. The 70,000 spectators who saw SC Dresden beat LSV Hamburg (the Luftwaffe club) might have been told that a few days earlier the first V1 rocket had landed in Britain. They would probably have been unaware that at the very moment they were filing into the Olympic Stadium, at Cherbourg the German garrison had been encircled by American forces. Playing in Dresden's forward line that afternoon was Helmut Schon. In February 1945, Schon was on duty as a factory air raid warden in Dresden when the Allies firebombed the city. Thirty-five thousand people perished that night, and 90 per cent of the city centre was destroyed. Many said it was war crime. In 1966, Schon's West German side lost to England in the World Cup final; in 1974 his team won the trophy against Holland. Schon was very much a postwar European; he never blamed the Allies for the destruction of his city, preferring instead to direct his anger at the futility of war in general.

The play-off final in which Schon had played in 1944 was necessary to decide the German championship because the country had never had a national league; instead, the champions of thirty-one regional districts qualified for the national play-offs. Each known as *Gauliga*, the regions had come about as part of a restructuring of German football by the Nazis after they came to power in 1933. Originally there were sixteen *Gauligen*, but as the Nazis swallowed up more and more territory, clubs from outside

Germany began to take part in the regional championships. Austria provided four clubs – and in 1941, the German national champions in Rapid Vienna – and six came from the Sudetenland. Clubs from Poland, Luxembourg and Alsace also featured in German football during the Second World War. In 1943, the German FA Cup, itself a creation of the Nazi era, was won by FK Austria. The 1944–5 season was started but not finished. The last official game in wartime Germany was the local derby between Hamburg SV and Altona 93, played on 29 April 1945; the following day Adolf Hitler committed suicide in his Berlin bunker. A week later the war in Europe was over; Germany was in ruins. There would not be another football championship until 1947–8, no national league until the formation of the West German *Bundesliga* in 1963, no truly national competition until after the fall of the Berlin Wall. Yet out of the ashes of the Second World War, German football recovered to such an extent that by 1954 the Federal Republic were world champions. Their success was all the more remarkable for the fact that the Germans had resumed international football only in 1950.

In 1946, Germany was a nation defeated and divided, its people struggling through the bitterest of winters, in towns and cities bombed to ruins. In England, the first snow fell in mid-December and it would be the end of March before the weather released its grip, which meant hard work for many Axis prisoners of war who were used to clear roads and dig through to isolated villages. They would also attempt to get more than a few football matches under way. German prisoners based at a camp on Wollaton Park in Nottingham were called upon several times to help with snow-clearing at the City Ground and Meadow Lane. Their efforts were not always appreciated. German POWs helping to shift snow from a railway line in Wales were pelted with stones by angry locals.

There was not always animosity, however, and it was football that helped to heal the wounds. In 1946, the Devon village of Bradworthy raised a team to play German POWs from the local camp. The Germans, who included former professionals in their ranks, won 10–1. At Poppylot POW camp in Feltwell, Norfolk, the prisoners were mostly infantrymen aged from 25 upwards. They had a very good football team and played against other camps. On one occasion, they, too, met the village team, on the prisoners' 'home' ground, a farmer's field opposite the camp. And footballing prisoners of war were not confined to village life. Brian Harris was an 11–year-old London schoolboy in 1946: 'I remember regularly playing football with the German POWs who were housed in Richmond Park. The gates were left open so they could come and go. Better than going home I suppose.'

For over a million Britons – and probably for quite a few enemy POWs too – there was only one place to be on Saturday, 31 August 1946: at a Football League ground. Unusually for the first day of the football season, the weather was cloudy and overcast, the forecast for rain. The previous week had seen gale-force winds and torrential downpours, rivers swollen, roads blocked by fallen trees. There were still 338,000 enemy prisoners of war in Britain and pressure was being mounted to repatriate them; they could not hang around playing football for ever. But conditions in Germany, where the agricultural industry had been all but destroyed, were appalling, and in Britain there was a shortage of labour, so in the meantime 2,000 German POWs had been put on standby to save the harvest. None of them were in a position to take advantage of the black market in nylons, perfume, chocolate and other scarce goods which, by the summer of 1946, was thriving in the UK. In Nuremberg, the war crimes trials entered their last day and that afternoon Goering, Hess and von Ribbentrop were among major Nazi leaders making their final impassioned pleas. And in Britain, the days when football matches were interrupted by air raids, and teams made up their numbers by borrowing from their opponents, or even from the crowd, were over. Now there were no guest players, but there was promotion and relegation. Now there was a return to the old ways of football.

The fixtures were a replica of the 1939–40 season, which meant that Blackburn Rovers and Sheffield United were making another attempt to establish themselves in the top division, seven years after they had been promoted. Twenty-eight thousand fans made their way to Bramall Lane, where Liverpool, fresh from a trip to North America, were Sheffield United's visitors. Liverpool's manager, George Kay, had prepared his players for peacetime football by taking them to play ten matches in the USA and Canada. Unlike the situation in austere postwar Britain, with its rationing and other shortages, food was in plentiful supply on the other side of the Atlantic; the well-fed Liverpool players returned home each half a stone heavier. Thanks to a last-minute goal from Len Carney, they started the postwar era in victorious fashion, but after losing 5–0 to Manchester United in mid-September, Kay signed a rising star in the North East. Albert Stubbins went from Newcastle United to Anfield for a club record fee of £12,000; he repaid Kay's faith with 24 goals in thirty-six games. Liverpool effectively won the title on 31 May, when they beat rivals Wolves on a scorching day at Molineux, but they had to wait another two weeks to be sure; thanks to yet another dreadful winter and a government ban on midweek football – it feared mass industrial absenteeism if matches were played on midweek afternoons – the 1946–7 season went on until 14 June. Stubbins had made a huge contribution to Liverpool's success, but so had the Scottish international winger Billy Liddell, who had still been awaiting his demob from the RAF when the season started.

The problem of getting players back from the forces affected everyone. During the war, Arsenal, who had dominated English football in the 1930s, had won relatively few trophies, hardly surprising since they were affected more than most by losing players to the war effort: in September 1939, forty-two of the club's forty-four professionals had joined the armed forces. The first postwar season would not be any easier. Players such as Hapgood, Drake, Crayston and Kirchen had retired. Cliff Bastin would hang up his boots in September 1946 and his statistics are a perfect example of how the war had damaged careers: he scored 176 goals in 392 peacetime appearances for Arsenal; during the war he played in a further 242 matches and scored 70 goals, but none of it counted. He was playing on the opening day of the 1946–7 season when the Gunners, £155,000 in debt, lost 6–1 at

Molineux. At one stage relegation was a serious threat but a club of Arsenal's stature would recover quickly.

So too would Manchester United. When Matt Busby was appointed their manager on 22 October 1945, he joined a club with an unimpressive pre-war record, no ground and many of its players still in uniform, including Johnny Carey, Stan Pearson, Johnny Morris – who had been involved in the crossing of the Rhine – and Charlie Mitten. There were men like Allenby Chilton, who had been wounded in Normandy, and Jack Rowley, and the emerging John Aston, Jack Crompton and Henry Cockburn, but Busby wrote later that most of his other options were players 'who after six years of war were regrettably too old to do the job I planned'. When all his players were back in the fold, Busby was on his way to becoming a legend. For each of the first three postwar seasons, United finished runners-up and won the FA Cup in 1948. These were indeed heady times for Manchester's football-followers. As United fought for the First Division title in 1946–7, City won the Second Division championship. Both clubs were playing at Maine Road and, by the end of the season, 2.2 million people had passed through the turnstiles there.

Manchester was not alone, however, in witnessing huge attendances. There was remarkable support everywhere, even in the lower divisions. On the opening day of the season, Notts County, fielding their Canadian centre-forward, Fred Whittaker, had a crowd of nearly 27,000 for the Third Division South match against Bournemouth at Meadow Lane. In the same division, Norwich City, at home to Cardiff City, and QPR, who entertained Watford, attracted 20,000-plus attendances as the fans flooded back. Those who poured towards Newport County's Somerton Park ground for the visit of Southampton were disappointed, however. Heavy rain had left the pitch unplayable. Newport, in 1939 promoted to the Second Division for the first time in their history, had already waited seven years to stake their claim; they would have to wait a few days longer and would then endure a dreadful season before finishing bottom of the table, their glory days quickly behind them.

Yet despite all the problems faced by the clubs, after seven years of war the overriding emotion was one of immense relief. When First Division football returned to Highbury on 4 September 1946, 'Marksman' wrote in the Arsenal matchday programme, ' . . . You who talked Arsenal with me over a campfire in Assam and the chap with the Italy Star on the train in India who informed me of Herbert Roberts passing on, the fellow in the Skymaster on the long hop from Ceylon to the Cocos Islands who told me about our cup final win, and all those who played with or against Tom Whittaker's Arsenal Arps in the very early days of the ARP. And the older ones who stuck to the job in London through bomb and fire and rocket, yet still made the long trek up to White Hart Lane to give the boys a cheer. We're home again now!'

It had been worth the wait. The biggest victory had been won.

BIBLIOGRAPHY

Books

Adrian, Alex. *Dunkirk Sportsmen*, 1st edn, London, Stockwell, 1944

Agnew, Paul. *Finney – A Football Legend*, 1st edn, Preston, Carnegie Press, 1989

Appleton, Arthur. *Sunderland AFC Centenary 1879–1979*, 1st edn, Sunderland, Sunderland AFC, 1979

Barnes, Walley. *Captain Of Wales*, 1st edn, London, Stanley Paul, 1953

Bate, Christopher and Smith, Martin. *For Bravery in the Field: Recipients of the Military Medal: 1919–1939, 1939–1945, 1945–1991*, 1st edn, London, Bayonet Publications, 1991

Buchan, Charles. *Charles Buchan's Soccer Gift Book 1954–55*, 1st edn, London, Charles Buchan Publications, 1954

Busby, Matt. *My Story*, 2nd edn, London, Sportsman's Book Club, 1959

Calley, Roy. *Blackpool: A Complete Record 1887–1992*, 1st edn, Derby, Breedon Books, 1992

Cameron, Colin. *Home and Away With Charlton Athletic 1920–1992*, 1st edn, Sidcup, Colin Cameron, 1992

Carter, Raich. *Footballer's Progress,* 1st edn, London, Sporting Handbooks, 1950

Chalk, Gary and Holley, Duncan. *Saints: A Complete Record of Southampton Football Club 1885–1987*, 1st edn, Derby, Breedon Books, 1987

Cheshire, Scott. *Chelsea: A Complete Record 1905–1991*, 1st edn, Derby, Breedon Books, 1991

Clarebrough, Denis. *The Official Centenary History of Sheffield United Football Club*, 1st edn, Sheffield, Sheffield United FC, 1989

Cresswell, Peterjohn and Evans, Simon. *European Football: A Fans' Handbook, The Rough Guide*, 1st edn, London, The Rough Guides, 1997

Crooks, John. *The Bluebirds: The Official History of Cardiff City Football Club*, 1st edn, Harefield, Yore Publications, 1992

Crooks, John. *The Bluebirds: A Who's Who of Cardiff City Football League Players*, 1st edn, Cardiff, Cardiff City FC, 1987

Cullen, Peter. *Bury FC 1885–1999 The Official History*, 1st edn, Harefield, Yore Publications, 1999

Dean, Rod. *Coventry City: A Complete Record 1883–1991*, 1st edn, Derby, Breedon Books, 1991

Dennis, Brian, Daykin, John and Hyde, Derek. *Barnsley Football Club: The Official History 1887–1998*, 1st edn, Harefield, Yore Publications, 1998

Downing, David. *Passovotchka: Moscow Dynamo in Britain 1945*, 1st edn, London, Bloomsbury Publishing, 1999

Downs, David. *Biscuits and Royals: A History of Reading FC 1871–1986*, 1st edn, Reading, Fericon Press, 1986

Dykes, Garth. *New Brighton: A Complete Record of the Rakers in the Football League*, 1st edn, Derby, Breedon Books, 1990

Dykes, Garth and Jackman, Mike. *Accrington Stanley: A Complete Record 1894–1962*, 1st edn, Derby, Breedon Books, 1991

Eastwood, John and Davage, Mike. *Canary Citizens: The Official History of Norwich City FC*, 1st edn, Sudbury, Suffolk, Almeida Books, 1986

Eastwood, John and Moyse, Tony. *The Men Who Made The Town: The Official History of Ipswich Town FC from 1878*, 1st edn, Sudbury, Suffolk, Almeida Books, 1986

Ekberg, Charles and Woodhead, Sid. *The Mariners: The Story of Grimsby Town Football Club*, 1st edn, Buckingham, Barracuda Books, 1983

Farmer, David. *Swansea City 1912–1982*, 1st edn, London, Pelham Books, 1982

Finney, Tom. *Football Round The World*, 1st edn, London, Museum Press, 1953

Garrick, Frank. *Raich Carter The Biography*, 1st edn, Cheltenham, Sports Books, 2003

Glasper, Harry. *Middlesbrough: A Complete Record*, 2nd edn, Derby, Breedon Books, 1993

Golesworthy, Maurice, Dykes, Garth and White, Alex. *Exeter City: A Complete Record 1904–1990*, 1st edn, Derby, Breedon Books, 1990.

Guthrie, Jimmy and Caldwell, Dave. *Soccer Rebel*, 1st edn, Pinner, David Foster, 1976

Halford, Brian. *Past Imperfect: The Story of Lincoln City FC*, 1st edn, Manchester, Parrs Wood Press, 2000

Hall, Ian. *Voices Of The Rams*, 1st edn, Derby, Breedon Books, 2000

Hapgood, Eddie. *Football Ambassador*, 1st edn, London, Sporting Handbooks, 1945

Hayes, Dean. *The Latics: The Official History of Wigan Athletic*, 1st edn, Harefield, Tore Publications, 1996

Hesse-Lichtenberger, Ulrich. *Tor! The Story of German Football*, 1st edn, London, WSC Books, 2002

Hilton, Chris. *Hull City: A Complete Record 1904-1989*, 1st edn, Derby, Breedon Books, 1989

Inglis, Simon. *The Football Grounds of England and Wales*, 1st edn, London, Willow Books, 1983

Bibliography

Inglis, Simon. *The Football Grounds of Europe*, 1st edn, London, Willow Books, 1990

Inglis, Simon. *League Football And The Men Who Made It*, 1st edn, London, Willow Books, 1988

Jarred, Martin and Macdonald, Malcolm. *The Leeds United Story*, 1st edn, Derby, Breedon Books, 1992

Jay, Mike. *Bristol Rovers: A Complete Record 1883–1987*, 1st edn, Derby, Breedon Books, 1987

Jeffs, Peter. *The Golden Age Of Football*, 1st edn, Derby, Breedon Books, 1991

Johnston, W.M. *The Football League: The Competitions of Season 1938–39*, 1st edn, London, Edson Printers

Kirkham, Pat and Thoms, David (eds). *War Culture: Social Change and Changing Experience in World War Two Britain*, 1st edn, London, Lawrence & Wishart, 1995

Knight, Brian. *Plymouth Argyle: A Complete Record 1903–1989*, 1st edn, Derby, Breedon Books, 1989

Korr, Charles. *West Ham United*, 1st edn, London, Gerald Duckworth, 1986

Lawton, Tommy. *Football Is My Business*, 3rd edn, London, Sporting Handbooks, 1947

Marks, John. *Heroes in Hoops, QPR Who's Who 1899–2003*, 1st edn, Harefield, Yore Publications, 2003

Marland, Simon. *Bolton Wanderers: A Complete Record 1877–1989*, 1st edn, Derby, Breedon Books, 1989

Marwick, R.W. *The Boys From The 'Brig: The Life and Times Of Albion Rovers*, 1st edn, Monklands, Monklands Library Services Department, 1986

Mason, Peter. *Southend United: The Official History of The Blues*, 1st edn, Harefield, Yore Publications, 1993

Morris, Peter. *Aston Villa: The First 100 Years*, Centenary edn, Birmingham, Aston Villa Football Club, 1973

Mortensen, Stanley. *Football Is My Game*, 1st edn, London, Sampson Low, Marston & Co, 1949

Murray, James. *Millwall: Lions of the South*, 1st edn, London, Indispensable Publications/Millwall FC, 1988

Nannestad, Ian and Nannestad, Donald. *Lincoln City FC: The Official History*, 1st edn, Harefield, Yore Publications, 1997

Neason, Mike, Cooper, Mick and Robinson, Doug. *Pompey: The History of Portsmouth Football Club*, 1st edn, Portsmouth, Milestone Publications, 1984

Northcutt, John and Shoesmith, Roy. *West Ham United: A Complete Record 1900–1987*, 1st edn, Derby, Breedon Books, 1987

Ollier, Fred. *Arsenal: A Complete Record*, 1st edn, Derby, Breedon Books, 1995

Peebles, Ian. *Growing With Glory*, 1st edn, Rangers Football Club, 1973

Peskett, Roy. *The Crystal Palace Story*, 1st edn, London, Roy Peskett, 1969

Phillips, Steven. *Rochdale FC: The Official History 1907–2001*, 1st edn, Harefield, Yore Publications, 2001

Purkiss, Mike, with Sands, Nigel. *Crystal Palace: A Complete Record 1905–1989*, 1st edn, Derby, Breedon Books, 1989

Redden, Richard. *The Story of Charlton Athletic*, 1st edn, Derby, Breedon Books, 1990

Rigby, Ian and Payne, Mike. *Proud Preston: Preston North End's One Hundred Seasons of Football League History*, 1st edn, Lancaster, Carnegie Publishing, 1999

Rippon, Anton and Ward, Andrew. *The Derby County Story*, 3rd edn, Derby, Breedon Books, 1997

Rollin, Jack. *History of Aldershot Football Club 1926–1975*, 1st edn, London, Jack Rollin & FKS Publishers, 1975

Rollin, Jack. *Soccer at War 1939–45*, 1st edn, London, Willow Books, 1985

Ryan, Sean and Burke, Stephen. *The Book of Irish Goalscorers*, 1st edn, Dublin, Irish Soccer Co-op, 1987

Schleppi, John Ross. *A History of Professional Association Football in England During the Second World War*, PhD Thesis, 1st edn, Ann Arbor, Michigan, University Microfilms International, 1980

Searle, Stan. *Mansfield Town: A Complete Record 1910–1990*, 1st edn, Derby, Breedon Books, 1990

Sedunary, Alan. *Heaven on Earth: The Official History of Reading FC 1871–2003*, 1st edn, Hatfield, Yore Publications, 2003

Sewell, Albert. *Chelsea Champions!*, 1st edn, London, Phoenix, 1955

Smailes, Gordon and Ross, Ian. *Everton: A Complete Record 1878–1988*, 1st edn, Derby, Breedon Books, 1988

Soar, Phil and Tyler, Martin. *Arsenal 1886–1986: The Official Centenary History of Arsenal Football Club*, 1st edn, London, Hamlyn, 1986

Staff, John. *Scunthorpe United Football Club: The Official History 1899–1999*, 1st edn, Hatfield, Yore Publications, 1999

Steel, Billy. *How To Play Football*, 1st edn, London, C & J Temple, 1948

Sumner, Chas. *On The Borderline: The Official History of Chester City FC 1885–1997*, 1st edn, Harefield, Yore Publications, 1997

Taylor, Rogan and Ward, Andrew. *Kicking and Screaming*, 1st edn, London, Robson Books, 1993

Taylor, Rogan and Ward, Andrew. *Three Sides of the Mersey: Oral History of Everton, Liverpool and Tranmere Rovers*, 1st edn, London, Robson Books, 1997

Turner, Dennis and White, Alex. *The Breedon Book of Football Managers*, 1st edn, Derby, Breedon Books, 1993

Turner, Dennis and White, Alex. *Fulham: A Complete Record 1879–1987*, 1st edn, Derby, Breedon Books, 1987

Walvin, James. *The People's Game*, 1st edn, Allen Lane, London, 1975

Ward, Andrew. *Armed With A Football*, 1st edn, Oxford, Crowberry, 1994

Ward, Andrew. *The Manchester City Story*, 1st edn, Derby, Breedon Books, 1984

Ward, Andrew. *Scotland The Team*, 1st edn, Derby, Breedon Books, 1987

Warsop, Keith. *The Magpies: The Story of Notts County Football Club*, 1st edn, Buckingham, Barracuda Books, 1984

Watt, Tom and Palmer, Kevin. *Wembley: The Greatest Stage*, 1st edn, London, Simon & Schuster, 1998

White, Eric (ed.). *100 Years of Brentford*, 1st edn, London, Brentford FC, 1989

Wright, Billy. *Captain Of England*, 1st edn, London, Stanley Paul, 1950

Woods, David M. *Bristol City: A Complete Record 1894–1987*, 1st edn, Derby, Breedon Books, 1987

Annuals and Newspapers

Athletic News Football Annuals, 1938–9, 1939–40, 1940–1, 1941–2, 1942–3, 1943–4, 1945–6

Sunday Chronicle Football Annual, 1946–7

Birmingham Post

Birmingham Sports Argus

Bristol Evening Post

Coventry Evening Telegraph

Daily Express

Daily Mail

Daily Mirror

Daily Telegraph

Derby Evening Telegraph

Leicester Evening Mail

Leicester Mercury

Liverpool Echo

Manchester Evening News

Manchester Guardian

Morley Observer

News Chronicle

Nottingham Evening Post

The Times

Sheffield Star

Sheffield Telegraph

South Wales Evening Post

Sunday Express

Sunday Graphic

Sunday Times

Western Mail
Western Morning News
Wolverhampton Express and Star
Yorkshire Evening Post
Yorkshire Evening Press

INDEX

Index